When Teams Work Best

To Barbara, Alex, Nick, Jon, Spencer, and Sarah. . . the greatest team of all.

F.L.

When Teams Work Best

6,000 TEAM MEMBERS
AND LEADERS
TELL WHAT IT TAKES
TO SUCCEED

Frank LaFasto
Carl Larson

Sage Publications
International Educational and Professional Publisher
Thousand Oaks ▪ London ▪ New Delhi

For information:

Sage Publications, Inc.
2455 Teller Road
Thousand Oaks, California 91320
E-mail: order@sagepub.com

Sage Publications Ltd.
6 Bonhill Street
London EC2A 4PU
United Kingdom

Sage Publications India Pvt. Ltd.
M-32 Market
Greater Kailash I
New Delhi 110 048 India

Printed in the United States of America

Library of Congress Cataloging-in-Publication Data

LaFasto, Frank M. J.
    When teams work best: 6,000 team members and leaders tell what it takes to succeed / by Frank M. J. LaFasto and Carl E. Larson.
        p. cm.
    Includes bibliographical references and index.
    ISBN 0-7619-2366-7 (c)
    1. Teams in the workplace. 2. Leadership. I. Larson, Carl E.
    II. Title.
    HD66 .L33 2002
    658.3'128—dc21   2001002424

01   02   03   04   05   06   07   7   6   5   4   3   2   1

Acquiring Editor:	Marquita Flemming
Editorial Assistant:	MaryAnn Vail
Production Editor:	Diane S. Foster
Editorial Assistant:	Kathryn Journey
Typesetter/Designer:	Marion Warren
Indexer:	Teri Greenberg
Cover Designer:	Michelle Lee

CONTENTS

Preface   xi
   How to Use This Book   xiii
Acknowledgments   xv

PROLOGUE: A BRIEF PERSPECTIVE ON TEAMWORK
AND COLLABORATION   **xvii**
   What's Going On?   xviii
    The Increasing Complexity of Problems   xviii
    The Evolution of Social Behavior   xix
   Not So Fast. What I See Is . . .   xx
   The Origins of This Book   xxi
   The Five Dynamics of Working Together   xxii

1. WHAT MAKES A GOOD TEAM MEMBER? THE ABILITIES
AND BEHAVIORS THAT MATTER   **1**
   Six Factors That Distinguish Effective Team Members 4
    Working Knowledge Factors   5
      Experience   5
      Problem-Solving Ability   6
    Teamwork Factors   8
      Openness: The Basic Ingredient for Team Success 8
      Supportiveness   14
      Action Orientation   18
      Personal Style   23
   Being Collaborative: Some Can, Some Can't, Some Won't 25
   Putting It to Work   28

2. TEAM RELATIONSHIPS: SIMPLE AND EASY VERSUS COMPLICATED AND HARD   **33**

Good Versus Bad Relationships   36

We Think We Are Better at Relationships
Than We Really Are   39

What Team Members Say About Team Relationships   40

*Question 1. What Behaviors Are Most Important in a
Team Relationship?*   41

*Question 2. What Is the Greatest Challenge in
Team Relationships?*   43

    Feedback Is a Gift   45

    From Poorly Managed Contention to
    Dysfunctional Behavior   47

*Question 3. How Do You Build and Sustain a
Collaborative Team Relationship?*   48

The Connect Model: A Proven Approach to Building
Effective Team Relationships   50

The Connect Model: Step by Step   53

The Benefit of the Connect Model to Team Relationships   60

Putting It to Work   61

**3. TEAM PROBLEM SOLVING: RAISING AND
RESOLVING THE REAL ISSUES**   **65**

What Factors Distinguish Good Problem-Solving Teams?   67

Focus   67

Climate   68

Communication   70

Focus, Climate, and Communication as Pervasive Issues   71

The Problem-Solving Dynamic: Goal, Energies, and the
Decision-Making Process   72

The Goal   73

The Team's Energies   75

    Mental Energy   75

    Physical Energy   77

    Spiritual Energy   78

    The Drain   79

Making Systematic Problem Solving a Priority   81

Five Steps to Effective Problem Solving 84
The Single Question Format in Action 86
Case One: Universal Product Numbers 86
Case Two: Improved Earnings 87
A Look at the Process 88
Cross-Functional Teams: The Challenge Increases 90
What About Process Problems? 92
Putting It to Work 93

**4. THE TEAM LEADER: WHAT WORKS/WHAT
GETS IN THE WAY** **97**
Six Dimensions of Team Leadership 98
Dimension One: Focus on the Goal 100
Define the Goal in a Clear and Elevating Way 101
Don't Play Politics 105
Help Team Members See Their Relevance to the Goal 105
Keep the Goal Alive 106
Dimension Two: Ensure a Collaborative Climate 108
Make Communication Safe 109
Demand a Collaborative Approach 110
Reward Collaborative Behavior 112
Guide the Team's Problem-Solving Efforts 113
Manage Your Ego and Personal Control Needs 116
Dimension Three: Build Confidence 121
Get Results 123
Make Team Members Smart About Key Issues and Facts 124
Exhibit Trust by Assigning Responsibility 125
Be Fair and Impartial 126
Accentuate the Positive 128
Say "Thank You" 129
Dimension Four: Demonstrate Sufficient
Technical Know-How 130
Know Your Stuff 132
Get Help 133
Dimension Five: Set Priorities 135
What Must Happen/What Must Not 136
When Priorities Change 137

Dimension Six: Manage Performance 138
   Require Results: Make Performance Expectations Clear 140
   Review Results: Give Constructive Feedback
      and Resolve Performance Issues 141
      Give Constructive Feedback 142
      Confront and Resolve Performance Issues 143
   Reward Results: Recognize Superior Performance 145
A Note on Contemporary Leadership Thought 147
Putting It to Work 149

5. **THE ORGANIZATION ENVIRONMENT: PROMOTING
    CLARITY, CONFIDENCE, AND COMMITMENT** **157**
What Is an Organization Environment? 158
What a Good Environment Produces:
  Clarity, Confidence, and Commitment 159
Three Dimensions of Organization Environment 160
  1. Management Practices 161
      Setting a Clear Direction and Priorities 161
      Balancing Resources and Demands 165
      Establishing Clear Operating Principles 168
  2. Structure and Processes 173
      Effective Processes Foster Effective Decision Making 175
      Effective Processes Keep People Connected 179
      Effective Communication Processes Align
         Information, Understanding, and Effort 182
  3. Systems 186
      The Necessity of Reliable Information 186
      Relevant Rewards Drive Required Results 187
      Team-Based Selling/Team-Based Rewards: A Short Story 188
      Standards Lead to Consistency and Fairness 192
Putting It to Work 195

A FINAL WORD **197**

NOTES **199**
  Prologue 199
  Chapter 1 200
  Chapter 2 201

Chapter 3   202
Chapter 4   205
Chapter 5   206

**APPENDIX: RELIABILITY OF THE COLLABORATIVE
    TEAM LEADER INSTRUMENT**   **209**

NAME INDEX   **211**

SUBJECT INDEX   **214**

ABOUT THE AUTHORS   **221**

PREFACE

Teams are everywhere: in business and industry, in government, in schools, hospitals, professional associations—indeed, almost anywhere people gather to get things done. There are executive teams, management teams, and teams within functional areas from R&D to customer service. There are also special-purpose teams, cross-functional teams, and even industry teams with members from different organizations. Indeed, the movement to collaborative teamwork has been one of the sea changes that have swept through organizations during the last two decades of the twentieth century.

Most organizational leaders and managers are well past the point of needing convincing that collaborative teamwork is an effective tool for managing complex tasks in a rapidly changing environment. They're sold on the value of teams. They've absorbed the theory. The trouble is that in real life, sometimes teams work effectively, but often they don't. No one knows this better than team members themselves.

This book is based on research in which we asked more than 6,000 team members across a variety of businesses and industries, in both public and private sectors, to assess their teams, their team leaders, and each other against a common set of criteria and to respond to the same open-ended questions. In the safety of confidentiality, they identified what encourages teams to succeed and what discourages teams into failure. A content analysis of their highly focused comments offers brisk and useful insight for senior managers building a team-based organization, team leaders, and members of teams.

Although the team members we surveyed justly praised their leaders, each other, and the organizations they served, they also straightened the line of sight on what gets in the way of team results. Their critiques are candid, honest, and not always understated. Their comments are also tentatively hopeful that someone will eliminate the speed bumps that compromise the path to the goal. Team members are concerned about the difference between their team's potential and the actual limitations they face. They clearly see the difference between what should be true and what really happens.

In their collective voice, team members offer five conditions that can either help or hinder a team in achieving its goal; these conditions correspond to the five chapters of this book. They are dynamics that, when left unattended, only widen the gap between what is promised and what can be accomplished. None of their suggestions should seem contrary to our sturdiest beliefs about working together. Indeed, as we will note from time to time, their insights are consistent with the most recent research and theory, as well as with our own extensive observations of hundreds of teams in scores of organizations. Briefly:

1. They told us that *team members* can be either collaborative and easy to work with, or dysfunctional and counterproductive, thereby diminishing and even ruining the entire team effort. They told us how to understand the difference and how to be a good team member.
2. They told us that good teams are highly dependent on *relationships,* which can be either simple and easy or complicated and hard. They told us how to build and sustain good team relationships.
3. They told us that what matters in the end is whether the right decisions are happening fast enough. They told us how *group processes* can help make good decisions or muddle them.
4. They told us that *team leaders* can either help or get in the way of a team's performance. They told us what leadership practices they find most helpful.
5. They told us that an *organization environment* can either encourage or discourage working together easily in terms of management practices, structure and processes, and systems and rewards. They told us what it takes for an environment to create a tailwind behind team effort.

In the end, they told us how these conditions, bundled properly, can bridge the distance between what we know is good team effort and how we actually go about achieving common goals. They told us that what is good for people working together is also good for an organization's bottom line. They told us how to blend cooperative spirit with a strong competitive desire to succeed . . . together.

In this book, we tell you what they told us.

▪ HOW TO USE THIS BOOK

We intend this book to be an eminently practical guide to success in collaborative teamwork, based on our analysis of the rich experience of thousands of team members and leaders. The five conditions of effective collaboration offer practical insights to people at a number of levels.

- *Executives and managers* who are responsible for the overall functioning of teams can use this book to ensure that teams throughout the organization understand what it takes to make collaboration work. They can learn what to look for in exemplary and less-than-exemplary teams, from the qualities of team members, to the processes that successful teams use, to the attributes of effective team leaders (Chapters 1-4). Senior managers may also want to pay particular attention to Chapter 5, which discusses organizational factors that foster or impede the work of collaborative teams.

- *Team leaders* will find specific practical guidance in every chapter that can improve their leadership of teams. The book can be an excellent training vehicle for team leaders, whether they are seasoned veterans or new to the job. In addition to learning valuable strategies and techniques for themselves, they can use much of the material in the book in managing team members to collaborate more effectively. Finally, team leaders can use the ideas in Chapter 5 on the organizational culture to assess organizational obstacles to their work and advocate constructive change.

- *Team members* can use this book to improve their own participation in teams, help their teams function more effectively, and prepare to become leaders themselves.

Our emphasis throughout this book is on practical, portable insight. At the start of each chapter, you will find a one-page "Snapshot" that provides a concise overview of the chapter. Then, each chapter opens with a real-life scenario that introduces the issues discussed in that chapter in concrete, familiar terms. Throughout the book you will hear the voices of actual team members through quotations that speak candidly and in down-to-earth ways about the difficulties and triumphs they experience in working in teams. Finally, to help you put the chapter's lessons into practice, each chapter concludes with a "Putting It to Work" section that includes specific suggestions and helpful instruments that you can use directly or adapt to suit your circumstances.

We think you'll find that you come away from this book with much more than a theoretical idea of what *should* make teams work best. You'll come away with the collective insights of thousands of team members and leaders on what really *does* work to bring out the best in teams. And you'll have in hand the tools that can help you put these insights to work.

ACKNOWLEDGMENTS

This book is based on 20 years of research and took more than seven years to write. As you might imagine, we are deeply grateful to numerous friends and colleagues who encouraged and supported us along the way.

Many professional colleagues and thinkers influenced our perspective on how people behave and work together in organizations. In particular, we owe a debt of gratitude to Dave Ulrich of the University of Michigan School of Business, Steve Kerr of Goldman Sachs, Len Schlesinger of The Limited, Alvin Goldberg of the University of Denver, Ronald Heifetz of the Kennedy School of Government at Harvard, and Tom Peters, management expert. Over the years, their seminal thinking played an important role as we shaped the content of this book.

Cardinal Health generously supported this project. In particular, we are grateful to Bob Walter, chairman and CEO, and John Kane, formerly president and COO, now retired. Lester Knight and Joe Damico, while at Allegiance Healthcare, embraced the concepts of teamwork and leadership in this book. Anthony Rucci, a friend and colleague for many years, believed in and supported this project from the very beginning.

Many people with whom we work—too many to mention—enthusiastically adopted teamwork as a way of doing business. The multidivisional salesforce at Cardinal Health deserve recognition for practicing teamwork in the best interest of their customers. We owe a special thanks to the Cardinal corporate sales team, formulated in the early 1980s by Terry Mulligan, who was among the first to see the potential for team-based selling. We are also thankful to John Hatcher for continuing this commitment within corporate sales.

This book is based on data collected during more than two decades. Susan Stein of Omni Research created the original database. Our gratitude goes to her and Laurie Larson for their numerous analyses, suggestions, and interpretive insights. In addition, we are grateful to Donna de St. Aubin for updating and maintaining the current database and for her continued commitment to applying the team excellence process.

We are indebted to Catherine Sweeney and Barbara LaFasto for their astute suggestions and unwavering support every step of the way. We also thank Alex LaFasto for his careful review of an early manuscript.

Three developmental editors left an invaluable imprint on this book. First and foremost, this book could not have been written without Liz Rimer. There are not enough words to express our gratitude for her unflagging commitment to the quality of ideas contained in this book throughout the entire process. We would also like to thank Barbara Steiger for work early on with the formulation and structure of the thinking of this book. Her sensitivity to the logical flow of ideas and to language is impeccable. Finally, John Bergez helped to smoothly combine our ideas into a meaningful focus. We are grateful to him for making the editing process a productive dialogue.

Geri Schulz deserves special mention and thanks. She exhibited absolute dedication and unremitting good humor from the beginning of this project to its end. She made a valuable contribution by conducting research in libraries and online. She prepared the final manuscript and made endless adjustments along the way. Her input was always candid, and her patience was exemplary.

We would also like to thank Marquita Flemming and Rolf Janke of Sage Publications. Their encouragement, enthusiasm, and support were meaningful and appreciated as we worked together to transform the manuscript into final book form.

Finally, this book would not have been possible without the candid feedback of the 6,000 team members and leaders who assessed their teams, their leaders, and themselves and shared their insights with us. To them we are extremely grateful.

PROLOGUE

A Brief Perspective on Teamwork and Collaboration

For the last 15 years, social scientists and observers of contemporary life have been commenting on a dramatic change in the way we do business in both the public and private sectors. The change that has attracted so much attention and commentary is a significant increase in teamwork and collaborative efforts: *people with different views and perspectives coming together, putting aside their narrow self-interests, and discussing issues openly and supportively in an attempt to solve a larger problem or achieve a broader goal.* By the mid-1980s, more than 6,000 identifiable partnerships among business, public sector, and nonprofit organizations had emerged.[1] A steady increase in collaborative teams was reported in the adoption of collaborative strategies in the auto, steel, and textile industries.[2] A similar pattern was noted in science and technology.[3]

Today, collaborative decision-making groups permeate education, especially in the management of schools. Collaborative problem-solving processes are embraced by the healthcare industry, as well as by institutions and agencies that fund social programs and initiatives. Community involvement groups dot the civic landscape and, in the private sector, teamwork programs are everywhere and in all forms.

Recognizing the strength of this trend, a U.S. Department of Labor report identified teamwork as one of five workplace skills that should be taught more aggressively in public schools.[4] The report suggests the teaching of these new skills is necessary both for the success of individuals in job settings and for the success of U.S. companies competing with foreign and domestic rivals.

■ WHAT'S GOING ON?

Why is this social transformation from individual work to teamwork occurring? Many people have offered numerous explanations, but our combined 50 years of working with organizations, both public and private, have led us to believe that two fundamental processes are at work: increasing complexity and social evolution.

The Increasing Complexity of Problems

In *Tales of a New America*, Robert Reich observes:

> Rarely do even Big Ideas emerge any longer from the solitary labors of genius. Modern science and technology is too complicated for one brain. It requires groups of astronomers, physicists, and computer programmers to discover new dimensions of the universe; teams of microbiologists, oncologists, and chemists to unravel the mysteries of cancer. With ever more frequency, Nobel prizes are awarded to collections of people. Scientific papers are authored by small platoons of researchers.[5]

The problems that confront us are complex and becoming increasingly so. For an organization to change or refocus its efforts in any significant way—in strategy, in design, or in structure—requires a coordinated effort among hundreds, or thousands, or even tens of thousands of individuals. Such private sector initiatives as improving earnings, boosting customer satisfaction, or competitors using the Internet to maximize efficiencies within an industry all require broad-based collaboration and ownership.

In the public arena, the problems are equally, if not more, complex. John Parr, former president of the National Civic League, declared:

> This is the time of rapid change in communities around the world. It may be easiest to see the radical changes affecting areas like Eastern Europe, Central Asia, and South America, but it is also clearly happening in the United States. Never in our history have there been more massive demographic changes, greater differences in socioeconomic well-being, and such alarming environmental and social

challenges. And never before has there been such a lack of confidence in the ability of our leaders and institutions to address these challenges.[6]

The relationship between the complexity of problems and the use of collaborative strategies can be seen clearly in the area of hazardous waste disposal. A 10-year study of the dispute surrounding the disposal of hazardous waste found that public cynicism and the absence of collaboration between states, scientific experts, waste producers, and the public led to the development of grass roots coalitions that blocked 75 out of 81 state and corporate attempts to site hazardous disposal facilities. In contrast, when policy-making institutions collaborate with the citizens of local communities, the likelihood of success is enhanced. For example, the researchers report that attempts to locate hazardous waste facilities in Bridgeport, New Jersey and Alberta, Canada were successful because policy-making institutions involved the citizens in a truly collaborative decision-making process.[7]

Whether the problem is hazardous waste, the homeless, the illegal use of drugs, the AIDS epidemic, or a massive organization turnaround, the fundamental conclusion seems to us quite clear: As problems become more complex, and as their solutions require the active participation of diverse perspectives, then teamwork and collaboration become increasingly necessary and valued.

The Evolution of Social Behavior

Evolution occurs at many different levels. Biological evolution in species is clearly the best known and the most widely explored level of analysis. However, anthropologist Gregory Bateson has gone on to describe the evolution of cultures,[8] and organization theorist James Moore describes the evolution of business "eco-systems."[9] Along this same line of thinking, a diverse group of scientists suggests that we, as individuals, may be evolving in the direction of a greater capacity for cooperative behavior.[10] Central to this analysis is evidence that suggests the following:

1. A social early-warning system in individuals allows cooperators to recognize and associate with each other, leaving self-oriented people to their own devices.

2. Humans have evolved an innate ability to discern cheaters in social transactions.
3. Groups are much better than individuals at making decisions, and they usually do as well as the best individual decision maker in the group.

We believe that the movement toward teamwork and collaboration is shaped by two societal forces. It is *driven* by the need to find new and more effective ways of dealing with complex problems. It is *made possible* by the increasing social capacities of individuals and collectives to use collaborative strategies when dealing with common problems.

■ NOT SO FAST. WHAT I SEE IS . . .

From the vantage point of any single individual, however, teamwork and collaboration may appear to be stumbling or falling. You may be a member of a team, or know of a team in your organization, that has problems or is experiencing outright failure. We have encountered or worked directly with many such teams. We have seen teams destroyed by individuals incapable of managing ego and control needs. We have seen large teamwork and collaboration initiatives fail: sometimes because compensation or performance appraisal systems worked in opposition to the very principles of teamwork and collaboration; sometimes because of hostile attitudes openly displayed by the managers; sometimes because individuals who were asked to work collaboratively were not given the training or support they needed to succeed. It is not difficult to point to problems or deficiencies in the principles or practices associated with teamwork and collaboration.

Many of us were raised in dysfunctional settings, acculturated with individualistic and competitive values, rewarded for capturing and controlling the resources of an organization, and self-aggrandized by successfully differentiating ourselves from others who were not as smart or, in countless ways, not as worthy. The deep-rooted habits and values that shape the way we work together and solve common problems change much more slowly than formal changes mandated by organizational structure and strategy.

It may be enlightening to reflect for a moment on our not so distant past. The organizations that we, the authors, entered at the beginning of our careers were dramatically different from those of today. The workers and, more so, the managers and directors, were far less multicultural. They were less gender-mixed. Organizations were run more by positional authority: People knew their places, and compliance was often gained by reminding them of their places. The norms for dress and demeanor were clearer, some might even say stifling. Very few people questioned the wisdom of decisions or the authority for making them. The structures were simpler; the problems were more easily defined; and the confidence that our formal leaders would do the right thing was higher.

We live and work in different times. These times require greater capacities for hearing and understanding. In our dot-com, twitch-speed world, we have little opportunity to reflect on and integrate different points of view. These times require strategies for coordinating and integrating the efforts of more people, relating to each other in much more varied ways.

■ THE ORIGINS OF THIS BOOK

We have both studied and worked actively with groups and teams throughout our separate careers. In 1981, we began working together on a systematic, long-term program, with a major part of our research centered on teams and teamwork, including high performance teams. We traveled throughout the United States, watching teams work, interviewing the leaders and members that had succeeded and teams that had failed.

Our sample included a wide array of teams: large and small, teams of short and long duration, creative teams and tactical teams—as mixed a group as we could find. The teams we studied included the team that designed the Boeing 747 airplane, the team that founded and planned the U.S. Space Command, the citywide teams that formed chapters of the American Leadership Forum, mountain-climbing teams (Mt. Everest and Mt. Kongur), the Presidential Commission on the Space Shuttle Challenger Accident, several cardiac surgery teams that are still regarded as among the best in the world, national championship athletic teams, epidemiology teams operating out of the National Centers for

Disease Control, executive management teams, landmark project teams, disaster teams, theater production teams, military teams, and presidential cabinets.

We reported our findings in a book entitled *TeamWork: What Must Go Right/What Can Go Wrong.* That book included extended discussion of eight characteristics we found to be particularly true of high performance teams: a clear, elevating goal; a results-driven structure; competent team members; unified commitment; collaborative climate; standards of excellence; external support and recognition; and principled leadership.

At the same time that we were doing the analyses that would ultimately be reported in our first teamwork book, we developed a set of measurements designed to assess the status of teams on these eight dimensions and evaluate the extent to which team members and leaders contributed to their team's success or failure. We used these measures to collect team data, to conduct team analyses, and to give teams feedback that would help them improve their performance. A summary of the reliability and validity of these measures, along with how they have been used by others in research has been reported elsewhere.[11]

Since 1987, we and our associates have accumulated extensive quantitative and qualitative data on a diverse range of teams whenever we have worked with them, assessed them, and consulted with them. These teams include executive-level teams, management teams, and project teams from several hundred organizations across a range of industries and a variety of countries (see Table 0.1).

With approximately 600 teams and 6,000 team members in this database, as well as corollary databases on individual team members, team leaders, and working relationships, we believe we can better understand why teams succeed, why teams fail, and what might be done to improve the ability of a team to work productively together. The voices of these team members can be heard in the team comments that appear throughout the book.

▪ THE FIVE DYNAMICS OF WORKING TOGETHER

Our conclusions emerge from the quantitative data and the tens of thousands of responses from the 6,000 team members in our database. Their insights are organized around what we call the five dynamics of

TABLE 0.1.   Industries in Our Team Database

Airline	Education	Pharmaceutical
Auto	Food	Publishing/Printing
Banking/Finance	Healthcare	Retail
Chemical	Industrial Equipment	Science/Engineering
Computer	Insurance	Sports
Consulting	Law Enforcement	Telecommunications
Distribution/Logistics	Legal	Utilities

teamwork and collaboration, as shown in Figure 0.1. These dynamics are the fundamental elements that need to be understood and actively managed in order to increase the likelihood of teamwork and collaboration succeeding.

Our conclusions about these five dynamics are presented in the five remaining chapters of this book. In all cases, the conclusions presented are those that we reached ourselves, those reached by the social scientists working for the research organization that maintained these databases (Omni Research and Training, Denver, Colorado), or those reached by independent researchers who have conducted their own analyses of our databases. Five questions have guided our efforts.

1. What are the attributes or behaviors of *individual team members*, as seen by their fellow team members, that help the team succeed, or interfere with the team's success?

To answer this question we gathered approximately 15,000 assessments of team members by their fellow team members. These assessments included quantitative ratings on a number of specific items and qualitative evaluations, or open-ended questions, that focused on what individual members of the teams did to help or hinder the team's success. What we have learned about team members is presented in Chapter 1.

2. What are the dimensions, strengths, and weaknesses of *working relationships* in teams?

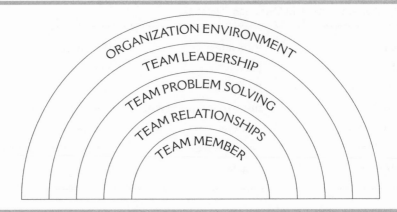

Figure 0.1. Five Dynamics of Teamwork and Collaboration
SOURCE: © 1998 Frank M. J. LaFasto, Ph.D. and Carl E. Larson, Ph.D.

To approach this question we accumulated, in a separate database called Interpersonal Impact, 35,000 assessments of 4,500 individuals by their direct reports, peers, and supervisors. These assessments include both quantitative ratings and qualitative evaluations of strengths and weaknesses of individuals in ongoing working relationships. What we have concluded about building or strengthening team relationships is presented in Chapter 2.

3. What are the behaviors of teams, as seen by their leaders and members, that make some teams more successful than others at *problem solving?*

To understand this question we accumulated more than 6,000 assessments by members and leaders of teams. These assessments include quantitative ratings and qualitative evaluations indicating in what ways the team is functioning well; what its problems are; in what areas it functions poorly; what norms or behaviors it accepts that keep it from functioning more effectively; and what one issue members of the team would like to discuss in an open and candid way. We add to these assessments our own experiential conclusions based on the hundreds of teams we have observed, advised, or coached. These conclusions are reported in Chapter 3.

4. What are the behaviors of *team leaders,* as seen by members of the team, that help lead the team to success or failure?

To explore this question we accumulated more than 6,000 assessments by team members of team leaders. The 6,000+ assessments describe, from all team members' points of view, approximately 600 team leaders. The assessments include both quantitative ratings and qualitative evaluations of what leaders do that promote either success or failure. Our conclusions are reported in Chapter 4.

5. What are the *organizational processes and practices* that increase or decrease the likelihood of teams succeeding?

The team members in our database often comment on some aspect of the organization in which the team functions. Our integration of these commentaries from 6,000 team members, along with our experience of specific organizations, is the basis for Chapter 5.

We offer these learnings in the spirit of improving teamwork and collaboration. We believe that a great deal depends on all of our collective competence in using these processes well. For this reason we have adopted two principles to guide our reporting of conclusions from our research.

First, we report only those conclusions in which we have considerable confidence based on our research and experience—not a lot of ideas that we think "may be true" or that "might be worth thinking about." A great deal has been written about teams on the basis of someone's "good ideas." We want to advance the discussion by presenting empirically based conclusions that you can rely on.

Second, we present those conclusions that will ultimately focus your attention on what you might do as a member or a leader of a team. Deliberately, we are very selective. One thing we have discovered in our work with individuals and teams is that if people or groups try to do too many things at the same time, they often end up doing nothing well, or even nothing at all. Change in individuals or groups is much more likely to succeed if it is very focused and is done incrementally. There may be dozens of things about individuals that make them effective or ineffective team members. We think you'll do well if you can remember and attend to two or three of them. Similarly, there may be hundreds of factors that influence the quality of a working relationship. But we think if you're going to start somewhere to promote healthy working relationships you should start with the way you give and receive feedback.

This practical focus is reflected in the section you will find at the end of each chapter entitled "Putting It to Work." Here we provide specific suggestions and tools that we hope will make the collective insights of thousands of team members portable to your own organization.

We turn now to what team members have to say about when teams work best. Together, they represent many valuable years of experience in actual teams. Listen to their voices—we're sure you'll recognize much of what they have to say, both good and bad, about collaborative teamwork. We've done our best to distill from their comments the practical strategies and behaviors that can help the teams in which you are involved realize their immense potential.

SNAPSHOT

1

A successful team begins with the right people. But exactly what qualities distinguish people who make effective team members? To find the answer, we gathered 15,000 assessments of team members from their fellow teammates across a wide range of organizations.

Team members tell us that the first thing they look for in a teammate is a *core competency*. We call this quality "working knowledge." It has two aspects: having sufficient experience to do the job at hand well and having the necessary problem-solving ability to overcome those obstacles that invariably arise on the team's path to its goal.

But team members also tell us that working knowledge alone is not enough. Four personal qualities, which we call "teamwork factors," contribute significantly to the team's success: *openness*, *supportiveness*, an *action orientation*, and a *positive personal style*.

Chapter 1 explores each of these factors. Although no one team member must possess each factor in optimal measure, assembling a critical mass of each quality is essential in building a successful team.

CHAPTER 1

WHAT MAKES
A GOOD TEAM MEMBER?

The Abilities and Behaviors That Matter

It's a problem that holds captive the entire planet. Since the invention of CFCs in the 1920s, there has been a steady depletion of the protective ozone layer around the earth. It's a problem of such gigantic proportion that it would be reasonable for any individual to ask, "What can one person possibly do?" Meet environmental strategist Stephen O. Andersen.

Andersen joined the U.S. Environmental Protection Agency in the 1980s to work on stratospheric ozone protection. A major focus was finding alternatives to CFCs and other ozone-depleting substances (ODSs). As Andersen explains,

> ODSs were used in more than 250 applications from refrigeration, to cleaning solvents, to aerosol propellants, many critical to economic well being. Society couldn't merely avoid these products; alternatives had to be found. The hard part was that every industry claimed there were no alternatives and urged the EPA to restrict some other sector.

According to Andersen, the EPA, acting out of "skeptical desperation," allowed him to try a strategy of using teamwork to resolve the most difficult issues. What did that mean in a practical sense? Andersen remembers, "I would imagine a small success and then set about to achieve it by involving others in the effort."

Recognizing the importance of collaboration, Andersen assembled a team of "respected, technically optimistic, influential experts with environmental attitude" to tackle critical problems. A dozen experts from around the world attended a groundbreaking meeting at their own expense, representing a variety of industries and companies. Some commented that it was their first opportunity to serve on a cross-organizational team. A typically modest Andersen explains, "We simply saw ourselves as a group of peers trying to address a significant problem that we knew something about."

Of course, assembling a high-powered group of experts was only the first step. The participants had different perspectives, interests, and allegiances. Whether they would achieve their objectives depended on how well they would work as a team. One key turned out to be the personal qualities of team member Stephen Andersen. As the team's work progressed, his unflagging commitment, his determination to address sensitive issues openly, and his efforts to deepen his own knowledge and expertise proved infectious.

Andersen also encouraged others by remaining determinedly supportive. "We gave people a second chance. We worked hard at understanding the point of view of people who were harsh to begin with. We then taught them how to be better team members before addressing the next problem."

Where others found problems and roadblocks, an ever-optimistic Andersen found solutions. When industry skeptics bristled at the prospect of technical collaboration focused on finding alternatives to CFCs, Andersen convinced the Justice Department to approve collaborative efforts aimed at protecting the environment, and he secured necessary EPA approvals himself. As Andersen notes, "Excuses resolved, the team pressed on with ultimate success."

Today, he says, the ozone hole is the largest ever recorded, but there is cause for cautious optimism. "If humans stay the course, the ozone hole will be gone in 50 years, and in 500 years the stratosphere will return to its natural condition."

The example of Stephen Andersen reveals a basic truth about teams. Among the top predictors of a team's effectiveness are the qualities of the individuals who make up the team: the skills and competencies they possess, the attitudes they display, the behaviors they engage in. In short, the type of people team members are and, more specifically, how they behave, is the most important quality they bring to the team table.[1]

The difficulty is that the specific qualities and behaviors it takes to be an effective team member are often unclear. People are brought together, placed within a team structure, charged with a goal or objective, and are expected to "act like a team." Unfortunately, exactly how they should behave in order to effectively "be a team" is frequently left undefined and unclarified. The team members are left on their own to figure out which behaviors are appropriate and productive to help the team accomplish its goal. If you have ever been a member of a marginal or dysfunctional team, you must certainly have wondered what would lead some people to behave the way they do, ostensibly in the name of good teamwork and collaboration.

> "He has integrity and openness—the courage to raise many unspoken issues."

Consider how team members we have surveyed describe the differentiating behaviors of effective team members.

- He has a disarming frankness without making people defensive. (Team 119)
- He has energy, clarity of purpose, and an ability to blend the talents of others effectively. (T175)
- She demonstrates a strong leadership initiative in raising issues. (T239)
- He facilitates communication among team members. He is competent, works hard, and is reliable. (T383)
- He has integrity and openness—the courage to raise many unspoken issues. He has leadership and clear goals. (T291)

In short, the effective team member adds value by addressing issues, building confidence and trust, demonstrating personal leadership, and bringing out the best thinking and attitude of everyone on the team. In contrast, the dysfunctional team member erodes trust and makes it harder to get at the issues, make decisions, and move forward.

- He belittles the efforts of others. (T175)
- He needs to be more collaborative in dealing with others. Many issues become win/lose, rather than win/win. (T4)
- I do not trust him to do what he says he will do. He is disruptive. He is "political." His personal goals are more important than the team's goals. (T67)
- He overcommits and underdelivers, which causes problems and a lack of trust. (T291)
- He gets stuck on an issue or a viewpoint and may hold such a position for a long time, even though the original reason that the position was taken no longer exists. (T140)

What type of person would you prefer to have as a teammate? What set of behaviors would you rather have in a work relationship and in your group meetings?

■ SIX FACTORS THAT DISTINGUISH EFFECTIVE TEAM MEMBERS

A team is a unique type of group in two important ways. First, a team has an objective—a specific goal that the team is trying to reach. The goal is usually thought of as a performance objective—that is, something the team is trying to *do*, rather than something the team is trying to *be*. And the performance objective is usually concrete or tangible: You can tell whether or not you have accomplished it. Teams are groups of people who design new products, stage dramatic productions, climb mountains, fight epidemics, raid crack houses, fight fires, or pursue an inexhaustible list of present and future objectives. Second, reaching the goal requires collaboration—a coordinated effort. Achieving the goal requires working together. Effective teams, then, are made up of members who are not only technically competent but also good at collaborating with one another to reach their common objective.

To shed some light on the specific qualities and behaviors that characterize effective team members, we collected 15,000 assessments of team members by their fellow teammates. We asked individuals two

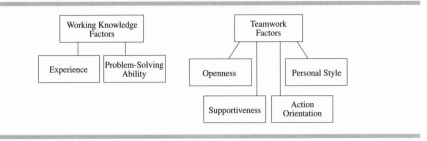

Figure 1.1. Factors That Distinguish Effective and Ineffective Team Members

questions: (1) What strengths does this person bring to the team? (2) What might this individual do to contribute more effectively to the team's success?

An analysis of these assessments reveals six factors that distinguish effective from ineffective team members. The distinguishing factors fall into two groups, as shown in Figure 1.1. The first group, "Working Knowledge," consists of two factors: *experience* and *problem-solving ability.* The second group, "Teamwork," consists of four factors: *openness, supportiveness, action orientation,* and *personal style.* Each of these factors is a key ingredient in a team's success—or failure.

Working Knowledge Factors

When it comes to helping a team reach its goal, the first two distinguishing characteristics that stand out among unusually effective team members are experience and problem-solving ability. Teammates who are important to their team's success are knowledgeable about the business they are in, and they are effective problem solvers. These two factors combine to form the quality we call "working knowledge."

Experience

Experience is the first thing a team looks for in its members. Whether the team is about to embark on cardiac surgery, mountain climbing, or building an airplane, once the goal is clear the question becomes "Who's been here before?" In other words, the team looks for practical knowledge that is relevant to its objective.

Typically, the team looks hardest and longest in the direction of the leader. The leader is usually there precisely because of his or her practical knowledge, breadth of experience, or record of success. But as the work continues, individuals rapidly discover that among the members of the team are those who know and those who don't, those who speak with the voice of experience and those who simply speak.

When team members are asked about their teammates' strengths and areas where improvements are needed, their comments highlight the value they place on experience.

EXPERIENCED

- Knows his business. Has a clear vision. (T4)
- The man has a wealth of experience and knowledge. (T68)
- Experience, sound judgment, good business sense. (T126)
- Long-term experience with international. (T128)
- Excellent grasp of our total technical capabilities and needs. (T175)
- Understanding of job and pulling together pieces to the big picture. (T278)
- Great technical background. (T360)

INEXPERIENCED

- Obtain more "product/business" knowledge. (T190)
- Poor functional knowledge. Tends not to see the big issues as she plows through the minutiae. Strategic issues are often avoided through lack of understanding. (T360)
- Develop an understanding of the business context in which decisions are made. (T375)
- Become more aware of the whole project picture. (T383)

Problem-Solving Ability

As a team's work progresses, another quality begins to emerge. Irrespective of their level of experience, some members of the team are good at solving the problems that inevitably arise as obstacles to a team's success. Problem-solving ability can be manifested in various ways. Some team members are adept at clarifying problems, bringing them into focus, getting them understood. Some are good at developing strategies for overcoming problems, figuring out what's likely to work and what isn't. Some know enough about the substance of the team's work to be able to make helpful or constructive suggestions about overcoming a problem. Whatever their specific contributions may be, team members who help the team resolve problems are seen as displaying strengths that keep the team focused on the issues and moving toward the goal.

> "Pay attention at meetings. You have a lot to contribute, but sometimes appear preoccupied with items other than the agenda."

PRODUCTIVE PROBLEM SOLVING

- Aggressive and proactive in problem resolution. (T126)
- Is an active, constructive participant in team discussions of operations issues. (T175)
- Tries to keep people together—focused. (T383)
- Provides thorough understanding of the key issues to the team and presents fact-based solutions very effectively. (T239)

On the other hand, ineffective approaches to problem solving typically involve carelessness, a lack of decisiveness, or an inability to focus.

UNPRODUCTIVE PROBLEM SOLVING

- Pay attention at meetings. You have a lot to contribute, but sometimes appear preoccupied with items other than the agenda. (T190)
- Research. Don't accept hearsay information. (T239)
- Stay more focused on the issue being discussed. (T298)
- Be more decisive. (T383)

Experience and problem-solving ability are the core competencies, then, that move a team toward its objective. It is easy to understand why these factors were identified early and often as characteristics of team members who are unusually effective in helping a team achieve its goal.

As important as these qualities are, however, they are not sufficient to make people effective team members. A recent analysis of what causes teams to get off track identified a variety of reasons why teams fail.[2] These reasons include people with private agendas working at cross-purposes; team members not getting along; an organization that is not really committed to a team philosophy; people being rewarded for the wrong things; people not knowing what they're supposed to do. We reached similar conclusions in our first book about teams. In *TeamWork: What Must Go Right/What Can Go Wrong*, we reported that when teams do get off track, the problems rarely have anything to do with technical expertise or content knowledge. Rather, teams experience their difficulties in the fundamental social competencies of working together effectively and productively. This brings us to the second set of factors identified by team members as describing those who contribute most to the success of teams.

Teamwork Factors

As much as team members value experience and problem-solving ability, they recognize that social competencies are essential for effective teamwork. More specifically, there are four "teamwork factors" that determine whether or not an otherwise competent and knowledgeable group of individuals will be successful in working together to achieve their common goal: openness, supportiveness, an action orientation, and a positive personal style.

Openness: The Basic Ingredient for Team Success

When team members describe those teammates who contribute most to attaining the team's goal, the characteristic that shows up most frequently is a pattern of behavior we call "openness." Team members who are open are willing to deal with problems, surface issues that need to be discussed, help create an environment where people are free to say what's on their minds, and promote an open exchange of ideas. These team members tend to be effective communicators, helping to create a climate in which communication flourishes and is used effectively to resolve whatever problems the team confronts to improve the team's performance.

The observations made by team members regarding the openness of their teammates focus on the ability to raise issues, offer a point of view, and be open to new ways of thinking.

"Be less defensive and more open to input from others."

OPEN

- Openly expresses his point-of-view. (T128)
- He is straightforward, and you don't have to guess what he's thinking. (T175)
- Willingness to bring up issues and offer possible resolutions. (T239)
- Willingness to discuss the delicate issues. (T298)
- Not shy about giving opinions and feedback. (T305)

Conversely, those team members who are not seen as open make it difficult to talk about the issues.

CLOSED

- Be less defensive and more open to input from others. (T297)
- Needs to be a little more open-minded, to try new ways of doing things. (T126)
- Be more honest with his feelings. He is unable to confront issues that are important to him. (T305)
- She is quiet and doesn't seem to interject ideas unless asked. (T390)

It may seem obvious that members of a team need to be able to talk with each other about how the team is functioning, how well the team is performing, who needs help, who sees problems coming that need to be addressed, and what they can do to improve their performance. Yet, whereas openness is the single most important feature of successful teamwork and collaboration, the very simplicity of the idea makes it easy to overlook or dismiss. In a previous book with Chrislip,[3] we published the results of a lengthy research project involving 52 cases of unusually successful collaboration. These cases were selected by the National Civic League, perhaps the most knowledgeable and informed organization about collaborative efforts in the United States. These collaborative efforts spanned a wide variety of objectives, time frames, and group sizes. Of the many features examined in these 52 cases, two properties were present in all the cases. These properties were labeled "a credible, open process" and "strong process leadership."

In a nutshell, the people involved in these 52 collaborative efforts were able to create and sustain a process in which people were free to say what was on their minds. Divergent points of view were listened to and valued; special interests were not in control; decisions had not already been made; people had confidence in their ability to have an impact on the root problem; and the group's leadership was committed to an open and collaborative process. These are the kinds of things that can make huge differences in the emotions and energies that characterize a team's efforts.

So What's the Problem?

For high-quality, lasting relationships, communication is important. For people to work well with each other on teams, they need to be able to talk things over. So what's the problem? Don't teams, in general, do a pretty good job of talking things over? The answer is absolutely not.

One of our databases provided responses from more than 5,000 team members to this question: "If you could discuss one issue in an open way, involving the team in the discussion, what would that issue be?" The overwhelming response from team members involved was the team's communication. Team members didn't trust each other to disclose the kind of information that was needed to solve the team's problems. In some cases, individuals were pursuing their own agendas rather than the team's goal—but no one was willing to deal with the problem. In other cases, the team leader's behavior was so degrading and alienating that the members of the team had become incapable of action. In still other cases, there was a performance problem with someone on the team and everyone knew it—but the leader wasn't doing anything about it and no one wanted to deal with the problem.

Problems of openness take thousands of different forms, but responses from team members point to some common themes. Here are the six categories of responses that occurred most frequently when team members were asked to identify one issue that they wished their team could discuss in an open way.

1. The communication climate. When we consult with or coach a team, one of the first things we assess is the team's communication climate. If people are inhibited, afraid to say what's on their minds, guarded, or generally apprehensive about talking openly with each other, then the team is likely to function at a level below its capability. Even worse, the team probably does not have the kinds of internal processes and emotional energy that will ultimately allow it to meet and overcome serious obstacles. Often fueled by low trust levels, the team is insecure or fearful about talking openly. Critical problems don't get discussed. People are inhibited about saying what's on their minds. Personal agendas fragment the team. Team meetings usually turn into fault-finding sessions.

2. Results. Team members are concerned about the quality of the product or outcome they are producing. Or they are unsure about what is happening with the outcomes, how their products are working, or what is being accomplished. Early warning signals are being ignored. The team's effort is being diluted by too many priorities.

3. Policies and bureaucracy. Organizational structure or politics are seen as deterrents to effective teamwork. Too many decision-making levels prohibit quick responses to problems. Territorial battles eat up time and energy. "We versus they" attitudes interfere with key relationships between the team and other groups. Organizational politics become higher priorities than the team's performance objectives.

4. Planning. Priorities are unclear or constantly changing. Goal setting and designing strategies to meet goals don't happen. The team is reactive rather than proactive. Forward-looking plans to meet problems, budgets, or scheduling are rare. Information is not shared in a timely manner.

5. Role clarity. Who does what? What is my role? What roles do other team members play? The lack of clarity appears in roles of self, of others, and often of the entire team as it relates to a broader objective. How the roles fit together and who deals with what kinds of problems are other issues in this category.

6. *Performance issues.* Someone is not performing well or is keeping the team from succeeding. Or people are denying their individual responsibility or accountability. Often the problem is seen clearly by everyone, including the team leader, but no one is dealing with it. Sometimes the problem involves the entire team's performance, but it is not talked about openly.

The "issues we should discuss" go on: the relationship between the team and other teams on a large project; the team leader is inhibiting performance or creating a defensive climate; problems with the performance feedback system. The key point is that the successful team has an open communication climate and is capable of dealing with any of these problems. The dysfunctional team has a communication climate that has closed down, rendering the team incapable of dealing productively with any of the problems.

So far we have been talking about the many routine, day-to-day problems that can affect a team's performance. If you want to get into the really dark side of closed communication, the following example will show how bad it can get. We did a post hoc analysis of an organization that was more than a year late and several million dollars in the hole on a set of units it was manufacturing for a large Department of Defense contractor. Everyone we interviewed in this organization told us the same story. There was long-standing hostility between the sales and manufacturing functions. The sales team had sold an ultra high-tech manufacturing process that the manufacturing function had already said it was incapable of delivering. Sales said, "We sold it; now you deliver it." Meanwhile, manufacturing did almost everything it could do to make the project unsuccessful and the sales function appear responsible. The project was so disastrous that it triggered a chain of events that ultimately led to the divestment of the organization. The people we talked to said that everyone in the organization knew what was happening but were afraid to talk about it. When we asked why, most people attributed the problem to a high-level manager who punished individuals for raising "negative" issues in meetings and whose personal motto was, "We have no problems here, only opportunities."

No matter how simple or simple-minded it seems, an open and healthy communication climate is not the norm—for relationships, groups, teams, or even societies. So when teams have members who are capable of creating the circumstances for surfacing, discussing, and re-solving problems, these people are extremely valuable members of the team. Moreover, their colleagues on the team recognize and value their contributions. As a matter of fact, these "open" team members are often acknowledged as possessing a valuable characteristic that many of us recognize as lacking in ourselves. This brings us to another reason why openness is the basic ingredient in team success: Teams are incredibly good at avoiding the "real problem."

The Passive Conspiracy

Often, teams engage in a passive conspiracy to avoid confronting the root cause of their dysfunction. By "conspiracy" we do not mean to imply that something overtly heinous is going on. Instead, an implicit and unspoken agreement emerges as a norm for the group. The implicit agreement may be to accept a condition as it is rather than to talk about it openly and address it directly. Even if the condition is one that affects the team's performance in a major way, ways are found around the problem.

There is some research that suggests that problems in organiza-tions are seldom approached in a problem-solving or collaborative man-ner.[4] Other ways of handling the problem predominate. People ignore the problem. Or they create activities and structures that maintain the il-lusion that the problem is being addressed. Or they accommodate by simply giving in to the conditions and avoiding them whenever possi-ble. Or they use the problem as a justification for adopting forcing strat-egies, attempting to impose some principle of power or position on each other.

We are amazed at the number of times we have encountered teams that operate under oppressive or stifling communication climates. Even more disturbing is the fact that when we've asked team members how long these conditions have been present, the response often translates roughly into "a very long time." The adjustments have been made, ac-commodations have been reached. The passive conspiracy is in place.

The conspiracy is not an intellectual one. Once, when working with a space exploration team that included some of the most competent scientists in the world, we were compelled to comment, "It doesn't take a rocket scientist to figure out that there's a problem here we need to talk about." Well, these were rocket scientists. Confronted by a science or engineering problem, they exhibited impressive abilities to identify the nature and dimensions of the problem; to locate sources of information to resolve critical issues associated with the problem; to identify people in the group who have had experience dealing with similar problems; to outline a variety of potential approaches for dealing with the problem; and so on. But if the problem involved humans rather than hardware, they were lost. As one team member commented:

■ He is less comfortable dealing with people issues than with technical issues. (T350)

Most problems that impair the performance of teams do not require superior or even above-average intelligence to solve. It's noteworthy that not once in our entire database is intelligence mentioned as a barrier to team success. The most complex problems besetting teams are rarely problems of intellect. Rather, they are problems involving emotions, attitudes, values, personal styles, and preferences.

For these reasons and many more that we will explore later, the basic ingredient for team success is openness. Individuals who are capable of managing their egos, surfacing problems, and creating a safe environment in which these problems can be addressed and solved give teams the basic competence they need to succeed. If, in addition to openness, the team also has members who exhibit the other three teamwork factors—supportiveness, action orientation, and positive personal style—then the team has the resources it needs to achieve unusual outcomes.

Supportiveness

The second teamwork factor that people see in effective team members is one that we have labeled "supportiveness." Although supportiveness can take many forms, at the core is a desire and willingness to help others succeed. Sometimes this means encouraging someone whose confidence is wavering. Sometimes it means placing a charitable interpretation on people's difficulties when they are trying but struggling. Sometimes it means figuring out how to help someone overcome an obstacle rather than taking advantage of a momentary failure. Sometimes it means defending someone who is being attacked. It always means putting the team's goal above any individual agenda, being easy to work with, and demonstrating a willingness to help others achieve. Whatever the specific behaviors, people who are seen as supportive are clearly interested in doing what needs to be done, in making whatever contributions they can so that the team succeeds. Team members characterize this strength in a variety of ways.

SUPPORTIVE

- Is dedicated to the team's success and wants what's best for the team. (T30)
- Works behind the scenes to aid the team. (T175)
- Willing to pitch in whenever necessary. (T298)
- Always willing to help out—a positive outlook. A willingness to take on more responsibility. (T360)
- Very easy to work with. (T383)
- Listens well to others' ideas. (T239)

By way of contrast, the nonsupportive team member is seen as focusing on "me" versus "we," often achieving objectives at the expense of others and usually appearing disinterested or insensitive to the concerns of other team members.

NONSUPPORTIVE

- Tends to run over people to get his job done. Doesn't seem willing to help with other people's projects when they overlap into his area. (T30)
- Be less controlling. (T68)
- Comes across as very "me" oriented versus "team" oriented. (T126)
- Get out and meet people in their office; make them feel they really count. (T175)

- Try to be more understanding of team members' feelings when he deals with a sensitive issue on the team. (T239)
- Invest more time to better understand others' perspectives. Be more patient when listening to others. (T291)
- Help his peers to excel. (T383)

"Invest more time to better understand others' perspectives. Be more patient when listening to others."

It is important here to be clear about what supportiveness does *not* mean. It does not mean that the supportive team member is a passive player who keeps his or her mouth shut, doesn't rock the boat, doesn't embarrass others by disagreeing with them, and doesn't make the team uncomfortable by suggesting that it could do better than it is presently doing. In short, the conventional notion of "team player" is not what we are talking about.

Supportiveness implies a much more active approach to the team in what it is trying to accomplish. Estimates vary, but we tend to agree with scholars who have argued or demonstrated that most of the significant work of a group is done by about a third of its members. Many people recruited onto teams are "social loafers,"[5] relatively passive members who let others do the heavy lifting. So the concept of team player often conjures up an unobtrusive person who goes along with whatever the majority wants. This notion of a team player is not even close to what team members tell us is the behavior of team members who contribute most to the team's success.

Supportiveness on the team also implies some degree of warmth or caring for each other. Warmth, affection, liking, and friendship are properties that are much more likely to be found in good teams than in poor ones. There is some recent evidence that old-fashioned notions about keeping friendship out of the workplace are ill-informed and extremely misguided.[6] In fact, friendships tend to move working relationships in the direction of higher quality and more productivity in work outcomes.

Supportiveness and Openness Together

Combining supportiveness with openness produces a cumulative effect that characterizes the most successful teams. The combination is key, because openness can go in either of two basic directions. We can use openness as an excuse for being caustic, insulting, psychologically cold and distant. In the name of honesty we can verbally slap each other around. We can obtain revenge for real or imagined past grievances. We can get even. So one way of being open is: "You want a little openness? I hope you can handle it. Are you ready? Here it comes." This combination—open and cold—can be destructive. The principle of openness implies that it is better to talk things over. The principle of supportiveness implies that it makes a great deal of difference *how* you talk things over.

The combination of openness and supportiveness takes the team in an entirely different direction. If team members can surface and discuss issues, that means things are likely to get better. And if the climate within which these discussions of problems occur is a supportive one, then the positive attitudes and the emotional energies required to sustain the collaborative effort through periods of frustration will be available to the team when it needs them. When we observe a team that is both open and supportive, we are very optimistic about the team's ability to handle any problems that come along.

Supportiveness, Aspirations, and Achievement

Research suggests that a group or team's performance level will be very closely correlated with its aspirations.[7] In other words, we usually achieve at the level we strive for. What we think we are capable of doing, we can usually do. As with many other aspects of behavior, most of it is attitude. The attitudinal climate of a team is more closely tied to its ultimate performance than almost anything else. Coaches and military commanders know that attitudes are often more important than tangible resources in determining outcomes. As the great general Dwight D. Eisenhower commented, "Pessimism never won any battle." In fact, one of the more highly regarded works on leadership identifies two of the most important functions leaders perform as "inspiring a shared vision" and "encouraging the heart."[8]

Early work on attitudinal climates of groups distinguished between "defensive" and "supportive" climates. Defensiveness is the opposite of supportiveness. A defensive climate is one in which people are inhibited, unwilling to share vital information, muddled, or unclear in their communication. Defensiveness is what results when people communicate in ways that are evaluative or judgmental, strategic or manipulative, condescending or superior. It is one of the primary contributors to dysfunctional group behavior.

Defensiveness is, for the most part, inconsistent with aspiration. Defensiveness implies energy invested in protecting oneself, digging in, putting up blockades, waiting for the attack. Aspiration implies setting high goals, creating new standards, doing things in ways that haven't been done before. Being open and supportive makes many things possible. Most importantly, it has a direct impact on whether team members will see an objective as achievable or not. Again, one of the best predictors of a team's performance level is the aspiration level of the team members. In the final analysis, what team members aim for and what they believe they can achieve strongly predict what they will actually do.

Action Orientation

The third teamwork factor that characterizes team members who are seen as contributing to their team's success is an action orientation. Not surprisingly, Bennis and Nanus found the same characteristic in their research on successful leaders.[9] Being action oriented means having a tendency to act, to do something. It also means encouraging others to take action. It means being willing to prod, to suggest courses of action, to be willing to experiment, to try something different.

Team members describe a distinct difference between an action orientation—a deliberate effort to make something happen—and a passive approach that favors waiting and hoping that others will do something about the problem or opportunity at hand.

ACTION ORIENTED

- Rises to the challenge. Achievement oriented. (T30)
- Reacts positively to immediate needs. (T175)
- Constantly has ideas to help the team bring in more business. (T278)
- An energetic worker, fast learner, organizes his work well, has courage to confront the issues. (T383)

PASSIVE

- Needs to demonstrate assertiveness and an active and enthusiastic investment in his role. Take a stand on issues. (T68)
- Take a more active role in team discussions of operations and issues. (T175)
- Procrastinate less. Take risks. (T278)
- Sometimes a little slow to act. (T297)

This is not routine action we are talking about. This is not the everyday, taking care of business kind of behavior. An action orientation falls more in the category of leadership, whether provided by a formally designated leader or by a member of the team. This is action that overcomes obstacles, breaks through barriers, and deals effectively with nagging problems.

Effective Teams Take Action

A couple of examples might help to illustrate the kind of action orientation that promotes team success. The first involves a "helpless" team in a tradition-driven, conservative financial organization. By "helpless" we mean a team that believes there is nothing it can do to significantly affect the condition under which it is operating. Team members believe this is the way it is; it's always been this way; it's always going to be this way; and there is nothing they can do about it. Whatever the problem is that's keeping them from functioning more effectively, it's outside of their range of control. When this happens to a team that is responsible for modifying and updating the entire product line for a financial services corporation, the future success of the company is seriously threatened.

This particular team was immobilized even further by the lack of a leader. Six weeks earlier their leader was moved to another position in the organization, and they were still without formal leadership. The team performed a very important function for the organization, and the importance of the team had contributed to the delay in designating a new leader.

In a very short time we saw this team turn around simply by "doing something." Team members identified the leadership roles that would be required for the team to succeed. They assigned individuals to these leadership functions. They wrote a job description for the team leader's position. They created a set of criteria to be employed in deciding who should fill the team leader position. They created a slate of candidates for the position. And they took everything to top management. Top management loved it. The moral is that the question with a helpless team is never "Are we doing the right thing?" The question is "Are we doing anything at all?"

The second example involves an "entrenched" team—a completely different animal. An entrenched team is one that usually performs well, even significantly above average. It's likely to have fairly confident people on it, often professionals or technically skilled people. Members of the team recognize that it's an above-average team. They begin attributing special status to the team and to themselves. They are good and they know it. They develop special relationships with each other, usually extending outside of the workplace. The down side is that their special relationships make them very close-knit, and they begin turning inward, ultimately isolating themselves from other teams or units in the same organization. They spend a lot of time complaining about the other individuals and units with which they connect. They start attributing blame for whatever difficulties they encounter to people outside the team.

We encountered an entrenched team whose relationships with other teams and units in the organization had completely eroded. Even some important relationships between the organization and its clients, and its relationship with other important organizations, had suffered to the point where the effectiveness of the organization, and its success, were jeopardized. We saw this team, led by a small core of its members, raise the problem constructively; develop a collective understanding of what happened and how it happened; and create a systematic program for acknowledging their own failures and for constructively rebuilding the team's relationships with other groups and teams. Of course, this kind of change will not occur unless someone surfaces the problem. Someone has to be willing to say "I see something happening that I think is keeping us from being as good as we can be." Once the situation is described, the team must develop a shared understanding of that situation, including how serious it is, and then decide what to do about it.

The First Law of Success

In the physical world, we have become accustomed to patterns and regularities that we depend on, often without thinking about them.

Regularities also govern the social world. Some things about human behavior are as predictable, or almost as predictable, as the events in the physical world. We have been observing one such pattern for years now, and we find it quite fascinating.

Consider two individuals, Allison and Kate. They have lived different lives and have learned different things from their experiences. Their personalities have been shaped by experiences of acceptance and rejection, the joys or agonies of growing up with different kinds of parents, successes and failures, and myriad other factors. As a result, confronted with the same situation, they look at it very differently. Allison sees the situation and talks to herself about what is possible: the ways she can succeed; the good things that can result if certain things are done well or right; the reasons why some kind of action makes sense. Kate, on the other hand, looks at the same situation and talks to herself about what can go wrong: the bad things that can result from doing things poorly or wrong; the reasons why certain courses of action won't work.

The interesting thing is that ever since Charles Morris's research almost half a century ago,[10] we have known that one or the other of these two views of the situation tends to prevail. That is, rarely are people likely to engage in a balanced comparison of both the good and bad outcomes. They are likely to see either the opportunity or the risk. So Allison and Kate sit in the same team meeting and respond to the same set of circumstances quite differently. Allison sees the problem, talks about it, tries to figure out what needs to be done, encourages other people to do something, and is convinced herself and tries to convince others that something that the team is capable of doing should be done and probably will work. Kate sits in the same meeting and tells herself all the reasons why the problem can't be solved and the action being contemplated won't work.

Now they leave the meeting, and a half hour later they are on their way home. On the way out of the building they see a job posting that represents what both of them would consider a terrific opportunity. Allison reads the posting and says to herself, "Why not?" It looks exciting. It's the kind of thing she's been wanting to do. She can do that job. And even if she doesn't get it, the process of going for it is going to be interesting and enlightening. Kate sees the same job posting and says, "Oh no." You have to know somebody to get a job like that. They have already got that thing all wired and lined up. They wouldn't pick her anyway. As a matter of fact, she is not sure she could do it even if they offered it to her.

Later that night the two teammates get together down at a club for a little music and dancing. At the end of the bar is a very attractive man. He's good looking, friendly, fun loving, a good dancer, mixes well with people.

Kate looks at the situation and says, "Oh my God. I couldn't handle it. I've never been any good at this kind of thing, he wouldn't be interested in me anyway. I'm not going to be rejected or make a fool of myself." Allison looks at the same situation and says, "Why not? Nothing ventured, nothing gained. Besides, the worst that can happen is he'll say no." So she walks down to the end of the bar and ends up on the dance floor having a great time with an interesting new acquaintance.

This scenario illustrates a law of human behavior that is as predictable as almost any law in the physical sciences. Simply stated, the law is: The guy is more likely to dance with you if you ask him. Or put another way: You're more likely to change conditions if you do something.

The reason why researchers keep finding an impulse toward action in leaders and successful team members is very simple. We are talking about two basic impulses: do something, or do nothing. "Do nothing" hardly ever changes anything. But "do something" changes the odds of success every time a new action is initiated. You try something, and then you step back and see how it's working. If it seems to be working, you figure out how you can sustain it. If it seems not to be working, you figure out how to increase the odds of it working. If it continues not to work and you abandon it, you learn what you can from the experience and try something new. As long as you continue to try something new, there is a good chance that you'll ultimately find something that works.

So the fundamental law of success is this: *Action is more likely to succeed than inaction.* That is why action-oriented people are so critical to the success of a team. The team can't solve the significant problems without them. These individuals change the odds in favor of success significantly and dramatically.

Personal Style

The fourth teamwork factor that characterizes effective team members is a positive personal style. As social scientists have known for a long time, there is a fundamental difference among people in terms of whether they convey a positive or negative attitude. Team members, too, are quick to notice that some people are energetic, optimistic, engaging, confident, and fun to work with.

POSITIVE STYLE

- Experienced motivator of people. He is a winner with a strong positive attitude and enjoys his work. (T4)
- Positive energy, new ideas, and lots of creativity. (T68)
- Has an infectious enthusiasm about the work. (T239)
- Gets along well with others. (T278)
- Well-liked, friendly. (T360)
- She makes everyone feel comfortable—staff, volunteers, donors, etc. I thoroughly enjoy sharing my day with her. (T390)

Others are cynical, defensive, hard-to-work-with whiners, who throw cold water on the noblest and most worthwhile of human impulses. It doesn't take more than one or two people with negative styles to seriously depress the emotional energy of a group or team. Cynicism, like a disease, constantly spreads, seeking new receptive hosts. The attitude and the behavior associated with it are contagious.

> "Be open to working with others to get the job done. Give the feeling of being approachable."

NEGATIVE STYLE

- Be a bit less competitive within the team. (T4)
- Be open to working with others to get the job done. Give the feeling of being approachable. (T33)
- Try to be a little more friendly. (T67)
- Develop more patience. (T68)
- Can be a little argumentative—lighten up and listen to the other guy's viewpoint. (T175)

- Don't always come across so negative. You have good points, but you could communicate them in a less angry manner. (T190)
- Reduce his "venting." (T291)
- He could be less cynical when making comments on various subjects. (T350)
- She is not a warm or outgoing person. She does not seem interested or willing to accept others' opinions or ideas that are not her own. (T390)

Almost all the social sciences have recognized that *behavior is contagious*. This principle operates by different names in different disciplines. It has been called "the interpersonal reflex," the "dyadic effect," the "norm of reciprocity," and "the lock-in effect," to name just a few. Although not always true, it is far more likely than not that people will treat you the same way you treat them. Smiles beget smiles; complaints provoke complaints; personal disclosures lead to further disclosure; and cynicism spreads faster than a cold.

How optimistic or cynical the climate of the team is greatly affects the first three behaviors of effective group members—openness, supportiveness, and action orientation. And that climate can be shaped and sustained by a very small minority of the members.

The problems posed by differences in the personal styles of the team members are complex and difficult. The issue involves what is often called "differentiation" versus "integration." Basically, the dilemma posed is whether we should celebrate individuals' differences so that everyone can feel comfortable with themselves the way they are, or whether we should pressure or require people to behave in ways more likely to promote collective success.

The fundamental choice goes back to the team's objective. If the team's objective is relatively trivial and the consequences associated with success or failure are relatively minor, then differentiation is certainly the way to go. Let everybody behave the way they want to behave, because people are pretty good at protecting themselves if the process becomes unduly painful. However, if the objective is vital and there are important consequences associated with success or failure, then some degree of integration is usually necessary. In particular, if cynical attitudes are draining off the emotional energy of the team, they must be dealt with. *How* to deal with these kinds of issues is the focus of the next chapter.

▪ BEING COLLABORATIVE: SOME CAN, SOME CAN'T, SOME WON'T

What team members tell us about effective and ineffective behaviors is, in many ways, straightforward and commonsensical. In fact, other researchers have discovered similar patterns to those we have identified. For example, Driskell and Salas found that collectively oriented members (team players) have a very different impact on performance than do egocentric members (nonteam players). Collectively oriented team members are more likely than egocentric team members to improve their own performance and to enhance the performance of their teammates.[11] Similarly, Cooke and Szumal discovered that across a variety of problem-solving groups, constructive individual styles—as opposed to aggressive and passive styles—are associated with higher quality solutions.[12] And some interesting research on high- and low-ability team members has found that low-ability members are at their highest motivation to perform better when they are explicitly told that their performance level will directly determine the level of success that the team achieves.[13]

Clearly, the attitudes, styles, and interaction patterns of team members have a direct impact on performance outcomes. We suspect that your own experience working with or on teams has brought you to a conclusion similar to ours. Some people are good at it, some aren't.

To be more precise, there is a continuum of collaborative attitudes and competence along which people tend to fall. At one extreme are the kinds of gifted people encountered during the three-year research project conducted on unusually successful, broad-based, community collaborations cited earlier in this chapter. Chrislip and Larson studied 52 successful cases, and in every single one of them there were individuals whom others identified, usually by name, as having been essential to the success of the effort. In many cases, those involved in the efforts stated that they would not have succeeded without these individuals. Sometimes these high-impact team members were professionals brought in from the outside. More often they were individuals who emerged from the group to exercise a strong leadership role over the process itself, maintaining an open and credible process, encouraging other people to express their views, exhibiting the kind of patience that helped people overcome the frustration involved in working together on complex problems. In short, they did all the things that leadership theorists mean when they talk about "encouraging the heart."

These people had the same doubts, uncertainties, and human frailties that we all have. But they made an effort to transcend their limitations rather than indulge them. They stayed focused on the problem rather than pursuing their own individual agendas. We have seen these people investing their energies in literally hundreds of teams with which we've worked. And just about everything worthwhile we've seen happen in teams originated in the mind of a single individual who then had the courage to express it.

A second group of people is more middle-range on many of the dimensions we have been discussing. They are people with good intentions and a desire to work collaboratively, but they have difficulty fitting their behaviors to their intentions or desires. Some are high-voltage style or fast-paced personalities who become impatient if people think too long or reflect too carefully on the options available to them. Some display the kind of self-confidence that borders on closed-mindedness; others seem fearful and reluctant to share ideas. Some may have grown up in confrontational, competitive families, have mastered that style reasonably well, and feel most comfortable in situations where their style provides an edge. In short, we've seen a lot of people who seem to have good intentions, and who genuinely want the group or team to succeed, but whose normal way of doing things creates obstacles to success. For some reason, things keep coming off track.

As a matter of fact, some of these people we really like, and we might even try to be helpful to them. We might give them some feedback; we might try to move them in the direction of some increased understanding of the impact they are having on others. Indeed, conclusions reported elsewhere, in a specific team context, show that if these well-intentioned people pay attention to the feedback from the rest of the team and actually try to do something to improve, then the rest of the team is likely to support them and to continue to value their membership on the team.[14]

Unfortunately, there is another group of people, at the other end of the collaboration continuum, who simply "won't." They come in various types. Some seem to have found a comfortable niche. They are into what Katz calls "stabilization."[15] Most of their time and effort is directed toward securing their position in the organization structure. They want to perform their job or manage their function effectively, and they will do it in a way that provides stability for them even if the consequences are disastrous for others and decrease the likelihood of the whole organization achieving its goal. These are people who each march to a drumbeat that only they hear. Their priorities are "me first," then the people around them that they rely on for security, then the rest of the organization.

A second type of noncollaborative individual is simply playing a different game. This is the person whose life experiences have led to the conclusion that other people are relatively easy to intimidate, made to feel defensive, kept off balance. Not only have these individuals grown accustomed to contention and strife, but they also have discovered they are a little better at it than most other people. If they see relationships in terms of winning and losing, they also win often enough to find the process of competing very rewarding. For these people, the principles involved in teamwork and collaboration range from annoying to downright stupid. Some of them even adorn their identities with anticollaborative proclamations. They enjoy being thought of as capable of intimidating others.

These individuals are usually overt about using people to achieve their own personal aspirations. They usually have a bloated ego and a thick skin. Sometimes their arrival offers an interesting change of pace, and their candid and blunt style can offer a breath of fresh air. But with this type of noncollaborative person, the breeze soon degenerates into a maelstrom, and in the eye of the storm is a competitive bravado: high control needs and a constant seeking of confirmation of their personal superiority. As you might imagine, often this is an issue of maturity. Although these individuals have moved into adulthood, they have retained some of the noncollaborative features of a child.

In the most severe case of those who "won't," the individual has placed himself or herself beyond the ethical and moral boundaries within which most of us live. We're not talking about criminal behavior, but rather about people who really do think they are better than others and have, therefore, been given some kind of almost divine latitude in using other people in particular ways, for their particular motives.

We have sat in meetings while these people bragged about how "their people" have worked every weekend and most evenings for the last six months. We've heard these people talk about the ones that matter and the ones that don't. We've seen them drive a wedge between other teammates and destroy any sense of trust that others held for one another. Perhaps you too have seen people who will sacrifice any sense of integrity just to maintain a personal advantage. These people embrace teamwork and collaboration only if it creates an illusion of fairness or equity. But they avoid genuine teamwork and collaboration because the outcomes are too unpredictable for them to maintain control.

Some can, some can't, some won't. Unfortunately, we are all part of the mix. We are all involved in the pursuit of objectives that are best obtained, and sometimes only obtainable, through the collaborative efforts of everyone. If we are dealing with people who are open, supportive, action oriented, and positive, the job is a whole lot easier. But given the incredible variety of people in the workplace, those we work with will have attitudes, behaviors, and personalities that blend with ours to varying degrees. So, in the next chapter we move up one layer of complexity and turn to the issue of team-based relationships and how they can be made more collaborative and productive. As we consider relationships, however, keep in mind that the quality of every relationship begins with the individual.

■ PUTTING IT TO WORK

Everybody thinks of changing humanity, and
nobody thinks of changing himself.

Leo Tolstoy

Now that we've summarized what 15,000 team members had to say about the behavior of their teammates, you may want to pause and reflect on how to apply their findings. One way to do this is to look at the Collaborative Team Member rating sheet we have created from our results (Figure 1.2). We've used this rating sheet ourselves, and some of the teams we've worked with have used it to give feedback to each

	1	2	3	4	5	

1. Inexperienced
- Lacks understanding of the business
- Inappropriate technical background
- Unsure what needs to be done
- Narrow perspective

1. Experienced
- Understands the business issues
- Appropriate technical background
- Knows what to do
- Understands the broader picture

2. Unproductive Problem Solver
- Uncertain of direction or outcome
- Avoids seeking input
- Indecisive
- Does not volunteer information
- Drifts

2. Productive Problem Solver
- Clear direction and expectations
- Consults with others
- Decisive
- Shares information in timely manner
- Stays focused

3. Closed
- Ignores Issues
- Silent
- Guarded
- Biased
- Doesn't listen

3. Open
- Surfaces issues
- Talks it over
- Straightforward and candid
- Open minded
- Listens

4. Nonsupportive
- Defensive
- Withholds effort
- Finds fault with others
- Commanding and controlling
- Rigid or inflexible
- Intimidating and competitive

4. Supportive
- Challengeable
- Helps the team
- Encourages others
- Manages ego and control needs
- Adaptable to changing team needs
- Makes it safe for others to contribute

5. Passive
- Waits for others to act
- Gives up quickly
- More of a spectator
- Avoids risk
- Safety in numbers
- Seeks easy way out

5. Personal Initiative
- Takes action
- Repeated efforts
- Likes being involved
- Takes risks
- Seeks personal accountability
- Sets high standards

6. Negative Style
- Draining
- Creates tension
- Emotional
- Self-focused
- Insecure
- Cynical
- Cold and distant

6. Positive Style
- Energizing
- Fun and relaxed
- Level headed
- Other oriented
- Confident
- Optimistic
- Warm and approachable

Figure 1.2. The Collaborative Team Member
SOURCE: © 1999 Frank M. J. LaFasto, Ph.D. and Carl E. Larson, Ph.D.

other. To begin with, you can use the sheet to explore your own potential for effectiveness as a team leader or member. As a team leader, you may also want to use this instrument as part of team training.

You'll notice that the broad dimensions that were covered in this chapter have been broken down into more specific items on the rating sheet. You can rate yourself according to how close to one or the other end of each continuum you think you are. Consider, for example, the continuum for "surfaces issues" versus "ignores issues." If you *almost always* surface issues, mark the 5. If you think you surface issues *more often than not*, mark the 4. If you think you are equally likely to surface issues and to ignore issues, mark the 3. If you think you ignore issues *more often than not*, mark the 2. If you think you ignore issues almost always, mark the 1.

When you have marked all the scales, go back over your responses and look for any 2s and 1s (especially the 1s). See if your self-ratings form a pattern. Pay particular attention to those ratings in which several items were rated 2 or 1 within one of the six broad categories. Think about the tendencies you seem to have toward noncollaborative behavior. In light of the general profile we have drawn of effective versus ineffective team members, what are your own strengths and weaknesses? What one or two changes might you want to make to be a more effective team member? How might you go about making those changes?

Having thought about your tendencies on these very important dimensions, as you see yourself, you may be willing to take a major step toward self-improvement. This step involves getting feedback from your teammates. Comparing your self-rating with those of your teammates will give you the most valid picture of how you do on these key qualities of good team members. The most important thing to keep in mind, if you ask for feedback from your teammates, is that the quality and, therefore, usefulness of the feedback is affected by how "truthful" their ratings of you are. You should create a process that guarantees anonymity and that allows your teammates to be comfortable with providing feedback. Perhaps using a third party to collect the feedback, one who is trusted by the team, will make it easier for your teammates to respond.

SNAPSHOT
2

Although the qualities of each team member form the basic building blocks of team success, how well members work together plays a major role in determining how effective the team will be. Our work with hundreds of teams has shown us that working well together does not come easily to most people. To find out more about what makes for productive team relationships, we gathered 15,000 assessments of team members by their teammates. We also asked team members to describe the strengths and weaknesses of the working relationships of their subordinates, peers, and supervisors—in effect, a 360° perspective.

In more than 35,000 such assessments, team members have told us that two behaviors stand out as consistent problems: *giving feedback* and *receiving feedback.* Put another way, the vital variable is the ability of a relationship to be constructively self-correcting.

To foster this key characteristic, Chapter 2 presents what we call the Connect Model. Used by more than 5,000 team members in a wide variety of organizations, the model offers a simple, step-by-step process for giving and receiving feedback and, ultimately, building more productive team relationships.

CHAPTER 2

TEAM RELATIONSHIPS

Simple and Easy Versus Complicated and Hard

The attitudes of the scientists and project team members were so depressed that you could feel them as a physical presence when you walked into the buildings. People were getting physically ill, coming to work depressed, uprooting their families, and moving out.

The results of our interviews clearly traced the problem to two high-level managers. These individuals managed two important functions for the organization—but they had problems with each other. The problems openly spilled over and cascaded down through the organization. Members of the two functions usually worked together on project teams. But if there were problems on the teams, the teams were prevented from resolving the problems themselves. The problems had to be taken up through the levels of the organization to these two senior managers, who would then make a decision and pass it down through the organization to the project team. If you were a member of one function and were caught talking or socializing with a member of the other function, you were in trouble. In fact, memos were circulated, listing by name, members of the other function to whom you were not allowed to speak! If a product or project idea originated in one function, the other function would try to kill it.

Unfortunately, the organization's products were closely tied to scientific research completed by the project teams. These project teams were typically grossly overdue and over budget. The product pipeline was drying up.

Sound familiar? One of the most common reasons why teams fail to achieve their potential is a problematic relationship. Individually, team members may be highly knowledgeable, competent, and well intentioned. But a team is more than a collection of well-intentioned individuals. At its core, it is an intricate network of relationships between two or more people interacting in pursuit of a common goal.

On paper a team looks rather tidy, with names and titles denoting special talents or expertise. In reality, however, the names and titles have faces, personalities, and feelings, as well as motives and agendas. An effective team results from these individuals coming together, identifying opportunities, sharing information, solving problems, and building collaborative capabilities. As your experiences have probably taught you, team relationship issues are highly complex. This situation is further complicated because we have lived our lives constantly immersed in relationships. We have had so much experience with so many kinds of relationships that we feel comfortable about our ability to function within them—even though we may often fall short of maximizing their potential.

The difficulty, of course, is that people vary in their ability to work well together. Long before we reached the full 35,000 assessments of relationships in our database,[1] we noticed something about the data. Of the 19 behaviorally anchored dimensions we studied, two surfaced as consistent problems: giving feedback and receiving feedback. The mean scores on these items were well below those of the other 17 items. This same pattern emerged from the 12 quantitative team member ratings in the 15,000 assessments of fellow team members, with feedback once again appearing as the lowest competency. In other words, as reflected in the following comments by team members, the most common relationship shortcoming revealed in our data is the ability to be self-corrective in a constructive way.

■ We need to give feedback and confront each other more directly. (Team 368)

■ We need a climate of feedback between peers and from our leader. (T150)

- We must learn to constructively criticize each other's performance. (T4)
- People must be more open about the way they feel and more comfortable giving honest criticism to peers, subordinates, and superiors. (T400)
- Create a level of trust to foster mutual feedback. (T7)
- Team members are often reticent about approaching one another to resolve differences. (T116)

Tandem to this observation, we noticed a surge in the number of people asking for outside intervention to resolve team relationship problems. One recent study, polling 150 executives from the nation's 1,000 largest companies, noted that work relationship issues have doubled during a 10-year period. According to the study, 18% of management time was wasted on resolving workplace personality conflicts during 1996, compared with 13% in 1991 and 9.2% in 1986.[2] Relationship problems in the workplace have been found to be associated with absenteeism,[3] damage and waste,[4] and decreased organization commitment.[5] You could probably add a few more to the list, based on your own observations. Relationships are so critical that it's easy to understand how a survey of 500 professionals revealed that "95 percent agreed that pay and benefits were not the main motivators in their decision whether or not to stay with a job. The key issue was the ability to develop trusting relationships with upper management."[6]

"Create a level of trust to foster mutual feedback."

Heaven forbid if any shareholder of any company or any donor to any institution should ever quantify how much money is wasted in organizations on relationship disorders! May they never know how progress is impeded by issues not addressed properly, or information not transferred effectively, or problems not resolved rationally—all because two individuals cannot deal with each other effectively. A dysfunctional team relationship brings a high cost—both tangible and intangible—to the team and the organization it serves. Moreover, such relationships are frustrating to everyone who must watch them and deal with the fallout.

There are many examples of organizations that have suffered tremendously, or even failed, because they never found a constructive way to address serious relationship issues. The case described at the start of this chapter is not unusual. Other examples may be more or less dramatic, but debilitating nonetheless. As you may have observed, it takes only one ineffective relationship to get in the way of a team's success.

Conversely, effective relationships, built and nurtured over time, are apt to "be there" in a supportive way, at some critical moment in the future when a team might need to discuss a difficult issue or address a crisis in a rational way. Why is this so crucial? Because, as the old adage goes, "When you really need a friend, it's too late to make one." Indeed, effective team relationships are the best insurance against hard times. In fact, the acid test of an effective relationship is whether it will contribute to the solution or add to the problem during a trying time.

All of our research, as well as empirical observation in working with more than 1,000 teams, have led us to a hard-and-fast conclusion: Healthy team relationships are characteristic of unusually successful teams. And bad team relationships are the most frequent source of the destruction of a well-intentioned team effort.

With these kinds of findings it was natural for our attention to be drawn to the question of how to improve team relationships, and more specifically, how to improve the process for giving and receiving feedback that stood out as the single greatest deficiency. Drawing on our database, available research on relationships, and our field observations with hundreds of teams, we developed a simple process we call the Connect Model, which is described later in this chapter. To date, this process has been tested and used by more than 5,000 team members in 15 organizations. We believe that it provides a valuable tool that you can use to significantly improve your own team relationships.

■ GOOD VERSUS BAD RELATIONSHIPS

What is a good relationship? How does it differ from a bad one? To make this distinction, we ask you to invest 60 seconds in the following exercise. Take a sheet of paper and divide it into two columns, as shown in Figure 2.1. Now, think of the best relationship in your life. It might be a work relationship, a friendship, or an intimate relationship. It could be a current relationship or one from your past. Once you

Best Relationship	Worst Relationship
•	•
•	•
•	•

Figure 2.1. Characteristics of Good and Bad Relationships

have focused on this "best" relationship, write down three words that describe it.

Next, focus your attention on your "worst" relationship, whether past or present. Write down three words that describe this relationship. Take a minute to complete this exercise before you read on.

We have conducted this exercise with thousands of people. If you're like most of them, you probably included such words as *trusting, caring, helpful, open, honest,* and *respectful* among your descriptors of the best relationship you've ever had. Conversely, the list of characteristics of your worst relationship probably included such words as *unreasonable, unfair, selfish, threatening,* and *inflexible*—words that stand in stark contrast to those that describe your best relationship.

Our research has led us to make four overarching observations. First, good relationships are *constructive* for both people. They embrace characteristics that acknowledge and protect the value of the relationship to both parties. They are mutually respectful, honoring the feelings of both people. They embody trust and, because they are non-threatening, offer a sense of safety.

Second, good relationships are *productive.* When necessary, they allow us to focus on real issues—the ones that matter—and to do so in a way that makes a difference. They rarely cause us to waste time and energy on defensiveness because they rarely force us to face anything we feel we need to defend. Instead, good relationships allow us to stay centered. They bring out the best in us—the best in our thinking, our attitudes, and our values—increasing our effectiveness as a coworker, spouse, parent, or friend.

Third, good relationships are characterized by *mutual understanding.* They encourage us to focus on and understand the other person's perspective, and they offer us the satisfaction of being understood. Good relationships emphasize mutual clarity and minimize the frustration of uncertainty.

Fourth, good relationships are *self-corrective.* Both parties are committed to making adjustments that will improve the relationship. There is confidence that any agreed-upon changes will be honored mutually, not in passing, but in concrete, observable terms.

These four observations form the foundation for the Connect Model, the step-by-step relationship-building process presented later in this chapter. Bad relationships, as you might expect, produce opposite effects. Rather than being constructive, they are destructive, with one or both parties typically bending the relationship to their own benefit. There are usually threatening undertones and reasons for defensiveness that, rather than allowing us to remain centered, take us out of our rhythm, inhibiting our ability to be productive or hit our stride. Clarity is replaced by ambiguity; we don't really understand each other or each other's underlying motivations. And bad relationships are not self-corrective. Either the real issues cannot be discussed, or promises and commitments are unaccompanied by concrete changes.

> "She needs a far more positive attitude toward other team members and to improve her rapport with others in the group."

- He does not listen to others or value any of the other team members' input. He is not focused on our team's goals and has been very detrimental to our team since he joined it. (T360)
- He could be more open to listening to what team members say. His way is not always right. Sometimes he comes across as though he thinks he knows more than other team members, when in fact other team members know just as much. (T278)
- She needs a far more positive attitude toward other team members and to improve her rapport with others in the group. (T350)

Good relationships bring people closer together over time. Bad relationships eventually result in minimal or total elimination of contact. Did you walk away from the bad relationship you described earlier? Our experience tells us this happens about 80% of the time. After all, we come to know and define ourselves through relationships. We are attracted to those who bring out our best and are polarized from those who force us onto an alternate track of behavior.

▪ WE THINK WE ARE BETTER AT RELATIONSHIPS THAN WE REALLY ARE

In biblical terms, it's much easier to see the mote in our neighbor's eye than in our own. In other words, it's difficult to find fault with ourselves, and this can make it hard to grapple honestly with issues in relationships, whether on teams or in other parts of life.

If you are an introspective person, you probably spend a good deal of time trying to understand why you have the feelings you have and why you behave the way you do. In your pursuit of self-discovery, you may find yourself seeking professional advice, risking true feelings with a close friend, reading self-help books, or simply contemplating the kind of person you are. You probably struggle to understand the influence people and circumstances have had on shaping who you are: the presence or absence of parents, grandparents, or siblings; the effect of losing a family member or loved one; the impelling nature of an alcoholic parent; the effect of divorce; the pressures associated with wealth or poverty, or with an overachieving or underachieving environment; or perhaps the effect of some traumatic event that changed your perspective.

Such influences have made each of us different. But our attempt to understand these influences underlies our common struggle to confirm that we are, or at least can be, healthy and happy individuals. It is our effort to believe that all of our experiences, the good and the bad, have somehow led us to be a good person who is trying to do the right thing in the right way. The catch is that everyone else believes this as well.

The responses of team members in our research reveal a glaring difference between how people see themselves and how others with whom they share a work relationship see them. The self-assessments of more than 4,500 people, as compared with the 360° assessments of them by more than 35,000 other people, reveal that people rate themselves far more favorably than they are rated by others.

Our findings clearly suggest that most people believe they are better at relationships than they really are. Even as you read the words,

"We think we are better at relationships than we really are," you might tend to remain detached and nonreflective. You may say to yourself, "You're right. In fact, I know a lot of people like that!"

It's difficult for most of us to think that we can be part of the problem in a relationship. We are predisposed to believe that we are more constructive in our approach to relationships and more effective with our skills than we really are. We readily bestow more credit on ourselves for our ability to build a relationship than others would acknowledge. In addition, our research strongly suggests that, even when we are aware of our interpersonal shortcomings, we still believe they are not as severe as others find them. Indeed, we have a built-in inability to recognize how we might be responsible for a relationship falling short of its potential. When we do acknowledge a personal shortcoming, we tend to minimize its role—figuring that those people who know us well should be willing to make a minor adjustment, "cut us a little slack" to make the relationship work. For all of the good qualities we bring to a relationship, our shortcomings are a small price for anyone to pay.

This observation suggests an inherent problem in relationships—the tendency to take our role in a relationship for granted. This tendency, in turn, can cause the relationship to be less than desired, typically without either party having a clear understanding of why it isn't better. For the most part, objective introspection regarding team relationships simply is not our forte. We encourage you to grapple honestly with this tendency as we explore what team members have to say about their relationships.

■ WHAT TEAM MEMBERS SAY ABOUT TEAM RELATIONSHIPS

In an attempt to add clarity to the process of building effective team relationships, we explored team members' viewpoints on three practical questions.

1. What behaviors are most important in a team relationship?
2. What is the greatest challenge in a team relationship?

3. How do you increase the odds of building and sustaining a collaborative team relationship?

Here is what they told us.

Question 1. What Behaviors Are Most Important in a Team Relationship?

If you were to ask enough people to describe what's important in a relationship, you would find an incredible variety of behaviors deemed as absolutely critical. Their experiences would offer up such insights as "It's important to be equal partners." Or "It's important to trust each other." Or "You have to share the same interests and activities."

We addressed the question, *"What behaviors are most important in a team relationship?"* in three ways. First, we gathered data on more than 35,000 work relationships in a variety of organizations. These relationships were both peer and hierarchical. The relationship assessments focused on a consistent set of 20 dimensions of interpersonal capability, as well as open-ended suggestions for behaviors that would improve the relationship.

Regardless of whether it was a working relationship with a peer, a superior, or a direct report, the result was the same. The two factors identified as most important were *openness* and *supportiveness.* As you may recall from the discussion in Chapter 1, openness refers to the ability to surface and deal with issues objectively. Supportiveness refers to bringing out the best thinking and attitude in the other person.

Second, we examined a random sample from 15,000 assessments of team members by fellow team members in terms of the behaviors that contributed most to, or interfered most with, the success of the team. Once again, the top two behaviors cited were openness and supportiveness.

Third, although the consistency of our results was dramatic, we wondered to what extent our findings agreed with those of other researchers. After all, over the years, thousands of social scientists have devoted millions of hours to the study of relationships. To better understand the cumulative insights from this body of research, we performed a meta-analysis of those empirical studies conducted during the past 20

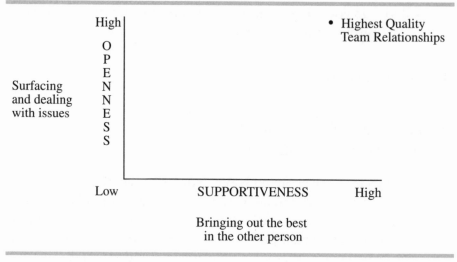

Figure 2.2. Two Factors of Collaboration

years that measured quality, performance, or both in all types of relationships.[7]

The results of the meta-analysis identified two factors critical to the success of any relationship as measured by satisfaction with the relationship, accomplishment of the relationship's objectives, or both. The first factor identified was the quality we have described as openness. Some of the studies refer to this behavior as a willingness to communicate, some studies as communication frequency, others as the ability to raise an issue. The second factor identified by the meta-analysis was supportiveness. Some of the studies refer to this behavior as acceptance of other people, other studies as the confirmation of the worth and value of others and, still others, as showing affection toward others.[8] However the behavior was described, it always focused on the deliberate attempt to treat others positively, to make them feel confident about themselves, and to try to bring out the best in their abilities.

The results are clear and compelling across all three analyses. The two most important behaviors for building and sustaining a collaborative team relationship are the synchronous presence of openness and supportiveness (see Figure 2.2). It is the ability of two people to talk over the real issues in a way that brings out the best thinking and attitude in each other. So important are these two relationship factors, they continue to determine the quality of relationships as long as we are alive. Degman has found, in examining the relationships between elderly parents and their care-giving daughters and sons, that even in the last stages of life, the quality of the relationship varies dramatically with capacities of the individuals to surface and deal with issues in an open and caring manner.[9]

Question 2. What Is the Greatest Challenge in Team Relationships?

Openness and supportiveness: If the path to collaboration is this simple, and this obvious, what's the problem? The problem is dealing with contention.

There are many things in life that are hard to do well: playing a sport or musical instrument; balancing work and family needs; achieving financial security. But all of these demands, challenging as they are, pale by comparison with doing well at managing some difficulty between you and someone else, a problem that makes it hard to work together effectively. Notice, that we said this is difficult to *do well*—not taking a blind stab at it, or taking care of it by ignoring it, or venting to others, or striking back.

Two reasons make it difficult to deal with contention, and these involve the inherent pitfalls of openness and supportiveness. Openness, unfortunately, is a painful process. Most of our experiences with openness are negative because they usually occur while managing contention. They deal with giving and receiving feedback, or trying to resolve differences or, in exasperation, finally stammering out some deeply guarded feeling.

Openness is usually experienced with some degree of tension, and most of us prefer to avoid such tension. If there is a problem, we prefer to ignore it or hope it will go away on its own or through the efforts of others. Let's face it, it takes time and emotional energy to deal with tough issues in a relationship. Most people in organizations feel it's not what they are supposed to be doing. They say, "All this process crap is not how I'm supposed to be spending my time!"

The second reason it is difficult to manage contention focuses on an inherent pitfall of supportiveness. The desire to bring out the best thinking and attitude in the other person is in continuous struggle with, and is often compromised by, our ever-present urge to be defensive. All of the issues that interfere with or draw attention away from collaboration begin with behaviors that arouse this impulse to be self-protective.

- If each of us were less defensive, we would all benefit. (T332)
- We must be able to challenge each other more without becoming defensive. (T76)
- Many of us are very defensive and not very open to criticism. (T436)

"We must be able to challenge each other more without becoming defensive."

It is an unavoidable truth: Our basic nature wants us to remain safe, to feel confident, to be in control. No one wants to feel threatened. No one wants to feel attacked. No one wants to have to defend *anything*. And when we feel attacked and hemmed in, our response is often more primal than rational.

The two most common forms of defensiveness are, ironically, very opposite behaviors: counterattack or withdrawal. This is the famous "fight-or-flight" syndrome. We get most intense and are most apt to be defensive about issues important to us, especially when the outcome is not what we think it should be, or when our sense of fairness has been violated. It is at this point that we may feel compelled to fight—to counterattack. Almost always, the counterattack will escalate into a head-knocking disagreement. Alternatively, we may choose to flee—to deal with the threat by withdrawing from the confrontation. Although this defensive behavior is passive, it is just as debilitating to teamwork and equally potent at stifling collaboration. Because the essence of collaborative teamwork is the ability to identify, raise, and resolve issues in a way that integrates different perspectives, the folded arms response of withdrawal—like counterattacking—squelches any hope of an open and supportive process.

Both counterattacking and withdrawal draw attention to themselves as extreme behaviors. They divert energy away from real issues and take over the communication environment. In either case, the interaction, rather than rising to collaboration, degenerates into senselessness. Let's face it, it's too confusing to unravel a legitimate issue or manage a feedback process while engaged in the swordplay of defensiveness. Suddenly the issue changes from whatever was under discussion to a struggle for self-preservation. New ideas don't come forward, and simple issues don't get resolved. Rarely can we bring out the best in someone, let alone change his or her mind, by aggravating or silencing that person.

The question is, where does our justifiable passion for a point of view end and defensiveness begin? The answer lies in our willingness to soften or even change our stance on an issue when presented with more compelling information. As with many behaviors, the problem is that we don't always know where to draw the line. This point brings us to the value of feedback from others.

Feedback Is a Gift

Somewhere along the way every relationship requires an adjustment to get back on track or to meet growing expectations. In this regard, feedback is a gift. As the slogan goes, "Friends don't let friends drive drunk." If a teammate is headed down a path that may be debilitating for the team, it takes caring and courage for a fellow team member to step into the tension and offer a "gift" by pointing it out. Likewise, it takes courage and maturity to accept the gift of feedback with a sense of appreciation. As team members recognize, this openness is the opposite of defensiveness.

- Be more open to feedback, rather than being defensive. (T4)
- Take more time to listen to what people are saying. (T239)
- Be more open to constructive feedback and less defensive. (T291)

Received in the proper frame of mind, feedback is simply finding out something about oneself that others already know. The gift is the opportunity to do something about it.

As you probably know from your own observations and experiences, such an ideal outcome is rare. Typical approaches to feedback usually devolve rather quickly into some version of "I'm right. You're wrong. Here's why!" Such approaches to feedback rarely work, and when they fail the price can be the relationship itself. In fact, most of us "resort" to giving feedback only when the situation is so bad we are willing to risk the entire relationship to try to save it.

Our difficulty with openness and our natural tendency toward defensiveness explain why traditional feedback doesn't work well or often enough. The openness of feedback is threatening. Imagine that you are told that your manager wants to see you because he or she has some "feedback" for you, without any indication whether the feedback is good or bad. Chances are your hands will become clammy; your heart rate will increase; or you will feel the need to get up and walk around. These are telltale signs of an approach-avoidance syndrome. You want to know what the issue is and get it over with, but at the same time you don't want to face anything negative. And if your manager anticipates resistance to whatever the feedback is, he or she may experience some of the same reactions. Feedback typically is performed under a cloud of anxiety for both the recipient and the giver.

Supportiveness is compromised because people's skills at giving and receiving feedback vary greatly. Sometimes we know the right thing to say when giving feedback; other times we blunder horribly. We may know the right words but struggle with our explanation, only to invoke defensiveness and exacerbate the issue we're trying to correct.

Similarly, the way people receive feedback varies. Most of us have attempted at one time or another to give feedback to someone who is very important to us, only to find that his or her response to our well-intentioned attempt was highly defensive. As the receiver of feedback, it's easy to argue with and intellectually complicate the message: "I don't understand. I don't know what you mean. How can you say that?" In fact, when all is said and done, the receiver actually has more control over the success of the feedback than does the giver.

In short, feedback is threatening. It is difficult to give well, and it is hard to receive objectively. Indeed, the ability to give and receive feedback constructively is our greatest deficiency in relationships. This is especially troublesome when we consider the importance of feedback in working relationships. Good feedback is associated with a heightened sense of personal accountability,[10] a wide range of worker satisfaction factors,[11] and enhanced performance, especially in groups whose goals demand extensive interpersonal relationships.[12] Because feedback is the lifeblood of growth in a team relationship, we need a set of tools that will move us closer at the end of an attempted relationship adjustment, not farther apart.

From Poorly Managed Contention to Dysfunctional Behavior

> *A long dispute means*
> *that both parties are wrong.*
>
> Voltaire

What begins as a "small" failure to deal with issues openly and nondefensively can soon spiral into something much worse. When contention between two or more individuals is poorly managed, a team relationship can become dysfunctional, putting the entire purpose of the team at risk. Unfortunately, it happens often enough that the behavioral tendencies are fairly predictable. Publicly, the relationship problem is usually ignored or openly denied, and dysfunctional feelings are suppressed. It is typical for one person to avoid the other or for both people to avoid each other. (Interestingly, an avoidance approach to the relationship problem is usually exacerbated by the presence of diversity, such as gender, race, or culture.)[13] Interaction is minimized and usually strained. Communication becomes less direct, finding its way through alternate routes like voice mail, e-mail, memo, or even other people.

When both people find themselves in the same team meeting, their communication tends toward one of two extremes. There's either a superficial conversation filled with polite insincerities or a contentious atmosphere thick with tension, messages within messages, and unusual attention to all the "interpretive cues"—facial expressions, eye contact, vocal intonation, strategic pauses—that accompany the words exchanged. At such a moment, teamwork becomes theater.

It's only fair to note that at one time or another, each of us has felt the need to keep our true feelings hidden for the moment. We may have put aside feelings that our work was unappreciated drudgery and instead played the role of the admiring, devoted subordinate. Or we may have set aside feelings of anger over the way someone was treating us at the moment and reacted matter-of-factly to their behavior so as not to unravel our poise. We have all had roles that may have required a momentary adjustment in our openness and candor.

The focus here is a bit different. We are referring to the dysfunctional team relationship—not an acute, momentary difficulty between two team members, but a chronic team-relationship problem. Such relationship theatrics, no matter how well acted, are always a barrier to collaborative teamwork. They impede authenticity. A bad team relationship cannot be made good with public efforts at deception.

Whereas all of this occurs publicly, privately each person in the dysfunctional relationship seeks understanding somewhere, usually with another team member who is willing to serve as a sympathetic listener. This person gets to hear the uncut, X-rated version of the frustration. But such sympathetic listening soon translates into taking sides. Soon people are privately pointing fingers at others on the team, and eventually the team process is fractured.

At this point, the team's primary reason for existing—to identify, raise, and resolve the real issues that will move the team toward its objective—becomes compromised. Personal agendas come into play, and the team loses its objective, line-of-sight focus on its goal.

Apart from the disappointment of suboptimizing the team's talent and usually underachieving the goal, other team members always report severe frustration with such situations. They know the negative impact the dysfunctional relationship has on the team's ability to achieve, and they report feeling helpless while watching it unfold, unable to do anything about it. They're also resentful, and often angry, that the team leader didn't act soon enough, if at all, to prevent the dysfunctional relationship from undermining the team's effectiveness. Furthermore, if the team is an ongoing one, such as an executive management team, damage from the dysfunctional relationship can cause years, and even entire careers, to be marked by frustration, conflict, anger, and resentment.

So what's the best strategy for preventing this kind of dysfunction? The answer lies in preparation: Cultivate the ability of a team to make use of available insights for integrating thinking, giving and receiving feedback constructively, and managing differing perspectives. This leads us to our third and final research question on team relationships.

Question 3. How Do You Build and Sustain a Collaborative Team Relationship?

You will recall that the four underlying characteristics of good relationships are (1) they are constructive; (2) they are productive; (3) they embrace mutual understanding; and (4) they are constructively self-correcting. Thus, whenever we attempt to establish a new relationship or strengthen an existing one, it is important first to understand how the relationship measures up in terms of these four attributes.

To be more specific, intuitive assessments of specific interactions can give us a quick feel for how a relationship will or will not develop. Our research suggests that the following four questions form the basis for assessing the degree to which an interaction contributes to building a good relationship.

1. Did we have a constructive conversation? One of the first and most important observations we make during a conversation that is intended to build a relationship with another person is whether or not that individual affords us respect as a person. This largely determines whether we feel good or bad about a conversation once it has occurred. Were our feelings honored or trampled? Was our conversation couched in an atmosphere of trust or caution? Did we feel threatened, or was it safe for us to say what was really on our mind?

2. Was the conversation productive enough to make a difference? The second judgment we make is whether the issue we are dealing with is real or fluff. It is important for us to know that we are dealing with an issue that can really make a difference in the relationship or the task at hand if it is resolved positively. When all is said and done in a conversation, our intuition tells us whether we have identified and dealt with a "bull's-eye" issue or merely danced around the perimeter of the dartboard. Did defensiveness throw us off track, or were we able to stay focused? Did we feel that we were operating at our best?

3. Did we understand and appreciate each other's perspective? The third requirement for building a relationship is that each person understand and appreciate what is being discussed not only from his or her own perspective, but also from the perspective of the other person. It is seldom sufficient and rarely gratifying to reflect on a one-sided conversation. It also is disturbing when the other person shows little interest in or appreciation for our perspective, or puts little effort into helping us understand theirs. Once again, we know when we've walked away with just half a loaf of bread.

4. Did we both commit to making improvements? Last, we judge whether there is reason to believe we both will work at making the relationship better. When the conversation is finished, we intuitively assess whether we each will do what we said we would do. Is there reason to believe in a better future? It's important to be able to trust that the relationship can be self-corrective. This is best fulfilled when we know we have agreed on concrete changes, and we have committed to monitoring our progress.

You may notice that these four requirements for building a relationship reflect our assessment of how open and supportive an interaction *was* with a person. Our observations are post hoc and past tense. That is usually how and when we notice such dynamics. They draw our attention when we were not in a respectful or trusting conversation; when we did not deal with the real issue; when we were not given a chance to be understood or never received sufficient explanation to understand the other person; when we walked away knowing nothing would really change—that it was just a lot of words. Unfortunately, at that point it is usually too late to improve or even salvage the relationship.

On the other hand, anticipating and understanding the four requirements allows us to use them as a road map for building a collaborative relationship in a constructive way. This perspective forms the foundation of the Connect Model.

■ THE CONNECT MODEL: A PROVEN APPROACH TO BUILDING EFFECTIVE TEAM RELATIONSHIPS

The Connect Model is a step-by-step process for building and sustaining collaborative team relationships. It has been tested with several thousand working relationships in 15 different organizations.

The Connect Model aims to do two things simultaneously. First, it recognizes a relationship for what it really is—a paired experience between two people, not merely the demonstration of individual interpersonal skills. It is a process we do *with* someone, not *to* someone. Second, it is an attempt to use the four requirements for building a relationship as a proactive map to guide us toward a constructive conversation,

FOUR REQUIREMENTS	PROCESS MODEL
1. Can we agree to have a constructive conversation?	Commit to the relationship. Optimize safety.
2. Can our conversation be productive enough to make a difference?	Narrow the discussion to one issue. Neutralize defensiveness.
3. Can we understand and appreciate each other's perspective?	Explain and echo each perspective.
4. Can we both commit to making improvements?	Change one behavior each. Track it!

Figure 2.3. The Connect Model and the Requirements for Building a Relationship

rather than using the four requirements as an after-the-fact assessment of whether the conversation did what we hoped it would do.

In short, the Connect Model is an attempt to let our behavior catch up with our knowledge base. Figure 2.3 shows the elements of the model and how they correspond to the four requirements for building positive relationships.

As the model indicates, having a constructive conversation begins with two things: committing to the relationship and optimizing safety. When you commit to a relationship, you apply all the good qualities of that best relationship we asked you to think about earlier and avoid all the negative qualities of your worst relationship. In good relationships, people commit to the relationship by defining their place *in* the relationship, not over it. Any relationship in which the other person thinks he or she is more important than the relationship itself will not work. People optimize safety by committing to avoid doing anything that makes the other person feel uncomfortable and to work to understand what the other person has to say.

The second requirement for building a productive relationship also occurs in two ways: by narrowing the discussion to one issue at a time and by neutralizing the defensiveness. Each of us has some topics that, to us, are like a red flag to a bull. It's important to understand what will cause defensiveness in the other person and agree to avoid those subjects.

In this connection, it is important to acknowledge that language and attitude can either facilitate or inhibit an open discussion.

Facilitative language fosters a trusting climate, helps bring issues to the surface, and furthers the discussion. Examples of *facilitators* include the following:

- "Help me understand why you feel the way you do."
- "Please tell me more."
- "How so?"
- "What can I do to make our relationship better?"
- "Let me see if I understand what you're saying."

Facilitators, accompanied by a desire to improve the relationship, contribute to positive feelings and lead toward workable solutions.

Conversely, *inhibitors* restrict our willingness to acknowledge real relationship issues, lead to distrust, and create awkward discussions. Examples of inhibitors include:

- "You have no right to feel that way!"
- "What's your problem?"
- "What you have described is your fault, not mine."
- "I think you're making something out of nothing."
- "Sorry, that's just the type of person I am."

Unlike facilitators, inhibitors create a defensive atmosphere, generate negative or mixed feelings about the relationship, and lead to makeshift solutions that typically come unraveled.

The goal is to bring as many facilitators to the discussion as possible and to minimize the influence inhibitors might have on the relationship. Such a focus can shorten the distance between our good intentions and the behaviors that influence the results we are seeking.

The third requirement for building a relationship is mutual understanding. We create mutual understanding by explaining and echoing—explaining what we're saying and echoing what the other person is saying. This basic ability, referred to as "perspective taking" by social scientists, is fundamental to effective communication. There isn't much point in talking about relationship issues if neither partner is capable of seeing the other person's point of view. The parties must each be capable of stopping themselves—stop concentrating on their own position; stop listening to their own inner voice; stop rehearsing in their minds what they are going to say when it's their turn to talk; stop long enough to hear and understand the other person.

It isn't necessary to agree with the other person, although a willingness to agree always helps. But each person does need to be capable of *understanding* what the other person is saying. If neither partner can see the other's perspective, then "talking it over" doesn't necessarily make it better. Without a conscious effort to understand each other's view of a shared issue in the relationship, one or both people will believe their perspective is the only one that matters—a sure dead end. Perspective taking is fundamental to the process of adjusting and strengthening any relationship.

The fourth requirement in relationship building is that the relationship is self-correcting. In behavioral terms, this means committing to improvements by agreeing to change one behavior each and then tracking the changes. It's important to note that both people should agree on the behavioral change each person will make. Rarely do we embrace a change if we feel it has been handed to us or forced on us. Even the smallest behavioral change must make sense to both people as a useful adjustment, one that is in the best interest of the relationship.

In terms of tracking improvements, it's helpful to establish two or three checkpoints spaced appropriately over the following weeks or months. Such checkpoints should only take a few minutes if things are going well, longer if further clarity or renewed commitment is required.

The Connect Model: Step by Step

We will now walk through the Connect Model in more detail, step by step, to show how two people who want to build a relationship *together* can do so in a constructive way. For the sake of simplicity, we will imagine that you are applying the model to one of your own relationships (incidentally, a good way to really learn it), even though you may also use it as a training device for people on teams. We will also look at the model from the standpoint of the person who is initiating the conversation about some aspect of a relationship. Keep in mind, things are likely to go best when both people are familiar with, and adhere to, the same process.

As you work through the model, keep in mind that, in practice, these things may take you a little out of your rhythm. They may seem unusual. They may seem funny or make you feel a little uncomfortable. But if you give them a try, the benefits far outweigh any such discomfort. And if you are like the thousands of team members who have used the model, you should find any adjustments fairly easy to make.

We should explain that when we conduct training for companies, we give participants a laminated card that lists the steps in the Connect Model. We tell people to use the card because they should have enough respect for each other not to leave the conversation to chance and risk a worse relationship. If the conversation is left unstructured, you risk not getting the results you desire.

Step 1: Commit to the relationship. The first step is to commit to the relationship. Whoever opens the discussion signals commitment and invites it from the other person: "Sally, we have an opportunity to address an issue that would strengthen our relationship. Would you be willing to discuss it with me?" You can use your own words, but that's the essence. Then the other person can either say, "Yes, I would," or "No, I wouldn't." From our experience, it is rare that someone would say, "No, I don't want to have a better relationship with you." But if that does happen, we recommend that you reiterate your good intentions and leave the door open in case the other person changes his or her mind. If the other person does agree to have the conversation, you don't have to have it at that moment. You might schedule a time the next day or two days down the road. But you each commit to having a conversation because you know there is an opportunity to have a better relationship.

When you do sit down to talk, the first thing to tell the other person is *why you believe this is worth doing* and that *you are willing to work at it.* Don't talk about the issue; talk about the relationship first. That's what is most important. The issue will get solved one way or another. The relationship is going to go on. It will either be better or worse based on this conversation. Again, you may want to choose your own words but, essentially, you're saying, "I really value the opportunity to work together, and I am willing to invest my effort and energy to make the relationship as good as it can be."

Step 2: Optimize safety. After you commit to the relationship, help the other person to feel safe. Tell the person that *you will do your best not to* *make him or her feel defensive during the discussion* and that *you will make an effort to understand and appreciate his or her point of view*: "Sally, I want you to know that I will do my best not to do anything that makes you feel 'less' during this conversation. And I will do my absolute best to understand whatever it is you're going to tell me."

Creating this safety component is essential. It also is probably the most difficult step in the process. It may make you feel a little like you're getting married. It will likely make you feel a little awkward. But once safety is established, the rest of the process becomes easier.

Step 3: Narrow to one issue. At this point, you've established the platform for the conversation. The next step is to *identify one issue in a nonthreatening way.* It could be how you treat each other in meetings; how you keep each other informed; how you involve each other in discussions; how you show respect toward each other; the level of trust in your relationship; or how you each view different parts of the business. Notice the emphasis on "each other." The key is to state the issue in a nonthreatening way. Using "we" language can be a step in this direction. If you phrase the issue as "Sally, the issue I would like to talk about is how you treat me in meetings," you're inviting a defensive reaction. You're also signaling that you've already fixed the "blame" for what is going wrong on the other person. Instead, you can say, "Sally, the issue I would like to deal with is how we treat each other in meetings. Can we talk about that?"

Of course, sometimes you do need to confront someone's behavior. But even then you can use "I" language to express how you feel when the behavior occurs, rather than accusatory "you" language that puts the emphasis on the other person's capability. So you might say, "The issue I'd like to talk about is that I often feel put down in meetings, and that's really uncomfortable for me. I'd like to share with you the things I perceive that leave me feeling this way."

Step 4: Neutralize defensiveness. Before you have your conversation, think about those *words, comments, examples, or ways you might treat this issue that could make the other person defensive.* Then, when you do have the conversation, *ask the person to let you know if you do make him or her defensive* so you can discuss it before defensiveness itself becomes a full-blown problem.

You: Sally, is there anything I should stay away from during this conversation that might make you feel defensive?

Sally: Yes. I don't want to hear about that meeting we had the other day on strategy.

You: I can stay away from that. Anything else?

Sally: Yes, don't pin any labels on me in this conversation. I hate it when people do that to me.

You: Okay, no problem.

Sally: Is there anything that I can do so you don't feel defensive during this conversation?

You: Yes, there is one thing, Sally. Don't interrupt me or cut me off. Let me say what I have to say.

Sally: Sure, I can do that.

Step 5: Explain and echo. Next, tell the other person *what you observe, how it makes you feel, and the long-term consequences.* For example:

You: What I observe, Sally, is that you have a tendency to interrupt me in group meetings. In the budget meeting the other day, for instance, I had an idea that I tried to bring up a couple of times, and each time you interrupted me, and I had to wait. Eventually, the idea came out, but maybe we could have gotten to it sooner if I had been given a chance. It makes me feel less valued, like my ideas don't have a lot of merit. It makes me feel frustrated because I can't seem to get my ideas on the table. And I'm starting to feel resentful. The consequences are, if we don't change this, I don't think I'm going to want to be in meetings with you in the future.

Now check to see if the other person understands you. *Ask the other person to echo what you just said.*

You: So, Sally, what are you hearing me say?

Sally: Well, what I hear you saying is that I interrupt you in meetings. You gave me an example of that, and it makes you feel frustrated, not very valued, and kind of resentful. Is that right?

You: Yes, but you missed something—the consequences. If we don't do something about this now, the level of severity is such that I'm probably not going to want to be in meetings with you.

Sally: Ah, you're right. You did say that.

Then *ask for the other person's perspective.*

Sally: What I observe about this issue is that you talk so slowly, I often wonder if you're taking a breather or if you're finished. It's very frustrating for me because I tend to talk kind of fast, and sometimes I find myself finishing your sentences for you. I can't seem to get into the rhythm of the conversation. Then when I do, you slow things down again, and I never know if you're taking a pause or if you're done. As a consequence, I think it's going to get worse before it gets better if we don't do something about it. What are you hearing me say?

You echo back to Sally what she observes, what she feels, and what the consequences are. Once the two of you arrive at a mutual understanding of the issue, you're ready for the next step.

Step 6: Change one behavior each.   At this point you have had a constructive conversation leading to a mutual understanding of the issues. Now you're going to talk about what to do about it. What improvement can you make? If you each put your ego aside, what can you do that will be in the best interest of your relationship? In the best interest of the team? In the best interest of the company? Sometimes it involves changing a specific behavior—a way of acting, communicating, or even reacting. At other times, it might involve simply being more open-minded about an emotional or contentious issue—being a more thoughtful listener and looking at the issue from the other person's perspective.

If the conversation is going well, either of you might initiate this step. For example:

Sally: Let's both figure out what I can do differently.

You think about it for a minute and give her a couple of suggestions.

You: Maybe you could ask me if I'm finished. Or maybe you could jot down your idea if you're not sure I'm finished, so you don't forget it, and interject it later.

Sally: I can do both of those things.

You: What can I do?

Sally: Maybe you could give me a sign when you're finished. Look at me and smile or something.

You: I can do that.

You now have a strategy going, a way you can each approach the issue under discussion. "Let's each commit to doing these things," you say. Sally agrees.

Step 7: Track it!   To ensure that your mutual commitment is fulfilled, the final step is to track your changes in behavior. Pick some dates to check out how things are going. Maybe it's once every two weeks, once a month, once a quarter—whatever you decide. It can be done in person or even over the phone. For example, Sally calls a month later.

Sally: How are we doing?

You: We were doing great until that planning meeting last week.

Sally: I did interrupt you in that meeting, I know.

You: As long as you recognized it, Sally, that's okay with me.

As should be apparent, there is a flow to the Connect Model. You and your partner in the discussion focus on each other first, then on a single issue that you have framed in a nonthreatening way. The flow then leads you through an effort to understand and appreciate what you each observe, and how it makes you feel, and what the consequences are. You then each assume personal responsibility for correcting the relationship in an ongoing fashion.

The simplicity of this approach merely reflects the positive aspects of our "best" relationships. It is a process that helps us "stack the deck" in favor of a positive experience because we care about the relationship. Figure 2.4 summarizes the process in action.

How To Proceed/What To Say

Commit to the Relationship

Why do I believe this is worth doing?
- I value our relationship and would like it to be as good as possible.
- There is much we can accomplish together.
- We can learn from each other.

Am I willing to work at it?
- I am willing to invest my effort and energy to make our relationship better.

Optimize Safety
- I will do my best not to make you feel defensive, or make you feel "less" because of how I handle this conversation.
- I will make a rational effort to understand and appreciate your point of view.

Narrow to One Issue

Identify one issue in a nonthreatening way.
- I believe our most immediate/important opportunity is in the area of . . .
  —How we treat each other in meetings.
  —How we keep each other informed.
  —How we involve each other in decisions.
  —How we show respect toward one another.
  —The level of trust in our relationship.
  —How we each view . . . our marketplace, product development, and so forth.

Neutralize Defensiveness
- What are some ways I might treat this issue that would make you feel defensive? What words, comments, or examples should I avoid?
- If I do make you feel defensive, please let me know so that we can discuss it before it becomes a problem.

Explain and Echo

Explain what you observe, how it makes you feel, and the long-term consequences.
- I *observe* . . .
  —When we are doing "something" together . . . , or,
  —When you do/don't do "something" . . .
- It makes me *feel* . . .
- I believe the long-term *consequences* are . . .
- I feel there is a solution to this, but first let me *check* to see if I was clear and if you understand what I'm trying to convey to you.

Echo what the other person has said.
- Let me see if I can describe your perspective and your feelings.
- Do I understand?

Change One Behavior Each
- In light of our discussion, what reasonable change should each of us commit to making? Let's agree on one stop/start behavior for each of us.

Track It!
- What would be the most useful way to monitor our progress?

Figure 2.4. The Connect Model

SOURCE: © 1993 Frank M. J. LaFasto, Ph.D. and Carl E. Larson, Ph.D.

▪ THE BENEFIT OF THE CONNECT
MODEL TO TEAM RELATIONSHIPS

The Connect Model is designed to satisfy the definition of collaboration offered earlier: the integration of different perspectives in order to arrive at an agreeable solution to a problem of common interest. It is learned and practiced two by two, and works best when both people want to have a relationship and want to work at it. It also provides a safe climate for exploring issues and feelings in a way that emphasizes mutual understanding.

As applied to teams, the Connect Model shatters the traditional paradigm of team member relationships, which relies on individual skills, a haphazard match-up of interpersonal expectations, a hope that objectives will not be too conflicting, and a deep-down desire that two people will like each other enough to want to interact. The Connect Model goes beyond an emphasis on the individual and focuses on the process overarching the relationship.

Traditional team processes represent a paradigm of anemic preparation. With little or no guidance, team members are expected to figure out how to discuss tough issues, deal with peer problems, and often strive for excellence under less-than-adequate leadership. The only way to get beyond the past is to eliminate the process that got us there and all of the unempowering, uninspiring baggage that accompanies it. What is needed is a new process that is stronger and more durable, one that can sustain a neutral balance when dealing with difficult issues, a process that encourages confidence by its accessibility.

The Connect Model offers three promising features in this regard. First, it is a process based on the benefits of preparation. It is a rational guide that gives team members practice at surfacing and handling issues collaboratively. It is a concrete process, to be drawn on any time. It gives team members a simple collaborative approach and an ongoing readiness for working together constructively.

Second, the Connect Model takes team relationship problems out of the shadows. It accepts any issue and breaks it into its most salient and rational parts. It allows the issue to be discussed safely, exploring facts and feelings, without risking everything for the sake of a single opinion or event. It ensures mutual understanding and never loses sight of its end objectives—the best interest of the team, the organization, and the customers served.

Third, the Connect Model is much more than a skill. It is a process. It is not done to someone, but with someone. It focuses on the collaborative responsibility of each team member, each relationship within the team, and group dynamics. It requires everyone on the team to be well versed in and held accountable for the expectations and behaviors required personally, in one-on-one team relationships, and within group settings to sustain a collaborative climate.

Now that several thousand people in various types of businesses and organizations have used the Connect Model, we offer a simple set of conclusions regarding team relationships.

1. The presence of a structured approach for discussing difficult issues is always better than a random discussion.
2. The approach works best when both people understand it.
3. Both people must *want* to work through an issue in a constructive way that preserves the relationship.
4. Practice at a structured approach makes team members and teams stronger and prepares them for managing greater challenges more collaboratively.

The Connect Model is a fairer, more rational, more open, and more supportive process than the hit-or-miss crapshoot most of us step into every day. It replaces the blur of hindsight with the clarity of foresight. When a team possesses the genuine confidence that accompanies a reliable process for addressing relationship issues, it has the capacity to grow trust in new and profitable ways. As you might easily imagine, strengthening trust at the team relationship level, one-on-one, affords tremendous benefits, especially during group problem solving, which we will explore in the next chapter.

▪ PUTTING IT TO WORK

Think of a relationship you have with a team member that could be better. Plan a conversation—in writing—using the steps of the Connect Model. Think through each step, make notes that allow you to be clear on what you are trying to convey: from your intentions, to your observations, to your feelings. When you have worked through each step on paper, review your notes to see if anything you have planned is likely to make the other person feel defensive. If so, change your plan to reduce the chance that defensiveness will cause the conversation to come off track. Make sure your plan reflects your good intentions to improve the relationship.

Once you are comfortable with your plan, ask your teammate if he or she would be willing to have a conversation with you in which the two of you might strengthen your working relationship. Agree on a time and place: enough time so that the conversation is not hurried, and a place that is sufficiently private.

Remember, although your plan allows you to be clear and confident about what you want to say, your greatest opportunity to improve the relationship is by listening carefully to your teammate. Avoid being defensive yourself and guide the conversation in a mutually beneficial way.

SNAPSHOT
3

A major part of any team's work consists of solving problems to advance the team toward its goal. Team problem solving, however, is often an uncertain and complex process. To better understand what makes some teams effective problem solvers, we randomly sampled 1,400 team members from our database of 6,000 individuals.

Team members tell us that three key factors differentiate effective and ineffective teams: the degree to which team members are *focused* in their efforts; the quality of the *climates* in which they operate; and the extent to which their *communication* is open or closed.

To shed light on how these three differences affect team problem solving, we present a simple model of the *problem-solving dynamic*. This model tells us that success is much more likely if the team's goal is clear and compelling and if the team's various energies are focused on the goal in a positive way as it solves problems.

Our own experience tells us that teams are most effective at problem solving if they follow a structured approach. In Chapter 3, we offer a five-step process we call the Single Question Format. Two brief case histories provide real-life examples of how this approach has helped organizations address significant challenges by productively channeling and focusing their problem-solving efforts. Finally, we comment briefly on the added problem-solving complexities faced by cross-functional teams and how to deal with team-related process issues.

CHAPTER 3

TEAM PROBLEM SOLVING

Raising and Resolving the Real Issues

George McLeod was a member of the 1985 men's Mt. Everest climbing team. At base camp, which was at 17,800 feet, McLeod made an observation: The tents were too far apart. He knew the 20 team members were highly dependent on one another for the success of the climb and, indeed, for their own lives. They had to work together closely. Mt. Everest must be climbed in increments. It takes teamwork to move climbers and resources up the mountain. But McLeod, an experienced climber, could see there were issues—both team and technical—that needed to be raised and resolved at base camp. As McLeod put it,

> The expedition never met as a whole team of 20 people until we actually met at base camp on Mt. Everest. We had an assortment of new faces with unknowns. When we arrived at base camp we came in three groups, and we dug out a platform to set up our tents. People were camping on their own. We were not about to be part of a team. There were people on the expedition that I hardly knew, and I was there for almost three months. If you are not getting along with somebody, you're going to avoid him. If you don't deal with it, it can get in the way of working together to reach the top. Nobody can take Mt. Everest alone. You have to climb it together. If there are issues, you have to deal with them. It's as simple as that.

The men's mountain climbing team got within the last 800 feet of the peak. But they failed to reach the summit. Talking over the challenges that eventually kept them from their goal—reaching the top—might have improved the odds of success.

Whether they are trying to scale Mt. Everest, find creative ways to capitalize on e-commerce, or improve customer satisfaction, teams exist to solve problems to achieve a goal. As you can probably testify from your own experience, however, the complexity of group behavior often makes problem solving in teams an unpredictable experience. Teams and groups are complex to the point of testing patience and defying comprehension.

A major reason for this complexity is the diversity of team members' behavior on the dimensions we have already discussed. Different team members can be more or less open or closed in their willingness to communicate, supportive or nonsupportive in their treatment of each other, active or passive in pursuing the goal, positive or negative in their attitudes and energies. These and a number of other factors affect their working relationships with each other, pushing and pulling them through issues of control, coordination, understanding, feedback, and endless degrees of connectedness. When you put all those personalities and propensities, all those interpersonal needs and foibles into a group or team, the permutations are potentially dizzying. Advertising legend David Ogilvy reflected this often muddled tendency of collective effort when he penned the following poem[1]:

> Search all the parks
> In all your cities.
> You'll find no statues
> Of committees.

All teams, then, experience a collision of people, motivation, and ideas. But it is precisely the diversity of viewpoints that makes teams worthwhile. Team problem solving is not harmony; it is the constructive integration of diverse perspectives. Productive team problem solving consists of sharing different perspectives and shaping them into a reasonable decision. Good teamwork involves an understanding of how this integration occurs.

This chapter explores how teams can most effectively channel their various inputs and energies to identify, raise, and resolve those issues that they must resolve to advance toward their goal. We start by looking at the key factors that differentiate teams that are good at problem solving from those that are not. We then present a simple model that helps to explain how those differences affect the problem-solving dynamic. Finally, we offer a practical, step-by-step approach to problem solving that has been shown to work effectively across a wide range of organizations and circumstances.

■ WHAT FACTORS DISTINGUISH GOOD PROBLEM-SOLVING TEAMS?

To better understand what makes some teams better problem solvers than others, we randomly sampled 1,400 team members from our database of nearly 6,000 individuals and looked at what they said whenever they characterized effective and ineffective teams. Their perspectives suggest that three key differences consistently separate those teams that are productive and successful in solving the problems they encounter from teams that are less successful: differences in *focus*, in *climate*, and in *communication.*

Focus

The first distinguishing mark of effective problem-solving teams is focus. Effective teams are very clear about what they are doing at each moment in their work. Whether they are discussing a topic, considering a problem, weighing an idea, or testing a model, this process focuses their attention on the task at hand, much as a lens focuses light. The team members concentrate their thoughts on a single problem, issue, objective, or strategy. They are working together.

An ineffective team, on the other hand, is unfocused. Team members readily recognize when their effort is diffused.

- We need to stay focused on our goals. (Team 380)
- Increase the amount of focus we bring to bear on the most critical priorities. (T364)
- Focus priorities. Too many "new ideas" at once. (T436)
- Who is responsible for keeping the group properly focused? (T492)

"We need to stay focused on our goals."

It is often hard for a casual observer to tell exactly what an ineffective team is doing. The goal or performance objective isn't clear. The team doesn't seem to be following any systematic strategy. The discussion topics, though often interesting, don't seem to relate to anything in particular. Sometimes one gets the feeling that the team is just killing time until the meeting is over. There is very little pooling of effort or concentrating of energy. The most obvious pattern is a series of individual acts and utterances that are fundamentally unrelated to each other.

Climate

The second factor that distinguishes good problem-solving teams is climate. With rare exceptions, members of effective teams describe the atmosphere of the team in positive terms. The team is relaxed, comfortable, informal, fun, warm. Teams that are good at problem solving have a way of making their members feel accepted, valued, and competent.

Members of poor teams, on the other hand, tend to describe the climate as tense, overly critical, political, cynical, inhibiting, cold, or too stiff and formal.

Several factors contribute to a debilitating team atmosphere. Often a bad team climate is the result of individual team members elevating their personal agendas over the team's goal.

- The "my world" attitude has had a negative effect on our ability to be collaborative. (T176)
- A key team member injured the team by being very oriented to personal goals rather than team goals. This has had a very

negative impact on the team and fragmented the team's cohesiveness. (T360)

■ The majority of team members have their own agendas and are too concerned about their own power base to contribute effectively. (T126)

■ If team members would put the "team objectives" above personal objectives, this would lead to more trust. (T128)

Just as often, a bad team climate is due to the influence of politics.

■ Political issues keep us from achieving our goals. (T28)

■ Remove hidden agendas and political influence from objectives. (T371)

■ Team meetings are posturing sessions. (T126)

■ We should have decisions made on our P&L versus political considerations. (T552)

Ultimately, however, team members trace the causes of a bad team climate to the dysfunctional behaviors of specific individuals. Often the root cause is found among the team members themselves.

■ Eliminate the dysfunctional behavior. We have one member who tries to make himself look better by publicly putting other people down. We have another who loves the sound of her own voice. We have several members who collect a paycheck but add little or no value to the organization. (T400)

■ Cut out the dissension. (T197)

■ Remove two team members. They are truly standing in the way of having an excellent, cohesive team. (T436)

Unfortunately, a bad climate can also be traced back to the personal style of the team leader.

■ The team leader needs to be more open with the group. He needs to share the process of decisions and not keep so much to himself. (T28)

- Less politics and favoritism by the team leader. (T405)
- Get our team leader to trust people. (T156)
- We spend too much time reacting to the whims of the CEO. We need to become more proactive based on what is needed in the business. (T176)

Whether team members blame personal agendas, the politics of the organization, dysfunctional behavior on the part of individuals, or failures of leadership, ineffective teams usually have bad climates. Their efforts to solve problems are stymied by an atmosphere that is negative, cynical, and harbors some degree of animosity.

- Negativism breeds losers. We are not losers!!! (T28)
- We have a tendency to be overly cynical. (T140)
- The attitude of the team is one of animosity. (T96)
- Get people to have a positive attitude and not focus on the negative. (T420)

Communication

The third factor that distinguishes good problem-solving teams is a property that seems to describe some of the more positive features of all human relationships, from intimate relationships to organizations to governments: open rather than closed communication.[2] If something is interfering with the team's performance, it gets talked about. People say what's on their minds. Importantly, however, these discussions tend more toward problem solving than venting. The issues get surfaced within the context of the team's performance.

In contrast, teams that are less effective at problem solving tend to be aversive. Team members don't like to talk about problems. They would rather wait and hope the problems disappear. Communication is closed. Often it is inhibited by an aversive leader or by the memory of painful experiences in which such discussions have been managed poorly and have resulted in long-term negative fallout for the team. As team members recognize, an inability to talk openly about critical issues can lead to no decision or a bad decision.

- Team members are willing to let a function falter, rather than present differing views or confront issues head-on. (T188)
- We have decisions based on reasons not openly discussed. (T168)
- I feel, and sense in others, a reluctance to raise issues. (T184)
- We hesitate to challenge one another's thinking on ideas to avoid embarrassment. (T150)

The communication differences between good and poor teams, especially openness, have long been recognized as important factors that are directly tied to effectiveness or performance measures.[3] More recently, research involving problem-solving groups,[4] tactical teams,[5] and, especially noteworthy, global business teams[6] has found communication and openness to be linked to positive team performance outcomes.

> "We have decisions based on reasons not openly discussed."

Focus, Climate, and Communication as Pervasive Issues

Our own research and experience with teams suggest that these three differences between effective and ineffective problem-solving teams—focus, climate, and communication—are key differences for all types of teams. Interestingly, these three differences appear to have little to do with how smart the members of a team are. It's noteworthy that not once in our entire database is intelligence mentioned as a barrier to team success. There are some consistent factors that make a difference in *how* teams work together to solve problems, but raw intelligence doesn't seem to be one of them.

Nor is rank in an organization. When we divided our database of teams into upper and lower quartiles to measure how well top management teams work together collaboratively to achieve their objectives, nearly all of the executive management teams fell in the lowest quartile of collaboration.

In our work with hundreds of executive management teams, we are coming to appreciate why this is the case: The members of executive management teams are all experts who, intentionally or unintentionally, are difficult to challenge. Members of executive management teams are themselves leading and managing their own major parts of the organization. They got to the top because of a healthy belief in their own judgment and abilities. Getting such a group of accomplished experts to appreciate the nuances of working together collaboratively is a leadership challenge. In addition, members of executive management teams, by and large, receive little feedback from their team leader, typically a CEO or president, that focuses on their collaborative style. We have found that people in executive management teams do not always, or even often, demonstrate the collaborative behaviors we have come to associate with effective team problem solving.

In summary, differences in focus, climate, and communication help explain why some teams are productive in solving problems, whereas others fall short of the mark. A closer look at the dynamic of problem solving will show why these differences matter—and also point the way to achieving greater success in solving problems as a team.

■ THE PROBLEM-SOLVING DYNAMIC: GOAL, ENERGIES, AND THE DECISION-MAKING PROCESS

Problem solving in teams has a dynamic that we believe can be captured in terms of a simple model involving two main elements: the team's goal and the energies that either are focused on the goal or drain away for a variety of reasons. (See Figure 3.1). In our experience with teams, most cases of success and failure can be understood in terms of these elements.

The focal point of our model is the team's goal. In our earlier research, we found that the single most important determinant of a team's success is a "clear and elevating goal." We came to this conclusion after talking to members and leaders of some of the most successful teams in recent history—heart-transplant teams, mountaineering teams, space exploration teams, new product development teams. Others who have studied groups and teams have reached the same conclusion with a consistency that approximates consensus. The goal is what it's all about; it is the reason the team exists.[7]

The path to the goal, however, is likely to be strewn with a series of often complex problems that involve both substance and process. Successful teams, we have discovered, are able to focus their energies in a

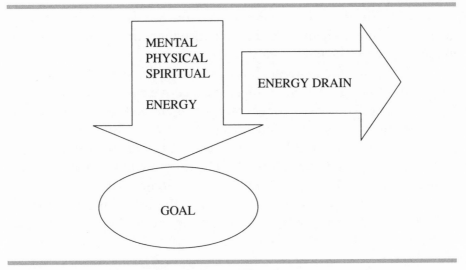

Figure 3.1. A Model of the Problem-Solving Dynamic in Teams

productive way to solve these problems. They both create and operate in positive environments. Unsuccessful teams, by contrast, allow their energies to be drained away in pursuit of peripheral issues. They often operate in negative, highly political environments in which there are winners and losers and success is comparative, coming only at the expense of others.

The ability of successful teams to focus energy on the goal can be observed in the processes they use for solving problems and making decisions. Successful teams have a more disciplined approach, which allows them to raise issues constructively, focus their energy on facts, and invite and reconcile differing perspectives, while their effort remains productive and aligned with the goal. Unsuccessful teams, on the other hand, are far less structured and much more random in their approach to solving problems and making decisions. A closer look at the elements of the model helps clarify why this is so.

The Goal

In our earlier work, we discovered that goals that are compelling to individuals and that unify team members in their commitment—giving them a sense of common identity and shared values—are the ones that are most likely to lead to extraordinary outcomes. Not surprisingly, goals vary immensely in the extent to which they draw us toward them, in the degree to which they are compelling.

Some goals, for example, have an almost magical ability to elicit hard and purposeful work. Think of the creative energy contributed by scores of people—actors, dancers, costumers, set designers, musicians—coming together as the curtain rises on opening night. Some goals elicit almost saintlike selflessness. Think of the public health workers who put themselves at risk, often without acknowledgment, in the front-line fight against disease. Some goals, like space exploration, inspire great effort even though the payoff is far in the future. And some goals derive their power from childhood dreams nurtured into adulthood: putting out fires, solving homicides, performing surgeries.

Goals may be compelling because of the tangible consequences associated with them: The environment is preserved; an abused child is rescued; a newly built house becomes a home. Or they may be pursued because of the psychological value that comes from the pursuit itself: meeting the challenge of climbing Mt. Everest or turning an idea into a flourishing new technology. And, of course, many goals elicit both these kinds of motivation.

> "Establish an overriding, compelling goal that can only be accomplished by the team working together."

Unfortunately, a team's goal might have none of the attributes that promote dedication, effort, and collaboration. The goal can be uninspiring, unchallenging, and of no consequence. Worse, it can be unclear ("What is it we're supposed to be doing here anyway?"). With amazing consistency, team members acknowledge the unease that comes with trying to achieve an ambiguous goal.

- ▪ We seem to have a lack of direction as to what we should be doing as a team. (T56)
- ▪ The team doesn't seem to have a common elevating goal which excites and motivates team members. (T180)
- ▪ Establish an overriding, compelling goal that can only be accomplished by the team working together. (T392)

- It's not clear what we are committed to, or working towards. (T428)
- We need a reason for this "team" to get together. (T384)

This first basic element in our model relates directly to the second, the energies that the team focuses on achieving its goal. If the goal is compelling, elevating, or simply engaging, it tends to generate energy. If the goal is also clear, that energy is more likely to be focused in a productive way. This power of clear and worthwhile goals is captured in Schrage's description of what he calls "Big Problems":

> Like a powerful magnetic field . . . a Big Problem draws talented people to it and forces them to subordinate their egos to the challenge at hand. Nothing builds creative community faster than a Big Problem. That's why monumental egotists like Picasso, Watson, Crick, Heisenberg, and Pauli were all willing to enlist in the enterprise of collaboration.[8]

The Team's Energies

The second factor that contributes to the effectiveness of team problem solving is the extent to which the energies of the participants are focused on the goal, rather than being dissipated on countless distractions. Notice the plural "energies." As the comments of team members reflect, there are different types of energies—mental, physical, and spiritual—that, when focused on the goal, make a team's problem solving much more likely to succeed.

Mental Energy

John Dykstra, who creates special effects for movies, most notably the "Star Wars" films, has this to say about the creative process:

> In an ordinary communication . . . you're trying to tell someone something you know: apples are apples and oranges are oranges. But when you say "let's make something you've never seen before," then apples and oranges take on a completely different significance.

Now, you're both trying to create something you *don't* know. So you try to get a communal mind going; you want to get people's minds to interact as components of a larger mind—one person's logical sense, one person's visual sense, another person's acoustic sense. You get a communal brain. What matters is not just the individual talents but the ability to integrate them.[9]

Katzenbach's recent analysis of top management teams has a similar theme as he discusses "the tangible result of several members of a group applying different skills to produce a performance improvement not achievable by any one member alone."[10] Scholars, too, in more controlled research endeavors, have marshaled convincing evidence that groups and teams, when working together, produce ideas, thoughts, and conceptualizations that might more properly be regarded as properties of the collective, rather than the individual mind.[11]

Team members recognize when they possess a collective mental energy.

- We have many creative people who join their ideas for terrific results. (T72)
- Our team, as a whole, functions as one. (T160)
- We have a proven ability to collectively meet challenging goals. (T140)

We have experienced this synergistic effect so many times that it hardly seems worth questioning. Groups and teams, especially the good ones, often end up with ideas, products, solutions, or strategies that no one even wildly claims to have been able to predict beforehand. And the more the mental energies of the group are focused on the goal or problem, the more extraordinary the outcomes are likely to be.

Conversely, when the mental energy of a team is not focused collectively on the goal, it becomes fragmented and the path to the goal more complex.

- We are not all pulling in the same direction, which definitely distorts our goals and objectives. (T38)
- We must act like one team with one goal in mind. (T56)

Physical Energy

A variety of theory and research demonstrates that individuals tend not to expend maximum (or optimal) physical effort while working in groups. As early as 1927, the German psychologist Max Ringelmann observed that the expenditure of individual physical effort decreased as additional people were added to the task of pulling on a rope. Two people pulled at 93% of the sum of their individual efforts, three people at 85%, and groups of eight at 49%. The "Ringelmann effect" has been described more recently as "social loafing," the tendency of some members of a group effort to slack off or take it easy, letting other members do the work.[12]

In most group tasks, then, it's relatively easy for individual members of the group not to focus all of their physical effort on the goal. But such slacking doesn't go unnoticed.

- Have everyone on the team pull their own weight instead of doing as little as they can. (T172)
- I don't have the feeling that some team members are willing to "inconvenience" themselves in the interest of the team's success. (T168)
- There is this tendency to let the "active doers" of the team continue to do, and the nondoers don't. (T400)
- Some people are only minutely involved, and we spend a disproportionate amount of time trying to encourage their involvement. (T320)

How much individual effort is focused on the goal is a key determinant of a team's success. Hackman, in *Groups That Work (and Those That Don't)*, identifies the amount of effort that individuals expend as the first factor in determining group or team effectiveness.[13] Hirokawa and Keyton, in their study of work teams, found that the willingness of team members to put forth the effort required for completing a task was one of the primary components of work-team effectiveness.[14]

Any first-line manager reading these observations might be tempted to say, somewhat sarcastically, "No kidding." Although the effects of social loafing may seem obvious, perhaps less appreciated is the extraordinary physical energy that characterizes teams at the upper end of the performance spectrum: These teams are unusually successful, ones that achieve extraordinary outcomes. For example, with new product design in aviation, or building the space lab, or developing a new artificial heart, or finding the cure for AIDS, the effort may take years. On a daily, weekly, or monthly basis, the expenditure of sheer physical energy may seem to be beyond the willingness, or indeed ability, of most of us to sustain. At the extreme of the performance spectrum, we have encountered teams that work all night, seemingly oblivious, and are surprised to discover that the sun has come up the next morning. Joe Sutter, team leader of the Boeing 747 airplane project, observed this phenomenon firsthand. Repeatedly, he directed individual team members to go home and get some rest while they worked through the excitement of building the world's largest airplane.[15]

Spiritual Energy

The kind of energy we associate most often with effective teams, and the kind we find most difficult to understand and explain, is spiritual energy. What most people think of as "team spirit" directly influences the amount of productive effort a team will expend: its persistence in the face of obstacles; the willingness of team members to set aside personal egos and cooperate with each other; the capacity of its members to challenge one another and accept suggestions and feedback; how hard it will try to find and correct "problems"; and a great many other important but elusive properties implied by the notion of "spirit."

The spiritual energy of a team is often labeled "group potency" or "group efficacy" by teamwork researchers. These terms refer to a team's collective belief in itself, its conviction that it can be effective. Silver and Bufanio have discovered that group efficacy is one of the best predictors (along with the team's past performance and goals) of a group's performance level.[16]

Team spirit is an elusive quality, yet we all recognize it when we see it. The team members display a collective sense of self-confidence, a belief that the team can perform at a desirable, unusual, or even extraordinary level. They seem to share a collective "will," a commitment to achieve the goal. And they seem to recognize, at an emotional level, that they are involved in something together that takes precedence over the pursuit of individual objectives. Team spirit seems to reflect a collective set of beliefs: We can do it. We're going to do it. And we're going to do it together.

Interestingly, this sense of team spirit can bring about heightened outcomes even when the outcomes are essentially individual ones, as Katzenbach observes:

> The "Magnificent Seven" women's gymnastics team that won the gold medal at The 100th Olympiad in Atlanta is a good example of an enabling team. The sole challenge of the group was to obtain the best possible gymnastic performance from each individual team member. There was no collective work product beyond the individual scores achieved on individual events.[17]

We also recognize when team spirit is absent. When a team is "dispirited," it shows in a number of consistent ways. There is a lack of confidence building among team members. There are low levels of cooperation and enthusiasm. There is a fear of speaking out, taking a risk, or making a mistake.

- We need a greater spirit of team unity. (T280)
- Remove the fear of retribution or punishment for speaking out on controversial issues. (T272)
- We need a feeling of "safety" that anything said is "O.K." (T384)
- It's very difficult to work on a team when you feel some members are just waiting for you to make a mistake so they can say you failed. (T400)
- Eliminate our common "fear of failure." (T136)
- A higher risk profile. We have a culture that survives by not "rocking the boat." (T236)
- Create an atmosphere where team members want to work together and help each other rather than work separately. (T140)
- Create a sense of cooperation and collaboration among the officers. (T168)

The Drain

So far, our model has said that if the goal is sufficiently engaging and energies are sufficiently focused, success is very likely. But, of

"Reduce the politics and direct that energy to getting the job done."

course, achieving this is not as easy as it sounds. If it were, all teams would be great teams—and that is far from the case. What often happens is that the energies, which presumably should be focused on the goal, end up being focused in other directions, usually self-protective thinking and counterproductive moves.

- There can be a lot of tension, which causes motivation to decline. (T280)
- We have back stabbing and back biting between team members. (T64)
- We obviously have team members who do not even like each other. What a waste of time for the rest of us. (T524)
- Reduce the politics and direct that energy to getting the job done. (T272)
- A tremendous amount of energy is spent on internal issues. Who's looking after the needs of the customer? (T400)

We've encountered rather strange situations in our travels among teams. One member of a disaster response team told us he was at a tornado site where one of the responding agencies loaded its people and supplies up and drove away, leaving victims unattended because it got into an argument with another agency about "whose tornado this was." A member of a mountain rescue team related that he was present when two teams reached a seriously injured accident victim at the same time, and the two captains stood over the victim for 15 minutes arguing about who was in charge.

We have both been involved in dozens of situations in which top-level managers have allowed personal conflicts between them to politicize their teams, creating complex and subversive strategies for attacking each other, and sometimes deliberately sabotaging other groups in efforts to make themselves look good. All of this, of course, results in a negative influence on the bottom-line success of the organization.

Sadly, this pattern of diverted energy is not at all unusual. In fact, in the not-so-distant past, the United States was embroiled in a massive energy drain: the Clinton-Lewinsky affair and all its assorted manifestations. For several years a dispute raged, but in its later stages two things seemed increasingly clear: (1) The dispute and its accompanying discourse steadily moved in the direction of traditional party politics and (2) much of the mental, physical, and spiritual energy of the U.S. Congress was focused on this embarrassing episode rather than on problems that most of the American people considered higher priorities.

Whenever you encounter a dysfunctional team, the first question you should ask yourself is: Where is the energy focused, if not on the goal? Most of the time, if the team isn't working well, you'll find something has been elevated above the team's goal. It might be office politics. It might be individual agendas. It might be ego and control needs. It might be competing goals or priorities. Whatever it is, it's draining the energy of the team away from the goal. And that's a recipe for failure.

▪ MAKING SYSTEMATIC PROBLEM SOLVING A PRIORITY

All teams encounter a range of problems on the way to reaching their goal. Whatever the problem, effective teams identify, raise, and resolve it. If it's keeping them from reaching their goal, effective teams try to do something about it. They don't ignore it and hope it goes away. They don't blame someone else for it and give up. They talk about it, figure out what can be done about it, and keep going. Good teams approach all problems, whether they're process problems or technical problems, with the same kind of attitude: Let's figure this out and change what we need to change.

The late Bud Sweeney, the team leader who helped revolutionize the fast food industry by bringing Chicken McNuggets to the marketplace for McDonald's, once told us that he had two principles for leading a team: First, make sure that everyone is clear about the goal and is ready to walk through walls to get there. Second, get team members huddled around a table talking about "Now how the hell are we going to do this?"

If a team consciously focuses on developing strategies and solving problems, the chances of success increase dramatically. Fortunately, it doesn't matter a whole lot how the team members are doing it, as long as they follow a systematic strategy. This brings up an interesting point.

Very early in relationship research, it was discovered that married people who have a plan for handling conflict are happier than those who handle conflict by trial and error. It doesn't seem to matter much how they handle the conflict, as long as they have agreed on a way to do it.[18]

We believe that the same principle applies in a variety of contexts. For example, almost any kind of strategic-planning process works better than none at all. Almost any kind of goal-setting process works better than none. And in the area of group problem solving, a number of different problem-solving strategies have been examined over the years, and they all work better than trial and error.

We have reason to believe that if groups spend time analyzing the problem, examining the issues and weighing the options, they'll probably make better decisions. But why do they have so much trouble doing these things? Because, as Donald Tabone, a retired senior executive from Merrill Lynch who is now a decision-making consultant, has so often reminded us, that's not the way the mind works. When analyzing a problem, the mind often changes the problem to something it likes better and can solve more easily. It ponders self-interests, personal threats, and safety issues. It leaps to solutions before the problem is well defined or even understood. When examining issues, the mind often pursues what's interesting rather than what's important in resolving the problem. When evaluating alternatives, the mind tends to emphasize the positive and de-emphasize the negative attributes of favored alternatives.

> "We need more effective decision making—identify an issue, resolve it, and move on."

Counteracting these tendencies in the team context requires a systematic approach to group problem solving. Team members recognize the need for this kind of structure.

- When a decision is made, it is done quickly without looking at all of the consequences. Too often, individuals walk away, and we all have heard something different. (T436)
- Require a more disciplined approach to management decisions. (T300)
- Formalize the structure of our meetings to move the group through issues more quickly and effectively. (T380)

■ We need more effective decision making—identify an issue, resolve it, and move on. (T492)

As these comments suggest, teams often fail in their core mission to
solve problems effectively. Fortunately, a simple and straightforward
line of research has demonstrated that groups can, with effort, significantly improve the quality of their decisions.[19] For example, in an experiment by Schultz, Ketrow, and Urban, both leader and nonleader members of groups were trained to remind groups about "vigilant problem
solving." For example, to help a group avoid premature decisions, the
reminder would be "Maybe we shouldn't decide on our choices until
we have spent a little more time analyzing other choices." The selected
leader and nonleader members were given checklists to assist them in
performing the reminder function. The researchers state,

"Reminders" were asked to intervene whenever symptoms of de-
fective decision-making prevailed. They were not to be aggressive;
rather, by their questioning, they were to assist the group in choosing an appropriate course of action.[20]

The researchers discovered that the presence of reminders, especially those who were not group leaders, significantly improved decision quality. In short, group members who are vigilant in promoting certain problem-solving practices can improve the performance of
problem-solving groups.

In a different investigation, a descriptive field study, the groups
were small collaborative groups planning strategies for addressing specific healthcare issues.[21] These researchers found very strong correlations between the performance of specific vigilant functions by the
groups and the quality of the group's decisions.

The key, then, is to equip team members with an approach to problem solving and to encourage them to be vigilant in monitoring how the
team is doing. As we have indicated, almost any strategy can improve
performance. We will discuss here the one we have found to work most
effectively across a wide variety of circumstances.

■ FIVE STEPS TO EFFECTIVE PROBLEM SOLVING

The problem-solving strategy presented here is a simple model with five steps. The model is designed to minimize the most common pitfalls to effective problem solving, allowing a team to focus its energies on the goal. We call it the Single Question Format, because it begins by concentrating the team's attention on one question (or problem).

We developed the Single Question Format from descriptive research on the thought processes of successful problem solvers. To test it, we compared it with other problem-solving formats in earlier research.[22] Over the past 30 years, we have evolved this problem-solving strategy into the simple structure shown in Figure 3.2.

We've used this problem-solving format over the years for a number of reasons. First, it promotes a sharp focus for the team's effort by getting the team to agree on one question that, if answered, will provide the solution to the problem at hand.

Second, this format delays consideration of solutions until a thorough analysis of the problem has been completed. One of the most widely recognized weaknesses in group and team problem solving has always been premature solutions. Like almost all effective formats, this format delays any active consideration of solutions until after problem analysis has occurred.

Third, because we're talking about a search for good decisions in situations where no clear-cut correct decision exists, good solutions depend almost entirely on how adequate the analysis was prior to a group reaching a decision. This format, in the third step, in effect asks: "What do we need to know before we can make a good decision? What are the issues we need to discuss before we can answer the single question we've agreed on? How can we be guided by as many facts as possible rather than relying solely on our opinions?"

The Single Question Format has the advantage of simplicity, and it approximates well the way successful problem solvers and decision makers naturally think. Importantly, it agrees with the results of solid field research on cross-functional project teams. Early and Godfrey, for example, studied cross-functional teams that floundered over extraordinarily long periods.[23] Interestingly, the process factors associated with floundering were a lack of clarity regarding the mission, jumping to solutions, and focusing too much attention on interesting

The Single Question Format

1. Identify the Problem

What is the *single question,* the answer to which is all the group needs to know to accomplish its purpose for meeting?

2. Create a Collaborative Setting

A. Agree on principles for discussion.

What principles should we agree on in order to maintain a reasonable and collaborative approach throughout the process?

Examples: We will:

1. Invite and understand all points of view.
2. Remain fact-based in our judgments.
3. Be tough on the issues, not on each other.
4. Put aside any personal agenda.

B. Surface any assumptions and biases.

What assumptions and biases are associated with the single question identified in Step 1, and how might they influence the discussion?

Examples: 1. We tend to assume we know our customers' needs.
2. We believe we have efficient processes.
3. We think our level of customer service is acceptable.
4. We assume our past approach should be our future strategy.

3. Identify and Analyze the Issues (Subquestions)

Before responding to the single question in Step 1, what *issues, or subquestions, must be answered* in order to fully understand the complexities of the overall problem?

- Limit opinions by focusing on the facts.
- If facts are unavailable, agree on the *most reasonable* response to each subquestion.

Issues (Subquestions)	Relevant Facts	Best Response

4. Identify Possible Solutions

Based on an analysis of the issues, what are the two or three *most reasonable* solutions to the problem?

- Determine the advantages/disadvantages of each.

Possible Solutions	Advantages	Disadvantages

5. Resolve the Single Question

Among the possible solutions, which one is *most desirable*?

Figure 3.2. The Single Question Format

SOURCE: © 1983, 2001 Carl E. Larson, Ph.D. and Frank M.J. LaFasto, Ph.D.

but minor issues. The Single Question Format helps the team avoid these pitfalls.

The Single Question Format in Action

Let us explore now two complex, real-life problems we've helped teams manage more effectively by following the Single Question Format. After describing each situation, we will discuss the problem-solving process that is common to both.

Case One: Universal Product Numbers

When a can of soda, no matter what brand name, is waved across the price scanner in the grocery store, the bar code system identifies the item as *soda*. This system of universal product numbers (UPNs) offers several benefits to the food industry, from product ordering to inventory management. Unlike the food industry, however, the accuracy and tidiness of a UPN system is not prevalent throughout the healthcare industry.

The Efficient Healthcare Consumer Response (EHCR) study estimated that approximately $11 billion each year is wasted within the U.S. healthcare industry supply chain.[24] A large portion of that waste is believed to be caused by the lack of universal product numbers on all healthcare products used by hospitals and nonhospital sites of care. To address the problem of waste, several attempts were made in the early 1990s to focus attention on the situation. Although each attempt gained ground, it neither was fast enough nor had enough consensus across the industry to make the needed difference.

In an effort to create a widely embraced initiative, the procurement leaders from 16 Group Purchasing Organizations (GPOs) and large healthcare systems came together. The GPOs represent healthcare systems and groups of hospitals, clinics, surgery centers, and so forth in screening and selecting the best-value healthcare products from the many manufacturers and distributors in the industry. The purpose of the group was to develop a unified perspective and, with one voice, agree on the use of UPNs in order to reduce waste within U.S. healthcare.

One of the reasons this face-to-face collaborative effort had not happened easily before is that the GPOs, as independent business entities, are in a sense competing with one another for the membership of individual hospitals in their groups. The UPN initiative required participants to reach beyond their individual group needs to address a healthcare industry need.

In November 1997, a task force meeting was held among the group of 16 organizations that, by their estimate, represented approximately 85% of the hospital beds in the United States. Within one month, four more organizations joined the initiative. Two months later, the 20 organizations, now representing more than 90% of U.S. hospital beds, reached 100% agreement on the issues central to the UPN challenge and constructed a prospectus on the necessary changes.

Their joint communiqué was submitted as support for two bills—one in the U.S. House of Representatives and one in the Senate—requiring the use of UPNs for Medicare claims. Because nearly all healthcare products are used by Medicare patients, this legislation would require all manufacturers to assign a UPN, which in turn would lead to the adoption of UPN usage throughout the industry. Although the UPN issue is yet to be resolved, this unified effort among independent GPOs has been a critical step in the ongoing attention devoted to unnecessary expenditures in healthcare.

Case Two: Improved Earnings

Allegiance Corporation became an independent, publicly traded company following its "spin-off" from Baxter International in October, 1996. As a distributor and manufacturer of healthcare products, Allegiance earned 1.4 pennies on a dollar. With slim margins and a marketplace that had demonstrated flat to low growth during the previous several years, Allegiance knew it had to reduce significantly its expense run-rate—the actual cost of doing business on an ongoing basis—and do so without damaging the company or its customer relationships.

As part of its initiative, Allegiance created a cross-functional task force of business unit and functional leaders from across the organization. Within 90 days, this group constructed and began implementing an action plan designed to eliminate $40 million from their expense run-rate.

The process began by eliminating activities that had outlived their usefulness. The reduction in people-related expenses was accomplished by leveraging the natural attrition—or voluntary turnover within the company—and then taking every opportunity to redeploy talent. Task Force I, as it came to be known, was so successful in strengthening the business and improving its responsiveness that the process quickly became part of the normal management of the company. Task Forces I through VIII eventually eliminated more than $150 million in expenses—significantly improving operating income—once again while strengthening, not damaging, the business. As a publicly traded company, Allegiance's stock grew presplit from $15 per share on its opening day on Wall Street to $100 per share as it merged with Cardinal Health, Inc., a leading provider of services supporting the healthcare industry. In 1998, Allegiance's total return to shareholders ranked 6th among Fortune 500 companies.[25]

A Look at the Process

Both of the initiatives we have just described depended on effective problem solving by the teams involved. Effective problem solving, in turn, depended on employing a process that allowed each team to focus its energies in a systematic way.

The process begins with the vital step of devoting whatever time is necessary to formulate the single question the group needs to answer (Step 1). Often it will take as much as several hours to reach agreement on what this single question is, but the investment is essential if further time and effort are to be well spent. As we have learned, and unfortunately relearned too many times, not having the right question at the beginning of the process invites divergent tracks of thought and unnecessary conflict along the way. In fact, if the right question is not identified at the outset, a series of false starts will often cause the group to backpedal in order to formulate the right question, and do it at a point when the team no longer has the luxury of a clean slate for thinking and interacting.

The UPN initiative, for example, formulated the following single question: "What should be the healthcare industry's response to implementing a universal product number database?" Allegiance's Task Force I decided to address this question: "How should we eliminate $40 million of expense in the run rate of the business?"

Step 2 is to create a collaborative climate for discussion. This step begins by reaching agreement on a common set of guiding principles for how people will participate in the process. Typically, this is a 10-minute discussion that generates 8 to 10 "We will" statements intended to ensure an open airing of the topic and encourage participation. The UPN initiative, for example, agreed that: "We will not allow any discussion to occur that might, in any way, inhibit fair business practice." This agreement meant they would not discuss such topics as pricing or group contracts, or any topic that might be construed as a violation of fair trade. They also crafted principles that required putting the "health of the healthcare industry above any other agenda."

Similarly, the Allegiance cost-reduction initiative embraced such principles as "We will not treat any expenses as sacred cows," "We will invite each other to examine the business for which we have stewardship," and "We will leverage attrition and not displace people from jobs." In both initiatives, the principles held people accountable for answering the overarching question while minimizing process distractions.

Once process principles have been agreed on, it's important to surface any assumptions and biases that participants bring to the question they are trying to answer. Again, this is a 10-minute discussion that offers an invaluable tailwind to the process because it usually allows underlying motivations to be diluted enough to steer the discussion in a more collaborative way. In the case of the UPN initiative, the discussion focused on assumptions and biases regarding who should be the keeper of the database, whether or not to use existing standards, and funding for establishing and maintaining the process. Task Force I at Allegiance took a hard stand on the need to eliminate cost. They assumed that their situation required the tough-mindedness demanded of a "turnaround" in order to revitalize earnings. They identified some fundamental assumptions about travel, outside consultants, and well-engrained benefit plans. They also identified strong biases regarding organization structure.

Agreeing on principles and surfacing assumptions and biases—creating a collaborative setting—at the beginning of a problem-solving initiative allows people to address the question they are trying to answer more objectively. This prepares the table for the most substantive step in the Single Question Format: Step 3, Identify and Analyze the Issues. This step requires identifying all of the issues, or subquestions, that the team must understand to respond meaningfully to the overall single question. Completing this step allows the team to avoid arriving at a solution too early, before understanding the critical components of the problem. The people working on the UPN initiative, for example, identified 24 issues. Several of these issues, such as "Should the UPN be cross-referenced to existing catalog numbers, and if so, how many?" and "How should we resolve the two sets of existing standards for a UPN system?" required a focused and factual examination to formulate a best response. The Allegiance task force addressed such issues as "How much Sales, General, and Administrative (SG&A) expense can the business afford?" and "Do we have the optimum organization structures for manufacturing, distribution, and corporate staff?" In both cases, once all of the relevant issues were identified, they were analyzed and best responses to each issue were agreed on.

In Step 4, each task force then proceeded successfully to formulate the two or three best solutions to the overall single question that represented their purpose for coming together. Finally, Step 5 involved selecting the best solution to the problem based on a shared understanding of all the relevant issues. In both cases, team members were collectively clear about the problem they were undertaking, the issues surrounding each problem, and how to best resolve each issue. This clarity, in turn, allowed them to proceed with sufficient confidence to their final decision and commit to it.

Cross-Functional Teams: The Challenge Increases

The universal product number case and the improved earnings case are particularly interesting because they are both examples of cross-functional teams—members from different disciplines or even organizations coming together to solve a problem of common concern. Although cross-functional teams bring breadth of perspective and expertise, they also bring fragmented loyalties, divided time commitments, and even conflicting demands. In cross-functional teams, both substantive and process problems become intensified.

For example, when a large and very complex organization redirects or refocuses its efforts, many changes may be made. Whole new systems may be designed and put in place. New structures may be created and new procedures invented. The changes usually require organization-wide effort, and the teams involved in the effort are almost certain to be cross-functional. Their members will come from different functions within the organization (e.g., marketing, product design, manufacturing), and they will discuss project issues that are broader than the interest of any one function.

In an organization-wide effort, there will be many such teams, connected to each other in different ways. You might not think that team members, all of whom work for the same organization and pursue, theoretically, the same goals, would have much trouble working together. But they do. We have spent an increasing proportion of our time in recent years dealing with relationships among teams, rather than issues within individual teams. Other researchers corroborate our experience. Barker and Thompkins have demonstrated that workers usually identify more strongly with their smaller functioning unit (team or work group) than with the organization.[26] Souder found that almost 60% of the new product teams studied reported communication disharmony.[27]

With cross-functional teams, the problems are big, broad problems, and clarity is difficult to achieve. It's hard to focus the energies of the individuals involved in these efforts. It's relatively easy for people to focus on their own individual responsibilities and not worry too much about the broad, integrating goal.

When people are told about the project or are asked to become involved in it, they usually respond with some degree of cynicism: What's really going on? Whose interests are really being served? Have the decisions already been made? Will anything actually happen?

Although these challenges are formidable, there is a way forward. We read with interest one of the conclusions from an investigation of development meetings between computer specialists and nontechnical users that pointed to the importance of "kicking around the problem" before trying to solve it.[28] We have found the same thing in studying citizen collaboratives.[29] We called the phenomenon "informal exploring" based upon some earlier research that had been done in negotiation.

The principle, in a nutshell, is that the more the problem is large, complex, and has multiple perspectives, the more important it is not to talk about solutions too early in the process. Rather, it is important to have people spend considerable time talking about the interests they have in trying to solve the problem, or the prior experiences they've had with similar kinds of problems, or the people they've known who have been directly affected by the problem. Far from being a "waste of time," this early informal exploring or "kicking the problem around," helps overcome much of the cynicism and mistrust that may drive the discussion off-track in the future. In the Single Question Format for problem solving, this approach is reflected in Step 2, which asks team members to surface any biases, assumptions, and perspectives about the problem before attempting to solve it.

In cross-functional teams, the fundamental principles of problem solving, such as goal clarity and issues analysis, are critically important to the quality of the group's outcome. Similarly, a communication climate that is open and supportive is essential for helping the group identify, raise, and resolve the many process problems that will affect the group's success.

▪ WHAT ABOUT PROCESS PROBLEMS?

Earlier we mentioned that a team's path to the goal is strewn with both substantive and process problems. In our own work with teams, we have found that the inability to solve the process problems accounts for the failure of teams as often as does the inability to solve the substantive problems. And research from the aerospace industry identifies "group process" factors as the most direct predictors of a team's performance.[30] How clear and elevating the goal is, how united the team is, how open and supportive the communication climate of the team is—these are process problems that show very strong correlations with team performance.

It's the process issues that often trip up otherwise competent teams. A case in point: We once worked with multiple groups of systems engineers who were designing and constructing a large integrated computer system for collecting massive quantities of certain kinds of information from all over the world, synthesizing and formatting it, and displaying it in real time and multiple locations. These were intelligent, talented people, the best in the world at what they did. They tackled engineering problems with fervor. But when a problem surfaced that had to do with the way they did their work together, these otherwise highly competent people were at a loss about what to do.

We finally convinced them that they should approach these process problems just as they would any other problem that had to be solved in order to achieve the goal. Put simply: Make sure everyone has a clear understanding of the problem. Do a thorough analysis. Explore the issues fully. Identify the options. Explore the pros and cons of the options. Choose the one that has the best chance of working. Decide what you can do to improve the likelihood that it will succeed. And get on with the work.

But aren't process problems different? Well, yes and no. Process problems are different in the sense that the decisions that need to be made are about the team itself, its members, and its relationships. The problems are the same in the sense that they have to be identified, discussed, and resolved—if they are affecting the team's performance. The same systematic strategy—and the same vigilance in applying it— works for resolving both types of problems.

As important as it is to implement a structured approach to solving both kinds of problems, the success of any problem-solving strategy depends on the key variable discussed earlier in this book—a communication climate that places a high premium on openness and supportiveness.

▪ PUTTING IT TO WORK

In order to explore the use and value of the team problem-solving ideas described in this chapter, we suggest a simple exercise that you may do yourself or with your team using the following model we presented earlier as a guideline.

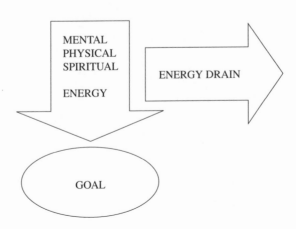

1. Describe your team's goal. What is the tangible, concrete out-come your team is hoping to achieve?
2. Describe the energies (mental, physical, and spiritual) that members of the team have focused, or should be focusing, on the goal.
3. Is the team's energy drained away from the goal? If it is, where is the energy focused (e.g., a noncollaborative team member, a relationship conflict, organizational politics)? Is this energy drain, in your opinion, seriously interfering with the team's success?
4. What might help the team regain its focus on the goal? Is there a role you can play in making this happen?

Next, put a problem-solving process in place. If you are the leader or member of an ongoing team, or if you have the opportunity to be on a task force or cross-functional initiative that is attempting to address a complex problem, try using the Single Question Format as the frame-work for your discussion. Before you get started, present everyone on the team with a copy of the Single Question Format (Figure 3.2). As the team proceeds through the five-step process, record the results of each step on a flipchart so that everyone stays involved and focused.

Once the team has reached a solution, debrief team members on how the process went and how the team can improve its problem solv-ing in the future.

SNAPSHOT

4

Although most people would agree that the right person in a leadership role can add the "spark" that drives a successful collective effort, defining the specific behaviors that characterize an effective team leader has proven more elusive. To better understand this issue, we asked 6,000 team members to describe the strengths and weaknesses of their own team leaders. Their comments go well beyond identifying the qualities of good or bad leaders to describing the specific leader behaviors they find most helpful as well as most intrusive.

From their written evaluations of some 600 team leaders, we developed a valid and reliable assessment tool that measures a leader's effectiveness across six key dimensions. In brief, team members told us that an effective leader:

1. Focuses on the goal
2. Ensures a collaborative climate
3. Builds confidence
4. Demonstrates sufficient technical know-how
5. Sets priorities
6. Manages performance

Chapter 4 explores each of these areas of leadership competence in more detail and invites you to gather feedback on your own leadership abilities and style by using the assessment tool provided at the end of the chapter.

CHAPTER 4

THE TEAM LEADER

What Works/What Gets in the Way

When we think about leadership, we are likely to see bold figures and striking deeds: Bill Gates building a cyber kingdom, Alan Greenspan stewarding a nervous economy, Mother Teresa ministering to the unfortunate, Jack Welch setting new standards for business performance, Steven Spielberg making movies in Hollywood, or Phil Jackson coaching championship basketball teams in Chicago and Los Angeles. Images of these leaders come readily to mind, and rightly so. But there are a great many equally remarkable though lesser-known leaders, like Alex Plinio of Newark, New Jersey.

In 1984, Newark was a city growing accustomed to quiet desperation, decaying crime-ridden neighborhoods, very high unemployment, and public assistance. After the 1967 race riots, neighborhoods had declined to slum level. In the 1970s, the city lost nearly 14% of its population. In the 1980s, it was losing many of its corporations.

In 1984, Alex Plinio was working in public affairs at the Prudential Insurance Company headquarters in Newark. He wondered what Prudential could do to help the city and whether there was enough leadership in the city to affect the root problems. "I started by just talking with people," Plinio recalls. He notes that,

> Over a period of three months, I talked with about 50 leaders from all the sectors, including board chairs, CEOs of corporations, college

and hospital administrators, city council members, the mayor, and state government people. In other words, a very wide cross-section of leadership.

Satisfied that there was enough genuine interest, Plinio created a process for Newark's citizen leaders to work together on community problems. It was an open process, genuine, and one that inspired confidence.

In 1985, the Newark Collaboration Group became an official nonprofit organization, with Plinio as its first chair. Within a year, *The New York Times* reported on the beginnings of a turnaround in Newark and attributed some of the progress to a hard-working core of people called the Newark Collaboration Group.

This is the kind of leadership that this chapter addresses. Bringing people together. Creating a process that is open, productive, and promotes confidence. Using the energies of everyone who is willing to focus on a common problem or opportunity, and keeping priorities straight. The often quiet, offstage leadership that usually gets important things done.

■ SIX DIMENSIONS OF TEAM LEADERSHIP

Leadership lends itself readily to metaphor. It's a natural subject for photographers, novelists, and filmmakers to fictionalize, romanticize, dramatize. Commonly, these images of leadership embrace the familiar formula of a challenging situation, personal gumption, astute keenness, unshakable purpose, and some degree of risk, all typically blended into a successful end game.

Of course, there is something to be learned from such mythical renderings of leadership. But eventually you must acknowledge that you and your situation are different. You are not the focused mountain climber or the placid rower in the photograph. You are not the spirited protagonist in the movie or the CEO in the business school case.

As a team leader, however, you *are* a key player in a setting that is fraught with meaning, challenge, and risk. Whether you are leading an executive management team in a Fortune 500 company or a team of frontline workers in a government agency or nonprofit organization, your interest is focused on what you can do, personally and specifically, to be more effective at leading *your team* and helping *your organization* succeed. Your purpose as a leader is to add value to your team's effort.

Unfortunately, leadership can be a frustrating and slippery topic to explore, offering little more than hints and promises of its innermost ingredients. Often, an examination of its properties can lead to dead ends, or be diverted and overpowered by sibling subjects such as charisma and character. From the outset, we must accept the fact that much of leadership may always remain elusive and nongeneralizable. How to be an effective leader isn't some calculable math problem. Perhaps the best we can hope for is the sketch of a shadowy profile, one that must be worked at, interpreted, and adapted to each person's unique qualities and the situation at hand.

But even if there may never be an established set of commandments for successful leadership, we believe that one way to get closer to the mark is to zero in on the way team leaders are seen and assessed by their teams—in both their strengths and their failings. To this end, we asked more than 6,000 team members to provide a written response to two questions about their team leader: (1) What are the strengths of the team's leadership? (2) What does the team leader do that keeps the team from functioning more effectively? From the responses to these two assessments of more than 600 team leaders emerged six consistent and useful leadership competencies.

1. Focus on the goal
2. Ensure a collaborative climate
3. Build confidence
4. Demonstrate sufficient technical know-how
5. Set priorities
6. Manage performance

As you read through this chapter, we urge you to ask yourself how many of these leadership competencies are a consistent part of your own leadership repertoire. Once you have done so, we encourage you to get some feedback from your associates as well. For without feedback, you are only guessing at your own effectiveness—and probably overrating it.

How do we know this to be true? When we compared responses of the 600 team leaders with those of the 6,000 team members in our Team Excellence database, the ratings by team leaders of their own leadership effectiveness were significantly higher than the ratings of them by team members. In fact, leaders' ratings were inflated over team members' ratings by an average margin of 50%.

What we've found is that, relatively speaking, team leaders tend to be out of touch with what's happening within their teams on a day-to-day basis. Incidentally, this is one of the reasons why two of the more consistent complaints voiced by team members are complaints about team leaders: The team leader is unwilling to confront and resolve issues associated with inadequate performance by team members, and the team leader dilutes the team's efforts with too many priorities.

Although it's important for team leaders to get feedback, the difficulty has always been what questions to ask yourself and your team to better understand the impact of your leadership. To help you, we have developed a list of questions from what 6,000 team members have suggested are critical accountabilities within each of the six major areas of team leadership. These questions are presented at the end of the discussion of each leadership dimension. At the end of the chapter, all six sets of questions are collected in the form of a diagnostic instrument for rating collaborative team leadership.

As we explore the six dimensions of team leadership, reflect on your own experiences with leading a team and watching others lead. Remain introspective. Take an active role. Make notes in the margins. Jot down examples. Recall feedback you have received in the past. Identify what you believe to be your strengths as a team leader and your opportunities for improvement. After all, leaders are always on probation.

▪ DIMENSION ONE: FOCUS ON THE GOAL

> *My responsibility is to get my 25 guys playing for the name on the front of their shirt and not the one on the back.*
>
> Tommy Lasorda
> Former Manager, Los Angeles Dodgers

Your first responsibility as team leader is to keep your team focused on its goal. You may refer to it as your team mission, vision, strategy, primary objective, or prime directive. Call it whatever you like as long as you keep it simple. The team goal is your team's reason for existence, and it should be clear and inspiring.

As team leader, you must help your team achieve as much clarity as humanly possible regarding its direction. You must help team members believe in that direction, whether the goal is of their own choosing or is handed to them by the larger organization. You must capture their imagination and help them see the goal as worthy of their devoted time and effort for half their waking hours. You must help them see the relevance of their activities to the master blueprint. Then you must keep the goal fresh and help them to understand and commit to inevitable adjustments in the team's direction.

This is a tall order—which is one reason good team leaders are in short supply. Let's take a closer look at what this essential part of your mission involves.

Define the Goal in a Clear and Elevating Way

Your first task as team leader is to clearly define the goal. Goal clarity is critical for team members to have confidence in their direction and to be committed to making it happen. Clarity also drives the alignment of activities and trust in the team leader's ability to lead.

Often a team goal is left undefined or, equally harmful, ill-defined. An undefined goal taxes the team's tolerance for spending valuable time and energy with no clear purpose. Similarly, an ill-defined goal—one filled with squishy ideas or one choked with a lot of language but lacking a coherent direction—taxes the team's tolerance for ambiguity. In either case, the team begins to drift aimlessly as the team members struggle to understand the importance of the goal and their role in achieving it.

- Our leader does not clearly articulate the goal. (Team 535)
- Our team leader doesn't communicate clearly the direction we are going. (T501)
- He needs to clarify our vision. (T581)
- More clearly define the purpose of our group and what it is to accomplish. (T196)

In addition, without goal clarity team members usually find themselves bumping into one another like Keystone Kops. Eventually, the collective priorities don't match or no longer make sense.

- ■ Establish a common goal for our team—an underlying target that will bind us together in a variety of efforts. (T192)

A team goal, then, must be firmly rooted in clarity. All team members must be able to describe, in syncopated rhythm, where the team is headed.

In addition to being absolutely clear, the goal must be articulated in a way that inspires passion and commitment. A model leader in this respect is Phil Jackson, coach of the world champion L.A. Lakers basketball team, and former coach of the six-time world champion Chicago Bulls. Jackson is superb at aligning individual talents with the collective goal. Throughout the wide range of behaviors demonstrated by his players—from the predictable finesse of Michael Jordan to the unpredictable flare-ups of Dennis Rodman—Phil Jackson keeps his team centered on a single, clear, inspiring goal: the NBA title. In his book, *Sacred Hoops*, he writes,

> "Establish a common goal for our team—an underlying target that will bind us together in a variety of efforts."

My first act after being named head coach of the Bulls was to formulate a vision for the team. I had learned from the Lakota and my own experience as a coach that vision is the source of leadership, the expansive dream state where everything begins and all is possible. I started by creating a vivid picture in my mind of what the team could become. My vision could be lofty, I reminded myself, but it couldn't be a pipe dream. I had to take into account not only *what* I wanted to achieve, but *how* I was going to get there.

At the heart of my vision was the selfless ideal of teamwork that I'd been experimenting with since my early days in the CBA. My goal was to give everyone on the team a vital role—even though I knew I couldn't give every man equal playing time, nor could I change the NBA's disproportionate system of financial rewards. But I could get the bench players to be more actively involved. My idea was to use ten players regularly and give the others enough playing time so that they could blend in effortlessly with everybody else when they were on the floor. . . .

Tex Winter's system would be my blueprint. But that alone wasn't going to be enough. We needed to reinforce the lessons the players were learning in practice, to get them to embrace the concept of selflessness wholeheartedly.[1]

Every team leader dreams of having a team goal that contains its own irresistible hook, one that tugs at the imagination: an objective that is, on the face of it, appealing because it is somewhere between difficult and impossible to achieve at all, let alone well—but at the same time an objective that will surrender its secret if properly explored by the right minds, with the right attitude, and with the ability to keep at it.

As the old saying goes, there is good news and bad news. The good news is that most team objectives contain their own magnetic appeal. The bad news is it takes work to flesh it out. For example, a surface view of Fannie Mae, the largest financing source for home mortgages in the United States, offers up a picture of just one more financial services company, one more organization that moves money around to serve up the best rates for its customers. But Fannie Mae sees itself as much more than a balance sheet. It sees itself at the center of the mortgage finance system, helping first-time and low- to middle-income home buyers to achieve the American dream of home ownership.

This self-perception is reflected in its mission, its goals, its organizational values, and even in its advertising campaign, which over the years has included a series of messages that reinforce this higher-order purpose. For example, one compelling ad offered the picture of a small white frame house with the caption, "Every nation builds monuments to its great accomplishments. This is ours." Another ad showed a half framed-in house with a picture of workers in tool belts along with the caption, "They work hard to build America's homes. Shouldn't they be able to afford one?" In a third ad the picture of a family photo on a nightstand was accompanied by the words "To measure our success last year multiply this family photo by 900,000." Continuing along their path, Fannie Mae provided financing to serve 2.6 million families in the year 2000.

Employees at Fannie Mae do not merely view themselves as people moving money around. They see themselves helping families achieve one of the most basic of human needs—and a big piece of the American dream.

It's captivating when a team goal is articulated with inspiration, but it doesn't just happen on its own. Someone—and it's usually the team leader—must unlock the higher order meaning that justifies the team's existence.

Time and again we have seen team leaders who are desperate for inspiration but have not come to grips with the elevating worth of the team's goal. Some of these leaders struggle because their imagination is earthbound at best. When this is the case, it is discomforting, and often embarrassing, to watch a team leader stammer out some incoherent, half-sculpted image of a goal, one that might as well have come from a Ouija board.

Most of the time, however, team leaders simply ignore the need to tap into why team members are willing to show up, day after day, and do their best work. By the way, it's usually not because they have a goal to grow earnings 15%, or to reach the next million or billion in sales. That's not what passes the alarm clock test the next morning.

On the other hand, we have met thousands of team members who are excited about the nobility and worth of their team's goal: Making a breakthrough in heart transplants; creating the biggest airplane in the world; pursuing new insights aboard the space shuttle; helping a newly married couple buy their first home. The social side of the team's goal is almost always where you will find the inspiration that can place a unique tailwind behind your team's effort and commitment.

This is particularly true when a team encounters extended hard times and unusually challenging barriers to reaching its targets. If a team is not putting results on the board, it must have something to believe in, a reminder of the reason for trying harder or finding a smarter approach. Team members must see how they are fulfilling an important social need, shouldering a responsibility that they are capable of performing better than anyone else. Whether it's a better automobile or better healthcare, they must see their need to rise to the occasion.

As team leader, it is up to you to animate the vision. You must paint a verbal picture that raises the team's understanding of the significance and worth of their purpose. Consider, for example, the litigation group within a Fortune 100 company. In the beginning, this team saw as their goals responding to internal business needs and identifying appropriate legal resources. As a broker of legal talent, they matched inside experts or outside firms with legal challenges. They saw themselves as coordinators. But after the team pushed itself to explore the elevating side of its goal, they described themselves differently. They saw their clear and elevating goal as "ensuring that litigation does not prevent our organization from selling its products and services worldwide." This shift allowed them to see their responsibility in a new and far more significant light. They saw that it was their responsibility to not allow litigation to be used as a strategic tool by competitors or by adversary groups trying to restrict their company's trade and ability to grow. They became the keeper of a different key, and they found this new purpose far more motivating and robust.

It takes courage and patience to unlock the elevating side of a team goal. It must be a credible extension from where the team currently stands—and it must tap into an emotional passion that is linked to a larger sense of responsibility.

Don't Play Politics

As team leader your primary responsibility is to ensure that the team reaches its goal. A cardinal sin of any team leader—one we have seen committed on many occasions—is allowing anything to weaken your focus on the goal. For example, a team leader can have a dysfunctional relationship with someone in another part of the organization that can cause the leader to become preoccupied with "maneuvering" around that individual in ways that fracture the team's efforts. Equally destructive is the team leader whose eyes are always looking upward for reasons of self-gain. It's worth noting that team members are always clearly aware when their team leader is compromising the team's objective.

- Our team leader lets politics get in the way. (T531)
- Create a good working atmosphere without political ambiguities. (T501)

Help Team Members See Their Relevance to the Goal

Being in sync with the team goal is crucial to team commitment. As a team member, or department, or function, or business unit, there is nothing worse than feeling isolated from the passion of the dream, grasping for relevance that seems slightly out of reach. It's difficult for team members to prove their worth or measure their merit if they feel marginal to the real action or in clumsy alignment with the grand plan.

A few words and a small investment of time can go a long way to influence the productive effort of an individual or function or business unit, depending on your scope of leadership. You must constantly work at concisely translating the vision from your private perspective so that others see the relevance and importance of their activities to the goal as you define it.

Keep the Goal Alive

The second law of thermodynamics tells us that anything left unattended will tend toward decay. Intuitively we know this to be true. So we reinvigorate our bodies with exercise, renew important relationships, and change the oil in our cars.

Conceptually, the team members in our research allude to this basic law. They tell us that team leaders need to continually reinforce and renew the team goal. No matter how bright and flashy, a team goal cannot be left unattended.

> ■ Our team leader is willing to openly and frequently communicate our goal. (T519)

As team leader you must look for opportunities to reinforce and breathe life into the team goal. We are not talking about running around with a hard sell. We're talking about finding fresh approaches for amplifying the meaning of the goal: Seeking examples that reinforce a sincere and constant pride in the opportunity to achieve a worthwhile objective; searching for events that create a clearer understanding of what the goal means and why it's worth team members pouring their hearts and souls into making it happen.

Moreover, it's important to recognize that a team goal is not always a fixed, single-minded focal point. Sometimes it's a focused but fluid direction, a credible trajectory toward a more strategic positioning, such as expansion into related products, services, or markets. But fixed or fluid, a team goal sometimes requires adjustment. The impetus for adjustment is pressure—either external to the team or self-imposed.

External pressure can be applied from a variety of sources. Sometimes it's the advent of technology, as exemplified when the microchip of the early 1970s drove down the price of hand-held calculators from $100 to under $10 almost overnight. Sometimes it's when new technology achieves its saturation point, such as the eventual impact of television's omnipresence on radio programming, or personal computers on typewriters, or electronic data on the paper information businesses, or on-line shopping on the retail industry.

Sometimes it's government regulation, or deregulation, as with carrier routes within the airline industry, or the length of time it takes for a pharmaceutical drug to reach its market. Sometimes it's the presence of stronger competition, as with foreign car competition on the American auto industry, or the impact of Nordstrom's service on the retail industry, or the reliability of Federal Express on the delivery services. Sometimes it's a decline in the perceived relevance of a product or service, as experienced by higher education during the 1980s. And sometimes it's the internal shift of growth within a marketplace, as seen in healthcare's shift from hospitals to alternate sites of care following the enactment of cost containment legislation in 1983. It's a rare team that does not at some point—and probably at many points—need to reconsider its direction because of pressures external to the team itself.

Occasionally a team will put significant pressure on itself to adjust and sharpen its direction. This happens when a team becomes increasingly dissatisfied with its own progress. This kind of self-imposed pressure is an attempt by the team to motivate itself toward constructive change to avoid ossifying into mediocrity or failure.

Whatever the source of the pressure that requires a change in the team goal, it is important for the team leader to think through how to effect change. Team leaders often become so wrapped up in the newer and more attractive direction that they move too quickly, neglecting to bring everyone along with them. They create problems of ownership within the team and problems with credibility for themselves.

If poorly managed changes in the team's goal happen often enough, they will rankle the team and generate persistent resentment. Time and again we hear team members complain about the "mission of the month," or the "vision du jour." They are referring to team leaders who make changes in the goal with almost no explanation and almost no reference to the past. Such cavalier and amnesiac behavior erodes faith in the leader, the goal, and ultimately, the team itself.

▪ Create a stable mission. (T126)

It's not unusual for a team goal to require reasonable adjustments along the way. As team leader, it's your responsibility to move skillfully within the goal. Make it clear that there is a wide latitude of possibilities on the path toward the team's objective. Leave on-ramps for new ideas and off-ramps to peel away approaches that have outlived their usefulness. And when it's necessary to make an adjustment to the team goal, do so in a way that helps team members understand the change as a reasonable and necessary one.

Box 4.1

The following items best represent the behaviors for "Focus on the Goal." (The items are numbered to correspond with the complete 40-item instrument presented at the end of this chapter.)

1. I clearly define our goal.
2. I articulate our goal in such a way to inspire commitment.
3. I avoid compromising the team's objective with political issues.
4. I help individual team members align their roles and responsibilities with the team goal.
5. I reinforce the goal in fresh and exciting ways.
6. If it's necessary to adjust the team's goal, I make sure the team understands why.

▪ DIMENSION TWO: ENSURE A COLLABORATIVE CLIMATE

Once the team's goal is established, the most important contribution a team leader can make is to ensure a climate that enables team members to speak up and address the real issues preventing the goal from being achieved. Anything less holds diminished promise for success.

Earlier we described collaboration as the dual presence of openness and supportiveness: the ability to raise and resolve the real issues standing in the way of a team accomplishing its goal, and to do so in a way that brings out the best thinking and attitude of everyone involved. It's too hard for team members to contribute, much less explore the possibilities, when it is not safe for them to say what's on their minds. They must be able to speak honestly. They must be able to deal openly with real obstacles, problems, and opportunities in a way that promotes listening, understanding of differing perspectives, and constructively working toward a solution.

There are few greater frustrations than sitting at a team table and being unable to openly discuss the real problems. It's disheartening to see team members leave the room without having raised—let alone discussed—the real issues, which are inevitably discussed later in hallways, offices, and carpools.

In fact, the best barometer for determining a collaborative climate is to ask a simple question: Once a meeting has ended, do team members meet informally to discuss their real thoughts and feelings about an issue that should have been addressed at the team table? If so, there's a problem. Furthermore, it takes only a few of these experiences to orient team members in the wrong direction and obliterate any team values worth building on. Worse yet, over time there's a numbing effect.

A collaborative climate is accomplished by talking about it, reinforcing it, and guaranteeing it. Most of all, the team leader creates a collaborative climate by demonstrating and modeling it through the behaviors and practices discussed in this section.

Make Communication Safe

The team leader has the greatest responsibility for making free expression safe—giving team members reason to believe that any issue related to the team's success can be discussed as long as it is done respectfully. It is the team leader's job to remove artificial barriers to communication and lower the real ones.

As a team leader, you have enormous influence over what issues get raised and how they get explored. Topics that may not appear to have your imprimatur will be considered out of bounds. Team members, in their own way, will be reluctant and even fearful to put you on the spot by raising a topic they think you might have difficulty discussing.

- There is a fear of questioning superiors regarding how to best do something. People just do nothing or blunder ahead. (T96)
- He squelches the free flow of ideas among the members of his leadership team. (T581)

A trademark of such fear is silence. It is up to you to break the silence. There is nothing that builds trust quite as sharply as a leader who deftly identifies the tough issue on everyone's mind. Incidentally, if it is a tough topic for you, you can be sure team members will know. Own up to your discomfort before you discuss it. It's not enough to say, "If it's really important to you, we can discuss this issue." Or "This probably is not as bad as we're making it out to be." Signals like these only make matters worse. Keep in mind, every team performs a biopsy on its leader. Team members want to know what makes you uncomfortable or what you feel a need to protect. If they discover that you treat some topics as sacred cows, their peace of mind will dissolve into suspicion and distrust.

Lingering issues offer one measure of a less-than-open and supportive climate. We are not referring to those issues that will always require regular and ongoing attention, but rather to issues that the team feels it should be able to resolve but just can't seem to. If we assume that all team issues can be addressed and resolved, then an issue that tends to linger may be a red flag regarding the team's collaborative capabilities.

Demand a Collaborative Approach

Ultimately, a collaborative climate is defined by individual behavior and the expectations that drive it. You can elicit collaborative behavior by making it clear that you expect it. This simplification is essential to collaborative leadership.

For example, sometimes a team member with a competitive approach or an overreliance on title, tenure, experience, or expertise inhibits participation by other team members. It's important that you, as team leader, refuse to tolerate behavior that detracts from a collaborative climate.

> "Hold each team member accountable for any nonacceptable behaviors."

- Our team leader allows inappropriate comments and behaviors to go unchallenged. (T527)
- Hold each team member accountable for any nonacceptable behaviors. (T296)

There is nothing more discouraging than a team leader who watches approvingly while a team member persists in knocking heads or remaining unchallengeable. Make it clear that no one is entitled to take an approach that keeps others from feeling it's safe to contribute. We suggest that you deliver this message constructively as feedback and then, if necessary, remove the velvet gloves.

Four social competencies of the collaborative team member—open, supportive, action-oriented, and possessing a positive personal style—were described in Chapter 1. These four factors, along with related behaviors, offer an effective formula for reinforcing a collaborative approach by individuals. Numerous team leaders, including a number of CEOs, have used these behavioral factors as vehicles for providing feedback to team members. First, the leader rates the team member on each behavior and asks the team member to rate himself or herself as well. Then they discuss their ratings and perceptions one-on-one. This process offers a very effective way to encourage the collaborative strengths of a team member and to discuss, constructively, opportunities for improvement. Furthermore, every time you, as team leader, focus on each team member's personal responsibility to be collaborative, you are shaping the collaborative climate of your organization at its most basic level.

In addition to requiring individual collaborative behavior, effective team leaders expect team members to build and sustain collaborative working relationships with one another. Most of the serious problems that we've encountered in organizations have been the result of people losing track of the goal and allowing their own relationship issues to overwhelm their good judgment. Effective team leaders make it clear to team members that they expect the energy of the team to go into meeting the performance objective—not competing with each other one-on-one.

As team leader it's up to you to keep this priority straight. The best way to accomplish this is to require team members to address constructively any relationship issues that threaten to interfere with the team's success. To help them accomplish this, it's a good idea to offer them a process for managing and resolving issues.

In our experience, the most successful team leaders ask team members to have a Connect Model-type conversation with each of the other members of the team, including the leader (see Chapter 2). Such teams usually afford themselves 60 to 90 days to have the 30-minute conversations with each of the 9 or 10 other members of the team, logging completion of each conversation on a matrix chart that is maintained by the team leader. This approach works best as a proactive attempt to strengthen team relationships, rather than waiting for problems to occur.

Such accountability helps assure that constructive conversations take place. These conversations, in turn, strengthen all of the relationships in the team. Leaders who use this technique know that for every relationship issue that is resolved, an obstacle—a piece of debris—is removed from the team's race track, allowing it faster and less hazardous movement toward its goal.

Reward Collaborative Behavior

Let's face it: We get what we encourage. It's important to clarify the cost-benefit ratio for people to participate collaboratively. If you are not rewarding effective teamwork, don't expect it to happen.

- There are no rewards for his team as there are in other departments of the company. (T551)
- We need team recognition. (T192)

Do make sure, however, that you're rewarding the outcome you desire. Rewards can send both right and wrong messages. One of the most frequent complaints by team members is that money, promotions, and titles often go to people who do not demonstrate collaboration. That tells everyone there are two different values at work—one for merchandising a popular philosophy about teamwork and one for managing the business. Effective leaders avoid this hypocrisy and keep these outcomes one and the same.

Assuming the right behaviors are being rewarded, other forms of acknowledgment are also essential. Privately, performance appraisals draw attention to collaborative capabilities—present or absent. Publicly, as we have observed time and again, recognition is still the most consistently effective reinforcement for collaborative behavior. Many organizations recognize teamwork at their national sales meetings, as well as within specific functional areas. Over time, several forms of attention focused on collaboration can effectively drive the right set of behaviors.

Guide the Team's Problem-Solving Efforts

As we have noted, teams typically face any number of obstacles and challenges that require the team to engage in effective problem solving in order to reach its goal. In this connection, the key is not to allow anything—including how the team leader guides the team in problem solving—to interfere with achieving the goal.

- Allow the team to participate in decisions. (T543)
- Greater democratic discussion before making major decisions. Fewer manager "secrets." (T197)

It's essential for a team to feel that its problem-solving efforts are meaningful and that it's capable of making good, timely decisions without having to go through drudgery to do so. When a team feels it's making the same decisions over and over, or undoing and redoing decisions again and again, or darting erratically from one crisis to the next, then the team knows it's remiss in its primary reason for existence—to raise and resolve those issues that move the team toward achieving its goal.

Effective team leaders do not leave this critical team capability to chance. They know that teams succeed or fail based on the worth of their decisions. As a leader, you have the ability to influence the productivity and effectiveness of your team's collective problem solving. Your responsibilities can be expressed in terms of the problem-solving model described in Chapter 3:

- Make sure everyone has a clear understanding of the problem the team is trying to resolve. Avoid taking it for granted. Write it on a flip chart in the form of a single question. Ask team members, "If we answer this question, will we have satisfied our purpose?"

- Make sure the team conducts a good analysis of the issues that are related to the problem rather than arriving prematurely at an answer to the primary question. The responses to the issues, or subquestions, should lead the group to a reasonable response to the primary question—one that considers all of the issues raised.

- Make sure that the solution is based on the best available information and collective judgment within the team.

- Make sure everyone feels it is safe to contribute and to challenge the discussion respectfully.

Beyond guiding the team's own problem-solving efforts, you may need to be watchful for other factors that can impede problem solving. When we refer to a collaborative problem-solving climate, we are referring to a specific psychological atmosphere or context in which activities are conducted and decisions are made. It is a facilitative atmosphere in which people have good, timely information and access to processes for offering their input and making decisions. Within most organizations, a lot gets in the way of this happening.

As a team leader, you should look for and work to overcome obstacles to collaboration even when these obstacles are inherent within the larger organization. For example, the organizational structure may make it difficult for some team members to be involved in decisions that should be made jointly with another part of the organization. Or the organization's systems might not be set up to provide accurate information or allow decisions to be made in a timely manner. Or decision-making processes—such as strategic planning, budgeting, capital expenditures, and acquisitions—may not bring together the right people at the right time in the decision-making process.

Effective team leaders look for and address speed bumps that are external to the team but that can slow down the team's ability to succeed. By the same token, they avoid creating obstacles for other teams within the organization.

Finally, guiding the team to solve problems productively means involving team members effectively in the decision-making process. One of the most important judgment calls for you as a team leader is to distinguish when it is necessary to require broad-based input from your team and when technical expertise is necessary and sufficient.

There are some issues and decisions that you, or someone on the team, will be expected to address because of experience or specific technical expertise. Such decisions might involve legal issues, specific technologies, or other matters that involve someone's unique knowledge.

On the other hand, there are some problems about which no one is expected to have special skill. For example, a problem such as juvenile crime is so complex that no one person, no matter how well informed, can resolve it. Such a problem requires enormous input and broad-based collaborative thinking by communities of people. So, too, with challenges like shrinking markets or declining morale. No one person is expected to know all of the dimensions involved in a solution. That's why such problems require data, discussion, and time to unravel.

As indicated in Figure 4.1, the more you can rely on technical competence, the less you have to rely on broad-based collaborative input. Conversely, the less that technical competence alone can solve a problem, the greater the need to solicit input from the entire team. We are talking about the relevance and appropriateness of the process to the decision being made. Erring too far to the left can cause overmanagement; erring too far to the right can involve the team in trying to resolve issues the members are not competent to solve.

A key to effective problem solving is to have the flexibility to choose the appropriate process. Such a choice can be available only if the team leader operates from a collaborative climate as his or her everyday way of doing business. Then, when it's necessary to turn over the decision-making reins to an expert on the team, the shift is discussed

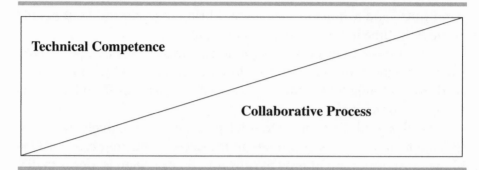

Figure 4.1. Technical Competence Versus Collaborative Process

and, with the blessing of the team, the primary shaping of the decision is carried out by the expert.

As you can easily imagine, the opposite approach does not work quite so well, if at all. We have seen many teams that have tried to create a collaborative climate only when they think one is needed. The rest of the time they operate out of "expert silos" or heavy decision making by the team leader. Trying to create an ad hoc collaborative climate, particularly during times of crisis, simply doesn't work as well.

Manage Your Ego and Personal Control Needs

In the musical *Pickwick*, the lead character sings, "If I ruled the world, every day would be the first day of spring." How true for most of us. The more control we have over our lives, the better we feel.

Consequently, it's no surprise that competing for control is one of the more natural and frequent points of conflict between team leaders and team members. In particular, team leaders with high control needs can send teams roiling. Furthermore, once team members identify a controlling pattern of behavior on the part of the leader, it becomes difficult for the leader to overcome the stigma. When high-control leaders attempt to ask facilitative questions such as "What do you think we ought to do?" or make acquiescent statements such as "Whatever we decide is fine with me," team members wait for the controlling shoe to drop. They know that the conversation won't be over, or a decision won't get made, until the leader is satisfied that the decision is one he or she would have chosen.

- He's a "control freak," and he keeps the team in a state of agitation. (T498)
- Our leader and God cover all knowledge, and it is important to hear from them both before we make commitments or finalize our conclusions. (T112)
- What the team leader says is gospel. There is no negotiating. (T38)
- All meaningful decisions must be made by the leader. (T108)

As team leader, you do need to provide guidance, share your ideas, and honor your convictions. You must also be able to demonstrate your passion and argue your point of view. However, it's much easier to show enthusiasm for an idea and argue for it on its merits if you haven't painted yourself into a corner as a control freak.

A useful way to think about managing your control tendencies is to focus on balancing and sharing the control between you and your team—as a group and with each member individually. In this regard, managing control tendencies is not so much high-wire walking as it is common sense.

In all relationships, including those on teams, controlling behavior appears to have a curvilinear relationship with satisfaction (see Figure 4.2). That is, too little or too much control can lead to the same outcome—low satisfaction.

On the one extreme, demonstrating no desire to influence a decision can be perceived as abandonment, abdication, or not caring. When this occurs, team members can be left guessing and wondering about your perspective. They may feel you don't value or trust them enough to share your ideas or that, for whatever reason, you don't want to offer guidance that will help them succeed. More than likely, they will begin questioning your ability to lead. Ultimately, their trust in you will decline.

On the other extreme, exerting too much control can be construed as overmanaging, not caring what other people think, and not valuing

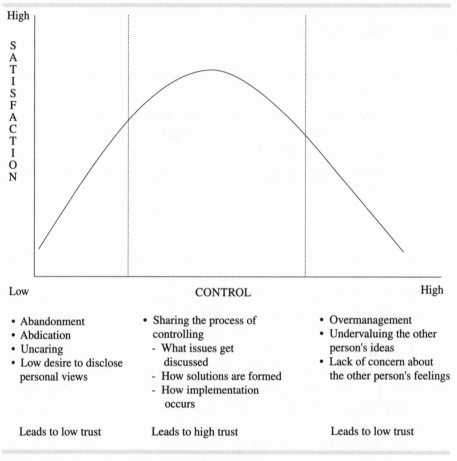

Figure 4.2. Control and Relationship Satisfaction

their ideas. Whether one-on-one or during group discussion, if you have ever been on the receiving end of someone who exhibited high control, you know what was really going on behind your own glassy-eyed response. While you were nodding, raising your eyebrows, and offering such utterances as, "That's interesting," your self-talk was not parallel with your visible responses. Silently you were probably saying to yourself: "Why are we having this discussion? This isn't a real give-and-take conversation. Just admit it. You already know what you want the decision to be."

In assessing the more subtle behaviors of the high-control team leader, it's important to look at the total package and ask these questions:

- Does the team leader only try to give the illusion of gathering input?
- Does the team leader limit the discussion by cutting it off while team members feel there is still more to say?
- Do team members ever feel hoodwinked or maneuvered into a decision?
- Does the team leader usually get annoyed when discussions dig into the issues, referring to the discussion as a "waste of time"?
- Does the team leader try to prescribe the taste or style of others?
- Does the team leader seem negative and overly critical of things in general?
- Does the team leader get unnecessarily immersed in details that could be entrusted to team members?
- Does the team leader make others feel defensive?
- Do team members feel they have to position a topic just right in order to avoid an abrupt halt to a discussion or being handed a solution?

Team leader behaviors such as these inhibit openness and supportiveness. They also dilute the confidence of team members and, more importantly, increase the chance of a poor decision getting made somewhere along the way.

An unfortunate feature of controlling behavior is that it is self-reinforcing. When we are right often enough, we can all become enthralled by our ability to make the right choice. It then becomes even harder to stop hugging our own ideas, especially when they differ from the ideas of others.

Eventually, as entrenchment deepens, it also becomes difficult to let go of control and have faith in the independent abilities of team members. Such hesitation and doubt can be devastating. After all, one of the more useful ways of building confidence is by trusting team members with sufficient autonomy—the freedom to think and the encouragement to act.

The best way to manage your personal control needs as team leader is to demonstrate behaviors that share control.

- *Stay focused on issues—as opposed to positions—during important discussions.* Allow the discussion to unfold at a pace that is comfortable for team members.
- *Ask well-thought-out questions more often than you prescribe solutions.* Ask yourself, "Will what I'm about to say further the discussion, inhibit it, or end it?" As you ask questions and listen, you'll acquire insights that may make a difference in the quality of solutions.
- *Repress the impulse to have the final say about every decision.* Determine which decisions are critical, and carefully choose the occasions when you use your power to influence outcomes. In the spirit of collaboration, avoid the urge to maneuver the team toward a predetermined solution.
- *Check with the members of your team during important decision-making processes.* Ask them if they feel all perspectives are being valued and whether they believe the solution will be the product of the team's best collective thinking—theirs as well as yours.

Remember, team members know when they are being asked to serve the team leader's ego versus the team's goal. Collaborative team leaders understand that leadership should be more than an ego-indulgent experience. They work at being well grounded in maturity, objectivity, and genuine self-confidence. They don't allow their insecurities to get in the way of the job at hand, and they don't labor to create their own persona. They know their leadership will be best characterized by others, based upon who they are as people, not what they are as a title.

Box 4.2

The following items best represent the behaviors for "Ensure a Collaborative Climate."

7. I create a safe climate for team members to openly and supportively discuss any issue related to the team's success.
8. I communicate openly and honestly.
9. There are no issues that I am uncomfortable discussing with the team.
10. There are no chronic problems within our team that we are unable to resolve.
11. I do not tolerate a noncollaborative style by team members.
12. I acknowledge and reward the behaviors that contribute to an open and supportive team climate.
13. I create a work environment that promotes productive problem solving.
14. I do not allow organization structure, systems, and processes to interfere with the achievement of our team's goal.
15. I manage my personal control needs.
16. I do not allow my ego to get in the way.

■ DIMENSION THREE: BUILD CONFIDENCE

The third dimension of collaborative team leadership embraces a rather common sense perspective: We like to be around people who strengthen our confidence, and we avoid those who weaken it. Consider the following experience, related by a member of an executive management team:

I arrived home after a long day at the office and sat down at the dinner table with my family. As we passed around the food, my wife asked me casually and without ever mentioning my manager's name: "So, what did *he* do today to make you feel bad?" At that split second, I realized how much I had been verbalizing my frustration with our team leader to my wife. In that same split second, I also realized it was time for me to make a job change.

Whether you like it or not, as a team leader you are the topic of dinner table conversation more often than you realize. In a relationship between a team leader and a team member, there is unequal footing. For the team member, the threat of insecurity or even diminished self-esteem is never remote.

Collaborative team leaders bolster the self-assurance of team members. They demonstrate personal confidence in individual team members, transporting each person to a higher self-expectation. They help team members succeed and achieve results by ensuring that the real issues are clear and that the important facts are understood. They build trust by providing meaningful responsibilities accompanied by the freedom to think and act. They encourage team members to stretch.

- ■ He inspires confidence in his leadership, the individual, and the team. Best leader I have had in 34 years with the company. (T585)

Collaborative team leaders demonstrate a positive attitude that focuses on opportunities and accomplishments. They are fair and impartial toward all team members, careful neither to reject nor to exclude. When all is said and done, collaborative team leaders believe leadership should enhance the confidence of others. Why? General Electric's CEO Jack Welch put it best: "Giving people self-confidence is by far the most important thing I can do. Because then they will act."[2]

As you think about your ability to build each team member's confidence to contribute, remember that team members are not only potential team leaders, they are coauthors of your own leadership. Their success is your success. With that thought in mind, let's explore the specific leadership practices that team members tell us build confidence.

Get Results

Building team confidence begins with achieving results. The most authentic confirmation of confidence is being part of a solid, well-earned, winning experience. It is the most preferred measure of leader effectiveness,[3] and as Ulrich, Zenger, and Smallwood argue in their book, *Results-Based Leadership*, it is the end game of leadership for the employee, the organization, its customers, and investors.[4]

- He has a passion for winning. Demanding. Inspires confidence among everybody he interacts with. (T519)
- He expects a lot but is not overbearing or intimidating in his style, which encourages people to work harder for him. (T551)

No matter how convincing the promise, a team goal is either achieved or it is not. If it is achieved, everyone's confidence is brighter and more buoyant. If it is not, the whole experience may fizzle. Even team members who were more successful than others in their personal contributions to the team goal can get painted with the same drab brush.

> "Our leader needs to create a sense of confidence that success will be achieved."

- Our leader needs to create a sense of confidence that success will be achieved. (T332)

Time and again we have seen teams, once bulging with confident individuals, drift into apprehension and indecisiveness because of a lack of results. Furthermore, although complete failure to achieve the team's goal usually has immediate consequences, mediocre achievement drags on and on as the team keeps trying to "believe" while watching commitment weaken and good people leave.

A member of an executive management team for an international airline made an interesting observation following the airline's decline:

> We missed our business plan so many times that it destroyed our confidence, our risk-taking, and our ability to grow the business. Eventually, we came to believe that our business plan would fall

short of the runway, and we would miss our landing before we even took off.

The feedback from team members is very clear: Confidence begins in the mind, but it must be nurtured by success. Results alone will not build a team's confidence, but they are absolutely necessary to the total formula.

Make Team Members Smart About Key Issues and Facts

A race car driver will test drive a track's conditions prior to a race to be as clear as possible about performance goals and margins of safety. It is clarity about the key issues that allows the driver to achieve the necessary confidence to commit to each turn and straightway. Without clarity there is doubt and apprehension.

In short, *clarity drives confidence. Confidence drives commitment.*

Conversely, if clarity suffers, so does confidence. Low clarity produces low confidence in many ways: in the team's objective or direction; in the team leader's ability to lead; in the capabilities of fellow team members. What starts out as a problem of clarity soon degenerates into suspicion and mistrust.

- The leader has got to lead! Open up. Communicate. Regain the trust and respect she must have had at one time. (T32)

As a team leader, you have the right to expect team members to be crystal clear about the critical issues and related facts affecting the performance and future of the team. Likewise, team members shouldn't have to muddle through vagaries or confusion in order to be confident that what they are doing is appropriately aligned with the key issues.

- He could improve the amount of communication he offers to the team concerning issues or roadblocks that he sees which could keep us from achieving our overall team goal. (T588)
- Withholds valuable information. (T549)

- The team leader discusses important issues with only select members and then communicates the "results" or "summary" to the entire team. (T308)
- Hold regular meetings with all team members to keep everyone up to speed on operations issues and share ideas. (T288)

In terms of keeping a team informed, a "need-to-know" approach by the team leader carries limited trust. Collaborative leaders work at making team members as knowledgeable and as smart as possible about the business and its underlying issues. This does not suggest a disregard for legally restricted communication and appropriate timing. But, with those limited responsibilities aside, team members should always feel that you, as a team leader, are putting extra effort into communicating the issues—and doing so in a way that leaves no mysteries to be uncovered, no surprises down the road.

The problem is this: You don't always know what team members don't know—and neither do they. It's essential to keep reinforcing, in as simplified a way as possible, the two or three pivotal issues and the relevant key facts. Encourage the team members to become deeply familiar with the issues. Ask them how the issues and the facts might influence their area of responsibility and decision making.

No one should be bewildered about the pivotal issues or in a fog about the facts. Be alert for signs that team members lack key information and understandings, and give them what they need to approach their task intelligently.

Exhibit Trust by Assigning Responsibility

There are few behaviors that build confidence as well as a personalized expression of belief in an individual. One of the most direct signals of such belief is trusting someone with important and meaningful responsibility.

Effective team leaders make good use of team members' talents. They leverage what team members can achieve at the present time and occasionally offer responsibility that helps them see beyond their current capabilities. They do so without making it seem like a high-risk venture or a long shot. Also, if a team member is understandably apprehensive about his or her ability to rise to the challenge, it's the leader who helps the team member to see a capacity for stretch.

- ■ We are each given an extraordinary amount of responsibility. (T583)
- ■ The leader allows the team members to be creative and provides a level of trust and backing that encourages team members to try new things. (T528)
- ■ Boldness. Invests real authority in each staff member to carry out responsibilities and make decisions. (T514)

A frequent complaint by team members is that their leaders often assign responsibilities on an ad hoc basis. Often such responsibilities involve after-the-fact timing, which precludes the team member from a chance to think and add value. He or she merely implements judgments already made by the team leader. As one team member put it: "I feel like a clerk assigned to busywork no one else wants to do. I would like something interesting to do—I would like to feel like an intelligent person."

- ■ Change the attitude of the team leader. Team members are capable of much more than their assigned responsibilities. (T32)
- ■ Let the members do their jobs without insulting their intelligence. (T197)
- ■ Our leader needs to work on overseeing the big picture and allowing his subordinates to control the day-to-day details. (T360)
- ■ Takes on too much alone, does not delegate!! (T549)

Be Fair and Impartial

We sense acceptance. We sense rejection. Acceptance feels better.

No team member wants to feel like an outsider on his or her own team. Unfortunately, our research tells us that team members can be made to feel slighted and treated unfairly by their leaders. Furthermore, when fairness and impartiality are at issue, the team leader is almost always unaware of the behaviors that are producing the problem. But team members are.

- Our team leader should not show any favoritism. (T276)
- Recognize that all team members are equally important to the team. (T355)
- Recognize that recent changes and improvements were a total team effort, not just one or two individuals. (T380)

As we have come to appreciate, team members look for ways in which the team leader either acknowledges or minimizes their value. We have already mentioned some of the ways a team leader can confirm the value of each team member, such as creating a collaborative climate, assigning meaningful and important tasks, and giving people the autonomy to act. But there is an additional cluster of behaviors that is far more implicit but sends equally potent messages, positive or negative, to team members. They are behaviors that signal to team members whether they are being treated fairly and whether they are included as valued members of the team. Such behaviors involve, for example, whether the leader includes or excludes individual team members in important meetings or activities; the amount of "air time" team members are given during meetings and where they are placed on the agenda; the extent to which the leader solicits the input of a team member rather than merely tolerating or avoiding it; the frequency of individual meetings between the team leader and team member; the ease with which an individual team member has access to the leader's calendar; and the frequency with which the leader visits a team member's office or work site.

- Quit sending signals about who he has faith in and who he doesn't. (T384)

Team members expect to feel acknowledged, valued, and treated fairly. If anything disrupts that feeling, particularly on a regular basis, they will begin questioning their personal worth in your eyes and their value to the team. As you think about the degree to which you value each of your team members, ask yourself how they think you feel about each of them. Better yet, if you want an unfiltered response, ask them directly.

When all is said and done, team members look to you as the team leader for an overarching sense of fairness and impartiality. They recognize, just as you do, that a team leader who is not fair and impartial can work in favor of some team members and against others—but he or she always works against the *team*.

Accentuate the Positive

> *Fear of failure drove me at first, but as I tackled each challenge, my anxiety was replaced by a growing sense of optimism. Once you overcome seemingly insurmountable obstacles, other hurdles become less daunting. Most people can achieve beyond their dreams if they insist upon it. I'd encourage everyone to dream big, lay your foundations well, absorb information like a sponge, and not be afraid to defy conventional wisdom. Just because it hasn't been done before doesn't mean you shouldn't try.*[5]
>
> Howard Schultz
> Chairman and CEO
> Starbucks Coffee Company

If you want to build confidence, display a positive attitude. There are many ways to do so. Some highly effective team leaders have an imperturbable sense of equanimity, whereas others are more passionate. Some frequently demonstrate ingenuity, whereas others work flawlessly at each step of a tried-and-true formula. From a ready wit to jolly laughter, from an extroverted personality to a muted mannerism, there are any number of traits that can be part of a positive attitude.

Responses from team members tell us, however, that among all the characteristics that can be part of a positive attitude, two qualities stand out: a desire to achieve and a "can-do" approach. Together, these two traits build confidence by maximizing the numerator and minimizing the denominator in the equation of risk.

$$\text{RISK} = \frac{\text{Desire to Achieve}}{\text{Fear of Failure}}$$

The first quality, a desire to achieve, is best demonstrated by a willingness to take on a challenging goal—to see its worth and want to do it. An achievement orientation brings with it a desire to do something that matters and an edginess to get at it.

The second quality of a positive approach, a "can-do" attitude, is more than cheerleading or a series of parlor tricks. An optimistic, "can-do" approach encourages. It is a frame of mind that is undaunted by adversity. Each difficulty or setback is just one more challenge to be surmounted. It's a durable confidence in the ability to succeed, compelling enough to be contagious.

- Increase the entire team's enthusiasm about their jobs. (T131)
- Minimize the complaining and concentrate more on the constructive things we can accomplish. (T76)

Say "Thank You"

We have seen many team leaders who possess all of nature's physical and mental blessings but are never eagerly embraced or widely accepted. Sometimes it's because they never seize the opportunity for accomplishment. Sometimes it's because they feel the best way to motivate others is to keep them on their toes by drip-feeding self-doubt. And sometimes, it's because they never say thanks for a job well done.

Effective team leaders have the capacity and the desire to acknowledge and appreciate team members for their accomplishments. Unfailingly, they acknowledge the contributions of team members. What's more, they not only notice such accomplishments, they actively look for them.

- He is good at letting the team, team members, and the company know when team members have done good work. (T549)

As the late Karl Bays, the highly successful CEO of American Hospital Supply Corporation, once said, "Good management is nothing more than good manners and common sense. In its simplest form, it's the ability to say thank you."

Box 4.3

The following items best represent the behaviors for "Build Confidence."

17. I ensure our team achieves results.
18. I help strengthen the self-confidence of team members.
19. I make sure team members are clear about critical issues and important facts.
20. I exhibit trust by giving team members meaningful levels of responsibility.
21. I am fair and impartial toward all team members.
22. I am an optimistic person who focuses on opportunities.
23. I look for and acknowledge contributions by team members.

■ DIMENSION FOUR: DEMONSTRATE SUFFICIENT TECHNICAL KNOW-HOW

"We all thought it would work. But when the curtain went up there was little talent on stage." Such was the lament offered by a peer of an executive whose successful track record as a line manager placed her at the head of a corporate staff function:

> She possessed all the capabilities imaginable—intelligence, good interpersonal skills, results oriented—except one: an understanding of the technical aspects of the new staff assignment. Everyone assumed learning would occur quickly. After all, how difficult would it be for a successful line manager to understand the fundamentals of a corporate staff job?

Unfortunately, an appreciation of the content within this staff function did not evolve as readily as everyone had hoped. The new function leader, in an effort to show results quickly, began making decisions without sufficiently understanding the consequences, or for that matter, heeding overt warnings by team members.

Eventually, the failure of this new assignment was a sizable one. For the individual, it was a failure that was hard to overcome, and eventually overshadowed an otherwise successful career. She ended up leaving the organization. For the organization, it undermined an otherwise well-intentioned attempt at lateral development. For the team members, it created emotional turmoil for nearly 18 months and sent them a multitude of negative messages about their capabilities and worth to the organization. Two of them resigned. And as for the function, it suffered a tremendous loss of credibility and an increased difficulty in attracting good people.

The fourth dimension of effective team leadership that emerges from the observations of team members is technical know-how. Broadly, having technical know-how means understanding the content, or body of knowledge, directly related to the achievement of a goal. Sometimes this means knowledge specific to a well-defined field. For example, if the goal is to lead a team in constructing the world's largest airplane, as was the case with the Boeing 747, understanding the discipline of engineering is essential. If the goal is to lead a team in creating a substitute for human blood that can be used during emergencies, it's necessary to understand the relevant science of biochemistry. If the goal is to lead a legal team as prosecution or defense in a legal case, it's necessary to understand the law.

But technical know-how also refers to understanding a product or service or marketplace. It could mean knowing a specific manufacturing process for a molded product, or the distribution requirements for food or medical supplies. It could mean understanding an organization's history, values, and culture. In short, technical know-how is a framework of understanding through which to identify and analyze key issues related to the team's objective. Usually it is knowledge comprised of study and direct experience.

> "He brings specific skills and experience, which are invaluable."

- He brings specific skills and experience, which are invaluable. (T519)
- He has knowledge of the business and industry. (T552)

■ Institutional memory. Depth of understanding of the company's business and strategy. (T581)

Lack of technical know-how doesn't mean that a team leader will automatically fail. People who are smart and who have excellent management and interpersonal skills can often hoist themselves to a credible stance. And, as we suggest in a moment, effective leaders know when to call on others' expertise. Nonetheless, in most situations, there is a minimum threshold of relevant knowledge that a team leader must possess in order to lead effectively.

■ Change our leadership—someone with more knowledge of what we do. (T296)

There are numerous reasons why a leader might be unable to demonstrate sufficient technical know-how. It might be because of lateral movement at a high level, lack of the necessary educational background, insufficient experience in an industry, or insufficient familiarity with products and services. Whatever the reason, a team leader who doesn't sufficiently understand the "content" can easily produce frustration on the part of team members, performance slippage, and an erosion of the team's influence within the broader context of the organization.

Know Your Stuff

In our first book we studied unusually successful, high-performance teams. Time and again, the impact of technical know-how was apparent and critical. For example, the surgeons selected for Dr. Michael DeBakey's or Dr. Denton Cooley's pioneering open-heart surgical teams were the most technically competent that could be found. The members of the project team that developed VHSIC (very high-speed integrated circuitry) computers for the strategic defensive initiative—commonly known as Star Wars—were selected from the best science and engineering talent in the country. The naval pilots who, after completing Top Gun School, gather at a remote naval installation in Nevada to learn and develop coordinated strike tactics, are the best people available.

This same observation was made recently by leadership scholar Warren Bennis in his book *Organizing Genius.*[6] He reported on six teams, including the original animation team at Walt Disney Studios, the Manhattan Project, and the Skunk Works team at Lockheed. This analysis of what Bennis called great groups—groups that had influenced history—arrived at an early conclusion: Great groups are made up of people who are very knowledgeable about the topic.

But what about the team leader? What is the connection between the leader's technical competence and goal achievement? Simply put, an intimate and detailed knowledge of how something works increases the chance of the leader helping the team surface the more subtle technical issues that must be addressed to accomplish an objective. As you might imagine, technical competence can be quite focused, as in the need to understand engineering to lead a team building an airplane, or law to lead a legal team, or medicine to lead a surgical team. Other times, technical competence can be in the form of broad experience. For example, over time, curiosity and accumulated experience can lead to a well-rounded understanding of the technical aspects of a goal. Think of the technical expertise possessed by someone like Jack Welch, who as CEO of General Electric, masterfully leads a highly diversified set of businesses—from household appliances, to jet engines, to a major television network, to financial services. Imagine the comprehensive insight he must possess to ask the right questions and provide guidance to the experts who run these individual companies.

A leader's technical know-how, however acquired, is essential. It doesn't always need to be expertly deep, but it does need to be conversant around the key technical issues. If a leader does not possess sufficient technical know-how, there must be a willingness to seek out and rely on those who do.

Get Help

One of the marks of an effective leader is the ability to use technical resources that the leader doesn't possess but that other people do. Effective leaders know what resources are available and then integrate them and maximize their use. In fact, given the complexity of most projects today, it would be difficult to conceive of a team leader attempting to achieve a goal or solve a problem without being open to the technical insights and perspectives of others. Think of a leader for an information technology group attempting to design and implement a new system. It would seem impossible to accomplish such an objective without being surrounded by competent people and being open to their advice.

Asking for what you need to guide the team's problem solving displays strength, not weakness. Leaders who use technical input skillfully are impressive. Dr. Don Wukasch served for 9 years on the open-heart surgical team of Dr. Michael DeBakey and 10 years on the surgical team of Dr. Denton Cooley, universally regarded as two of the most brilliant open-heart surgeons in the world. During our interview with him, we asked Dr. Wukasch about his perception of the difference in styles between the two renowned open-heart surgeons. Dr. Wukasch commented that Dr. DeBakey and Dr. Cooley had very different styles, but they were the same on the one issue that mattered most. Each of them was always deeply interested in having surgical team members bring in new ideas and propose new methods.

Effective leaders recognize that some knowledge is perishable. They know they must remain open to new ideas and challengeable on their technical assumptions. All we need to do is contemplate—for a nanosecond—how technical knowledge in the computer industry has been in a state of constantly accelerated evolution since the advent of the microchip. For all practical purposes, the computer industry has made its own base business obsolete several times during the past 20 years. For a leader to be out of touch with that reality could mean making a computer business extinct in relatively short order.

Bringing together people with different expertise and different perspectives is, of course, a primary reason for having a team in the first place. The leader's role is not to have all the answers, but to help the team analyze complex issues related to the goal. This usually means being open to technical advice from team members who may be more knowledgeable in a specific area. It means asking good questions, soliciting input, acknowledging a thin understanding of an issue, and demonstrating a willingness to listen and learn. It may also mean devoting blocks of time to being "tutored" by the experts on significant issues. Such time investments can pay huge dividends in the leader's ability to discuss key topics intelligently—and in the trust generated among team members. After all, one of the essential strengths of any leader is to be seen as credible and knowledgeable by people on and outside the team.

On several occasions we have seen leaders who stubbornly disregard the importance of technical know-how. They soon discover they can be ignored as easily as a substitute teacher. Occasionally, an obvious lack of relevant knowledge can take a leader completely out of the game.

Box 4.4

The following items best represent the behaviors for "Demonstrate Sufficient Technical Know-How."

24. I understand the technical issues we must face in achieving our goal.
25. I have had sufficient experience with the technical aspects of our team's goal.
26. I am open to technical advice from team members who are more knowledgeable than I am.
27. I am capable of helping the team analyze complex issues related to our goal.
28. I am seen as credible and knowledgeable by people outside our team.

■ DIMENSION FIVE: SET PRIORITIES

A leader's ability, or more correctly, inability to set priorities is the second most frequent complaint by team members. (The most frequent is an unwillingness to confront and resolve issues associated with inadequate performance.) The team

> "The team leader should have more focus, clear priorities, and be less ambiguous."

members we have surveyed contend that their day-to-day efforts get diffused, primarily by leaders who make everything a priority and by leaders who lack a steadfast commitment to critical initiatives.

- ▪ The team leader should have more focus, clear priorities, and be less ambiguous. (T384)
- ▪ More time spent on business strategy and client relationships. Less time spent on administrative matters. (T392)
- ▪ Focus on major strategic issues. (T545)

The key word in these comments is "focus." Let's explore further how focus can be achieved and maintained.

What Must Happen/What Must Not

How many priorities can a person be expected to sustain? How many ways of dividing up one's time will be productive? The answer varies. There is no exact number or even range across all types of industries, companies, jobs, and people. What is important is that a team leader strive for focus with relentless attention to one question: "What must be done to make the most systematic progress toward our goal?" Anything less invites a dilution effect. Everything gets done halfheartedly. Nothing is done really well. Some objectives are neglected and carried over year after year.

Broadly, a priority is determined when we are confronted with choices and decide which of two or more competing activities is most important. As a leadership trait, the ability to set priorities is the ability to reconcile competing demands for finite resources of time, money, and energy. And that means asking the question, "What need—business, organizational, social—does *not* get met if we postpone or don't do this particular task?" Although this may seem simple enough, being good at setting priorities requires a complex set of characteristics: knowledge of the business; decisiveness; confidence in the eventual outcome; and a psychological hardiness for taking the heat from those who disagree.

Effective team leaders understand the urgency of advancing toward the goal and translate that urgency into clear priorities. They scrape away the inessentials and concentrate on a handful of critical initiatives that will advance the team toward its goal. Equally important, they require each member of the team to do the same in their respective area. They ask: "What are the three most important objectives in your area that will drive us toward our goal?"

This approach sounds—and is—simple, yet team leaders often allow that clarity and focus to become diffused. Why? Because most team leaders want to be much more than curators of the team goal. They dream of being imaginative leaders who are full of surprises that are bold, creative, and strategic. To that end, it's necessary to explore ways of initiating change in the team's direction. The key is to explore change deliberately and selectively, not with flirtatious and diverted interests. We have seen many team leaders who seem hopelessly attracted to novel approaches and enticing possibilities, as if they were fearful of staying with basic priorities. If this happens often enough, the impromptu marshalling of resources required to explore every interesting opportunity can take a team out of its rhythm. Almost always, it's apparent when a leader's interest seems to be elsewhere. Furthermore, a leader's continually distracted attention can diffuse the team's energy and easily detract from results.

Although requiring a strong sense of heart and intuition for what must be done, leadership is more than improvisational passion. Above all else, it's a steadfast commitment to a goal and absolute clarity regarding the activities necessary to achieve it.

When Priorities Change

Being steadfast about priorities doesn't mean that priorities never change. On the contrary, rarely are priorities permanent. Often, the strategy for getting to the goal changes. That means priorities frequently evolve along the path toward a goal. Effective leaders see ways of reconciling what may be perceived as an apparent dichotomy in priorities. The key is that they do not allow priorities to simply multiply, thus diluting the team's effort. They understand the necessity of making choices and embrace choice-making events as opportunities to test the relevance of a priority and possibly upgrade to a better approach.

In fact, it should be noted that an effective leader will destabilize the priorities if the plan isn't working. To a certain extent, effective leaders are respectfully impatient with any speed of progress. They don't want to be like Moses, the great Hebrew leader, who worked hard for a glimpse of the Promised Land but died before reaching Canaan.

Often it's essential to adjust, change, and make trade-offs among priorities in order to attain the necessary speed and assurance for achieving the goal. During a crisis or strategic uncertainty, for example, coherent priority adjustment is indispensable. Whatever the reason, if it's necessary to change priorities, effective leaders carefully explain the reason for the change and ensure that everyone understands what the change means. After all, as any team leader would expect and want, there is an emotional investment that team members make in a set of priorities and the effort that goes into meeting them. A change in priorities, if it is seen as arbitrary, can be disruptive and discouraging. One way of checking for understanding is for the leader to ask each team member to describe for the team how the new priorities will change what they have been doing. The task of articulating a response to this question helps determine any necessary adjustments by each person. It is also more likely to further tighten the alignment of efforts. And, as we noted earlier, it's the alignment of *individual* effort that makes *collective* effort work.

Box 4.5

The following items best represent the behaviors for "Set Priorities."

29. I keep the team focused on a manageable set of priorities that will lead to the accomplishment of our goal.
30. Team members and I agree on the top priorities for achieving our goal.
31. I communicate and reinforce a focus on priorities.
32. I do not dilute the team's effort with too many priorities.
33. If it's necessary to change priorities, I make sure the team understands why.

■ DIMENSION SIX: MANAGE PERFORMANCE

The sixth and final dimension of team leadership that emerges from the insights of team members is performance management. Consider these two examples of written feedback to leaders from team members.

- Our team leader allows unacceptable individual performance to go unchallenged. (T76)
- Our leader needs to handle our one non-team-playing member directly and forcefully. (T380)

These statements capture the two most frequent types of feedback offered when team members see a failure by the leader to manage performance: Someone is seen as not pulling his or her weight, or someone is seen as being difficult to work with. In either case, the focus of the feedback is on the team leader's perceived inability, or unwillingness, to do anything about a performance problem.

In one team-building session with the CEO and executive management team of a Fortune 100 company, the team's feedback to the CEO focused on the CEO's apparent reluctance to address performance issues within the team. As an example, the team discussed how long it had taken the CEO to eventually remove a team member with a performance problem. After reviewing the team's feedback and listening to the discussion, the CEO commented:

> Yes, it seems I didn't move on that performance issue as fast as you would have liked. But let me ask you, if *you* were the performance problem, wouldn't you want me to take my time? Wouldn't you want me to make sure you were given a fair chance and the necessary help to turn it around?

The CEO's response offers a double insight. First, managing a performance issue takes time, at least to do it right: planning a well-thought-out message; having a discussion; creating an action plan; giving it sufficient time for progress to be observed. Second, even if the leader is addressing the performance problem, the team is unlikely to know it. For reasons of confidentiality—which is the way any of us would want the leader to handle it if *we* were the performance problem—something may be happening, but not publicly announced. All in all, during what appears to be an extended period, team members can easily begin to conclude, often incorrectly, that nothing is happening or that favoritism has occurred. Unfortunately, addressing the problem properly and confidentially can appear to take the same amount of time and leave the same impression as if the leader were ignoring the problem completely.

Perhaps the best way, and possibly the only way, to manage this dilemma is to clearly demonstrate a track record of managing performance effectively. To simplify, we would like to focus your attention on the 3 Rs of performance management: *require* results, *review* results, *reward* results.

Require Results: Make Performance Expectations Clear

Performance management begins with making expectations clear. Moreover, expectations should focus on *results* that are mutually agreed on by the team leader and team member.

- More standard expectation of performance and excellence. (T312)

Our experience tells us the following four categories of performance create a fairly comprehensive, results-oriented package.

1. Objectives. The first category of performance management consists of the *specific objectives* that must be achieved to accomplish the team goal. It's important not to confuse effort with results. To ignore this distinction is to invite disappointment. Everyone wants his or her effort to make a difference. It's unfortunate when good effort is misguided and misses the mark. It's even more unfortunate when effort goes to waste because of an ill-conceived objective.

A critical role of the team leader is to help each team member translate the team's goal into meaningful initiatives and activities. Specifying objectives helps team members construct a coherent perspective for how they focus their time and resources and assists them in prioritizing.

2. Collaborative Style. The second performance category includes the *skills* necessary to work within the team. Good performance expectations include an understanding that a collaborative approach is not an option. It's the leader's responsibility to hold each member of the team accountable—from the outset—not only for *what* they achieve but also for *how* they go about achieving it. The leader must make the collaborative approach an overtly stated requirement, not an implied preference. Each team member must be clear about demonstrating an approach that brings out the best thinking and attitude of everyone else on the team.

3. Management Skills. The third performance category measures the *ability to manage people and other available resources* effectively. It should be clear to each team member that managing is a privilege. No one has the right to chew up talent or make less than optimal use of resources. Any team member who manages other people must have a performance plan that guides each person toward achieving results. Effective team leaders take an active interest in how each team member, in turn, is managing his or her own team.

4. Personal Development. The final performance category concerns achieving sufficient progress in one or two well-defined developmental areas of *personal improvement, professional improvement, or both.* Personally and professionally, we're all works in progress. When a leader devotes attention to a team member's personal development, it's good for the individual and it strengthens the team, as well as the organization's talent pipeline. Working through a developmental opportunity with a team member can also be beneficial for the team leader.

Setting clear expectations doesn't involve anything that isn't already familiar or that is counterintuitive. Most managers know how essential it is to articulate their expectations for individual performance. What is important is the discipline of doing it.

Review Results: Give Constructive
Feedback and Resolve Performance Issues

Having stated expectations that emphasize results, effective team leaders tend to review results on a consistent basis. They know that what gets done is what they pay attention to. Accordingly, they put time into reviewing results with team members—not as an annual event, but on an ongoing and continuous basis. They offer constructive feedback that includes a well-rounded review of all four dimensions identified in setting expectations: specific objectives, a collaborative style, management skills, and personal development.

Most importantly, effective team leaders know that it is their responsibility to address issues of inadequate performance by team members. They know that a performance issue and the absence of feedback is a devastating combination. And they understand that failing to address a performance issue through constructive feedback is an evasion of leadership.

Give Constructive Feedback

■ The leader should provide more counsel and feedback. (T579)

Feedback can be uncomfortable for the person giving it as well as the person receiving it—so much so that it can be hard to find the appropriate balance of sensitivity and clarity. On the one hand, feedback can be softened or so vague that it produces a wrong response or immobilizes the receiver into no response at all. For reasons of personal comfort, the person giving the feedback might be ambiguous with the hope that the receiver will think about it and somehow greater clarity will soon follow. Needless to say, that hope is rarely fulfilled. On the other hand, feedback can be so point-blank that it leaves a powder burn. Even though the leader's intention is not to demean the receiver of the feedback or bruise feelings, when the feedback is brusque or consists of a blitzkrieg of shortcomings, it often has those effects.

Effective leaders know what feedback is not. They know that it's not a bucket dumping of frustration or a warning shot fired over the bow. They know it's not practicing psychiatry without a license: "You seem to not like yourself very much." They know it's not a tedious, moralizing lecture or admonition. They know it's not creating defensiveness that can wrong-size the commitment of the team member to make a change and turn a discussion into a messy melodrama. They know feedback is not a surprise or "gotcha."

When offering corrective feedback, effective leaders ensure that it is both unambiguous and as helpful as possible. They are direct, but with an approach that neither rejects nor threatens self-esteem. One way they do this is by always trying to land on the issue—that is, the behavior—not the person. (The Connect Model presented in Chapter 2 can provide a particularly helpful structure for giving constructive, highly focused feedback.) Even when the recipient of the feedback is "listening impaired," effective leaders still take the high road. And if the recipient of the feedback is having an unusually difficult time, an effective leader knows when to be soothing without compromising the message.

By the same token, effective leaders never compromise the feedback process—short term or long term—by how they give praise. When they offer praise, they do so without being mawkish, patronizing, or seeming insincere. Even when a team member's performance is unfaltering, they view feedback as an opportunity to recognize excellence and to stretch for growth in the individual and the team.

It's not always easy for a leader to see a team member's performance in 3-D. The best you can hope for is to ask the right questions: Are results being delivered? Is movement toward the milestones far enough and fast enough? Does the person take a collaborative approach? Is the person properly managing the people and resources entrusted to him or her? Is the team member addressing opportunities for personal and professional improvement? Asking questions such as these helps pinpoint where someone's performance is strong and where someone's performance needs adjustment. The bridge between identifying the need for an adjustment and making the adjustment is constructive feedback.

Confront and Resolve Performance Issues

For the team's collective effort to succeed, everyone must perform. When someone is not performing, everyone knows it. If the leader doesn't deal with it, everyone knows that as well.

How do we know? When we divided our database of team member responses into upper and lower quartiles on a collaboration index and compared the top and bottom teams on all of the numeric items in our instrument, the most powerful discriminator was the following item: *Our leader is willing to confront and resolve issues associated with inadequate performance by team members.* This item was the best discriminator of effective versus ineffective leadership and also the top complaint about leaders' shortcomings. On average, ratings on this item are the lowest that leaders receive from their teams on all the leadership qualities we have researched.

Most team leaders have had experiences that tell them it's hard to manage a performance issue. Dealing with a performance problem involves telling people they are not measuring up, which is emotionally difficult and often creates an uncomfortable set of circumstances. Legally, confronting performance issues requires a strong working knowledge of employment law and good management practices to reduce the risk of inappropriate and even actionable behavior.

But as difficult as it is to manage a performance issue, confronting the issue is usually better than letting the problem persist. Time and again we have seen what happens when a team leader ignores or ineffectively addresses an issue of inadequate performance by a team member. The team wastes time hand wringing. They watch impotently as collective effort comes unraveled. They criticize the team leader, usually behind closed doors, for not stepping up to the problem—all because they believe nothing is happening.

Excellent team leaders never knowingly ignore a performance problem; they are action oriented. They try to do something about the problem early enough and in a constructive way. The overall pattern is fairly straightforward. They take the team member aside and remind him or her of the goal and why it's important. They describe what the person is doing that is making it more difficult for the team to achieve the goal. They let the team member know they want the individual to be successful and that an adjustment is needed. They confirm their support and desire to help. They also let the individual know that, ultimately, the challenge for improvement is that person's responsibility. They negotiate a remedy with the person. They create a process for monitoring improvement, and they don't let it drag on forever. They articulate clear expectations. Then they watch. If the team member is trying, they'll tend to hang in there with the person. If the individual ignores the feedback, they'll remove him or her from the team—and do so rather quickly for the sake of everyone involved.

- Make the tough management decisions and replace certain team members. (T400)
- Eliminate the unmotivated team members and replace them with dedicated individuals. (T96)

Reward Results: Recognize Superior Performance

Having required and reviewed results, the final step is to reward the people who achieve or exceed the results desired. As you might expect, team members are highly cognizant of the importance of rewards and recognition.

- ▪ The leader positively motivates the team and individuals by giving sincere recognition. (T588)
- ▪ Not a glory hog—looks for ways to give credit to team members at the lowest level. (T585)

Team members' comments offer one simple but trenchant insight into the reward process. A reward carries with it a burden of proof. It must make sense. If it doesn't make sense—to the recipient as well as any observer—the reward is devalued and the entire process is suspect.

> "The leader positively motivates the team and individuals by giving sincere recognition."

A reward can take many forms. It can be money, a promotion, or an appealing assignment. It can be any form of recognition. What the reward *is* matters less than whether it can be rationally comprehended from a few different angles.

First, the team leader must ensure that rewards and incentives are aligned with achieving the team's goal. All too often, team members are asked to achieve one objective, but they are rewarded for achieving something else. For example, it's very easy to ask the people who make up the salesforce of an organization to work together collaboratively in order to take advantage of frequently missed opportunities with customers, but then reward them only on the achievement of their individual targets for sales and gross profit. Such clumsy alignment of the goal and the reward can easily fracture team effort. Some people work hard to honor the request; others don't. Because there are no consequences either way, the misalignment makes it very easy to create hard-to-forget disappointments within the team. Effective leaders are careful to tie rewards clearly and directly to those desired activities that make it possible to achieve the team's goal.

Second, a reward must be fair. It must uphold the first precept of Hippocrates, which is to "do no harm." A reward should feel fair and appropriate on its own and equitable on a relative basis. The following comment from a team member represents a perspective worth noting:

■ Sometimes the people who get rewarded are not deserving, and no explanation is offered. It's like watching all of your hard work dismantled right in front of your eyes. (T144)

A reward shouldn't complicate the feelings of the recipient or the observer. It should make reasonable sense to a reasonable person.

Often, deciding on a reward is not a hard-and-fast calculation. It usually requires judgment by the team leader. How difficult were the conditions for some objectives to be achieved versus others? What impact did the achievement have on the team goal? Rewarding fairly and appropriately also requires separating *what* was accomplished from *how* it was achieved. For example, if a team member achieves excellent results but along the way wreaks havoc within the team, the leader must take into account both parts of the equation. If team members are expected to work collaboratively with one another, there should be the appropriate rewards or consequences for how their results are achieved. Otherwise, at least for that moment, the credibility of the entire process falls apart.

Third, a reward should be a celebration of standards. It should never lead the team into a thicket of confusion and doubt about what constitutes excellence. Excellent results must be recognized and confirmed as pushing the standard. The imprimatur of excellence must be reflected in the reward, otherwise the performance process is underdemanding. At the same time, rewards should not be scaled in such a way to create apathy, as reflected in this remark from a team member:

■ There is no incentive for above-average performance. (T236)

Knowingly, or unknowingly, a reward evangelizes the performance culture of an organization. At that moment, the recipient and his or her accomplishments are held up as the desired standard—high or low. Over time, the performance standard is confirmed.

It is the leader's responsibility to recognize and reward superior performance. It is the most concrete way of giving substantive meaning to the word *excellence* and heightening the appetite for success.

Box 4.6

The following items best represent the behaviors for "Manage Performance."

34. I make performance expectations clear.
35. I encourage the team to agree on a set of values that guides our performance.
36. I ensure rewards and incentives are aligned with achieving our team's goal.
37. I assess the collaborative skills of team members as well as the results they achieve.
38. I give useful, developmental feedback to team members.
39. I am willing to confront and resolve issues associated with inadequate performance by team members.
40. I recognize and reward superior performance.

▪ A NOTE ON CONTEMPORARY LEADERSHIP THOUGHT

As we remarked at the start of this chapter, leadership is a subject that lends itself to metaphor, imagery, and even myth. By distilling what actual team members have to say about their experiences and perceptions of team leaders, we hope to have provided you with a more specific and helpful answer to the question, "What makes for an effective team leader?"

Although we have based this discussion on our analysis of team members' comments, you should know that our analysis of leadership is very consistent with what others are concluding. In particular, two recent reviews of leadership thought, one academic[7] and one "popular,"[8] taken together, reinforce our primary findings in this chapter.

First, leadership is about vision—having vision, articulating the vision, inspiring a shared commitment to the vision. Every contemporary perspective on leadership assumes that there is something of value we are pursuing and that attaining it will require us to work together.

Second, contemporary perspectives on leadership increasingly emphasize the relationship between leaders and constituents. There is clear movement away from understanding leadership as positional authority and toward understanding leadership in terms of the relationship between leader and constituent, such as the employee, the organization, its customers, and investors.[9] Aspects of the relationship that have been emphasized include trust,[10] confidence in followers,[11] intellectual stimulation of followers,[12] responsiveness to followers,[13] providing assistance,[14] and joint problem solving.[15]

To illustrate this emphasis on relationships, consider one of the better empirical studies of leadership we have encountered in the last several years.[16] A group of psychologists studied 1,264 members of 112 teams in the aerospace industry. Using a variety of measurements and some very sophisticated analyses, this research demonstrated that there were two very clear ways in which leaders influenced a group or team's performance.

First, the leader could directly affect certain group process variables, such as a collaborative (open and supportive) climate. These group process variables, in turn, led directly to heightened group or team performance. In other words, leadership was effective to the extent that it created circumstances or conditions that allowed the group or team to succeed. The leadership variables didn't correlate directly with group or team performance, but instead correlated directly with the group process variables, which in turn predicted group performance.

Second, leadership led to "group potency," the group's confidence in itself and its ability to achieve the goal. These potency variables enhanced group performance directly, as well as indirectly by positively influencing the group process variables described earlier. Either way, leadership can influence performance by enhancing the confidence that is felt in the group or team.

While we are on the subject of current thinking about leadership, we'd like to add a word about so-called leaderless teams. Although the principles of leadership discussed in this chapter focus on the formal leadership of a team, many also apply to the informal leadership that emerges in self-directed, or self-managed, work teams. After all, as Moment and Zaleznik[17] discovered nearly 40 years ago, when there is no formal leader, an informal leader will likely emerge. It could be someone who is exactly the right person for the team and its goal. It could also be someone who is authoritative, or someone who is well liked but ineffective, or someone who is pursuing personal gain. As this line of research tells us—and our observations agree—a team without a formal leader eventually surfaces a leader from the available talent, but in ways that are not always predictable.

Moreover, although it is not a hard-and-fast conclusion, we have observed repeatedly that teams without formal leadership are consistently poor at managing their own performance, as described in Dimension Six of this chapter. Experience teaches us that when such teams come off track, they are much less likely to be self-corrective. They are much less likely to address performance issues among team members and require excellence when excellence does not emerge naturally.

▪ PUTTING IT TO WORK

One way to begin putting the lessons of this chapter into practice is to evaluate your own leadership style and current capabilities, and to seek feedback from others. Comparing your self-perceptions with the perceptions others have of you is likely to be highly instructive.

To this end, we provide here a questionnaire that brings together the questions listed for each of the six dimensions described in the chapter (see Figure 4.3). The questionnaire is presented in two forms: a self-rating form and a form for team members to use in rating their leader. The validity and reliability of the instrument are described in the Appendix.

If you plan to seek feedback from the team you lead, it's important to ensure confidentiality and anonymity. Although this may be accomplished in many ways, we have found that such data gathering works best when the completed team member questionnaires are sent to a neutral third party—someone from human resources, or an external consultant, coach, or mentor.

Remember that people like to know you have taken their feedback seriously. Usually this requires that you share with them what you have learned from the feedback and how you plan to address key issues. Notice that we said sharing what you have *learned*: It isn't necessary to make public the numerical ratings you received. Simply focus on the two or three ways in which you are committed to improving your effectiveness as a team leader. Most often this discussion is accomplished in a team meeting. Whatever way you choose to review your action plan with the team, keep in mind the following suggestions:

- Try to give at least equal attention to negative comments as well as to the positive ones. In fact, more attention to the negative comments will help to counteract the natural tendency to soak up only the praise.

- Focus on the main message from the majority of comments. However, don't dismiss a negative comment simply because it seems to be an outlier. Maybe one person has particularly good insight, or is more honest or forthcoming than the rest. On the other hand, if after due consideration you can't see the justice in an outlier comment, then stay with the majority.

- When all is said and done, draw your own conclusions. Try to be honest and open with the feedback, and decide for yourself what actions to take.

- Finally, turn the evaluations as a whole into a personal agenda for improvement and review your progress with the team.

Although we believe that this questionnaire can guide your effort to become a more effective leader, it falls somewhat short of a recipe. Leadership can't be reduced to a finite "to-do" list.

The six dimensions of leadership emerging from our study are linked in a way that is yet to be fully understood. Although the exact blend will vary across individual leaders, there is little doubt that all six capabilities must somehow alchemize into collaborative leadership.

This much is clear. It's not a matter of being good at some parts and not others. It's a matter of being good enough at all of it, or at least not ineffective on any specific dimension. Moreover, the final ingredient in the alchemy of leadership is something only you can provide. In this respect, collaborative leadership is not only a matter of what you do but also a matter of who you are.

- ■ Our team leader has high moral values, and he genuinely cares about each individual. (T588)

The Collaborative Team Leader
(Team Leader Version)

I. Focus on the Goal

True	More True Than False	More False Than True	False	
☐	☐	☐	☐	1. I clearly define our goal.
☐	☐	☐	☐	2. I articulate our goal in such a way as to inspire commitment.
☐	☐	☐	☐	3. I avoid compromising the team's objective with political issues.
☐	☐	☐	☐	4. I help individual team members align their roles and responsibilities with the team goal.
☐	☐	☐	☐	5. I reinforce the goal in fresh and exciting ways.
☐	☐	☐	☐	6. If it's necessary to adjust the team's goal, I make sure the team understands why.

II. Ensure a Collaborative Climate

☐	☐	☐	☐	7. I create a safe climate for team members to openly and supportively discuss any issue related to the team's success.
☐	☐	☐	☐	8. I communicate openly and honestly.
☐	☐	☐	☐	9. There are no issues that I am uncomfortable discussing with the team.
☐	☐	☐	☐	10. There are no chronic problems within our team that we are unable to resolve.
☐	☐	☐	☐	11. I do not tolerate a noncollaborative style by team members.
☐	☐	☐	☐	12. I acknowledge and reward the behaviors that contribute to an open and supportive team climate.
☐	☐	☐	☐	13. I create a work environment that promotes productive problem solving.
☐	☐	☐	☐	14. I do not allow organization structure, systems, and processes to interfere with the achievement of our team's goal.
☐	☐	☐	☐	15. I manage my personal control needs.
☐	☐	☐	☐	16. I do not allow my ego to get in the way.

III. Build Confidence

☐	☐	☐	☐	17. I ensure that our team achieves results.
☐	☐	☐	☐	18. I help strengthen the self-confidence of team members.
☐	☐	☐	☐	19. I make sure team members are clear about critical issues and important facts.
☐	☐	☐	☐	20. I exhibit trust by giving team members meaningful levels of responsibility.
☐	☐	☐	☐	21. I am fair and impartial toward all team members.
☐	☐	☐	☐	22. I am an optimistic person who focuses on opportunities.
☐	☐	☐	☐	23. I look for and acknowledge contributions by team members.

Figure 4.3. The Collaborative Team Leader (Team Leader Version)

(Continued)

IV. Demonstrate Sufficient Technical Know-How

True	More True Than False	More False Than True	False	
☐	☐	☐	☐	24. I understand the technical issues we must face in achieving our goal.
☐	☐	☐	☐	25. I have had sufficient experience with the technical aspects of our team's goal.
☐	☐	☐	☐	26. I am open to technical advice from team members who are more knowledgeable than I am.
☐	☐	☐	☐	27. I am capable of helping the team analyze complex issues related to our goal.
☐	☐	☐	☐	28. I am seen as credible and knowledgeable by people outside our team.

V. Set Priorities

☐	☐	☐	☐	29. I keep the team focused on a manageable set of priorities that will lead to the accomplishment of our goal.
☐	☐	☐	☐	30. Team members and I agree on the top priorities for achieving our goal.
☐	☐	☐	☐	31. I communicate and reinforce a focus on priorities.
☐	☐	☐	☐	32. I do not dilute the team's effort with too many priorities.
☐	☐	☐	☐	33. If it's necessary to change priorities I make sure the team understands why.

VI. Manage Performance

☐	☐	☐	☐	34. I make performance expectations clear.
☐	☐	☐	☐	35. I encourage the team to agree upon a set of values that guides our performance.
☐	☐	☐	☐	36. I ensure that rewards and incentives are aligned with achieving our team's goal.
☐	☐	☐	☐	37. I assess the collaborative skills of team members as well as the results they achieve.
☐	☐	☐	☐	38. I give useful, developmental feedback to team members.
☐	☐	☐	☐	39. I am willing to confront and resolve issues associated with inadequate performance by team members.
☐	☐	☐	☐	40. I recognize and reward superior performance.
☐	☐	☐	☐	41. What are my strengths as team leader?

_____

_____

_____

42. What one or two changes are most likely to improve my effectiveness as team leader?

_____

_____

_____

Figure 4.3. Continued

SOURCE: © 1996 Frank M. J. LaFasto, Ph.D. and Carl E. Larson, Ph.D.

The Collaborative Team Leader
(Team Version)

I. Focus on the Goal

True	More True Than False	More False Than True	False	
☐	☐	☐	☐	1. Our team leader clearly defines our goal.
☐	☐	☐	☐	2. Our team leader articulates our goal in such a way as to inspire commitment.
☐	☐	☐	☐	3. Our team leader avoids compromising the team's objective with political issues.
☐	☐	☐	☐	4. Our team leader helps individual team members align their roles and with the team goal.
☐	☐	☐	☐	5. Our team leader reinforces the goal in fresh and exciting ways.
☐	☐	☐	☐	6. If it's necessary to adjust the team's goal, our team leader makes sure we understand why.

II. Ensure a Collaborative Climate

☐	☐	☐	☐	7. Our team leader creates a safe climate for team members to openly and supportively discuss any issue related to the team's success.
☐	☐	☐	☐	8. Our team leader communicates openly and honestly.
☐	☐	☐	☐	9. There are no issues that our team leader is uncomfortable discussing with the team.
☐	☐	☐	☐	10. There are no chronic problems within our team that we are unable to resolve.
☐	☐	☐	☐	11. Our team leader does not tolerate a noncollaborative style by team members.
☐	☐	☐	☐	12. Our team leader acknowledges and rewards the behaviors that contribute to an open and supportive team climate.
☐	☐	☐	☐	13. Our team leader creates a work environment that promotes productive problem solving.
☐	☐	☐	☐	14. Our team leader does not allow organization structure, systems, and processes to interfere with the achievement of our team's goal.
☐	☐	☐	☐	15. Our team leader manages his/her personal control needs.
☐	☐	☐	☐	16. Our team leader does not allow his/her ego to get in the way.

III. Build Confidence

☐	☐	☐	☐	17. Our team leader ensures that our team achieves results.
☐	☐	☐	☐	18. Our team leader helps strengthen the self-confidence of team members.
☐	☐	☐	☐	19. Our team leader makes sure team members are clear about critical issues and important facts.
☐	☐	☐	☐	20. Our team leader exhibits trust by giving us meaningful levels of responsibility.
☐	☐	☐	☐	21. Our team leader is fair and impartial toward all team members.
☐	☐	☐	☐	22. Our team leader is an optimistic person who focuses on opportunities.
☐	☐	☐	☐	23. Our team leader looks for and acknowledges contributions by team members.

Figure 4.3. The Collaborative Team Leader (Team Version)   *(Continued)*

IV. Demonstrate Sufficient Technical Know-How

True	More True Than False	More False Than True	False	
☐	☐	☐	☐	24. Our team leader understands the technical issues we must face in achieving our goal.
☐	☐	☐	☐	25. Our team leader has had sufficient experience with the technical aspects of our team's goal.
☐	☐	☐	☐	26. Our team leader is open to technical advice from team members who are more knowledgeable.
☐	☐	☐	☐	27. Our team leader is capable of helping the team analyze complex issues related to our goal.
☐	☐	☐	☐	28. Our team leader is seen as credible and knowledgeable by people outside our team.

V. Set Priorities

☐	☐	☐	☐	29. Our team leader keeps our team focused on a manageable set of priorities that will lead to the accomplishment of our goal.
☐	☐	☐	☐	30. Our team leader and the members of our team agree on the top priorities for achieving our goal.
☐	☐	☐	☐	31. Our team leader communicates and reinforces a focus on priorities.
☐	☐	☐	☐	32. Our team leader does not dilute our team's effort with too many priorities.
☐	☐	☐	☐	33. If it's necessary to change priorities our team leader helps us understand why.

VI. Manage Performance

☐	☐	☐	☐	34. Our team leader makes performance expectations clear.
☐	☐	☐	☐	35. Our team leader encourages the team to agree on a set of values that guides our performance.
☐	☐	☐	☐	36. Our team leader ensures that rewards and incentives are aligned with achieving our team's goal.
☐	☐	☐	☐	37. Our team leader assesses the collaborative skills of team members as well as the results they achieve.
☐	☐	☐	☐	38. Our team leader gives useful, developmental feedback to team members.
☐	☐	☐	☐	39. Our team leader is willing to confront and resolve issues associated with inadequate performance by team members.
☐	☐	☐	☐	40. Our team leader recognizes and rewards superior performance.
☐	☐	☐	☐	41. What are the strengths of the team leader?

_____

_____

_____

42. What one or two changes are most likely to improve the effectiveness of the team leader?

_____

_____

_____

Figure 4.3. Continued

SOURCE: © 1996 Frank M. J. LaFasto, Ph.D. and Carl E. Larson, Ph.D.

SNAPSHOT
5

The goal of any work environment is to ensure that people consistently take action to achieve the organization's goals. Not surprisingly, an organization can create many roadblocks to that happening—especially when it tries to implement collaborative teamwork. To shed more light on this issue, we asked 6,000 team members, including team leaders, to tell us about those environmental factors that either promote or get in the way of effective teamwork. Team members tell us that a productive work environment depends on the effectiveness of three overarching organizational dimensions:

1. *Management practices* that set direction, align effort, and deliver results
2. *Structure and processes* that ensure that the best decisions are made as quickly as possible by the right people
3. *Systems* that provide useful information and drive behavior toward desired results

Chapter 5 explores each of these dimensions, underscoring the message that a collaborative environment combines the three to maximize *clarity*, encourage *confidence*, and instill a *commitment* toward delivering results.

CHAPTER 5

THE ORGANIZATION ENVIRONMENT

Promoting Clarity, Confidence, and Commitment

If there is one consistent message that screams out from the popular Dilbert cartoon, it's that organizations are capable of overwhelming the best intentions and efforts that people have to offer. Some people may think Dilbert has only a tenuous connection with reality, but we know of an entry-level systems engineer who worked for eight years with a Fortune 100 company without ever having been part of a project that was completed by the organization. Somewhere along the way priorities changed, resources shifted, and each project was abandoned long before it was ever finished. As you might expect, in a fit of frustration, he quit. "Personally and professionally," he commented, "I needed to put my name on something. Our team goal changed so often that it didn't matter what we were working on. I lost faith in the organization. Nothing felt right." In its simplicity, his final comment is perhaps the best summary of organization environment. It either feels right or it doesn't.

Organization environment, the fifth and final dynamic of collaboration, has an enormous impact on teamwork. Opinion surveys have suggested that the primary reasons for team failures are organizational factors, particularly nonsupportive attitudes of senior management, noncomplementary systems for appraising and rewarding performance, and insufficient training for working as a team.[1] In this chapter, we draw on the responses of 6,000 team members and leaders to further illuminate the aspects of organization environment that have the greatest impact on the success of collaborative teams.

■ WHAT IS AN ORGANIZATION ENVIRONMENT?

Broadly, organization environment is the *psychological atmosphere* that emerges from the way an organization conducts itself. It's the intellectual and cultural climate that shapes attitudes and guides behavior, ultimately signaling whether the organization is a good or bad place to devote half of one's waking hours.

An organization environment has no particular location. It's pervasive. It can encompass and saturate everything we do: how we communicate; how we make decisions; how we interact with one another; what we celebrate; and what discourages us.

The environment is never neutral. It has compelling content. It shapes our ideas and perspectives. It can promote openness or silence. It can encourage risk taking or risk aversion. It can allow for differences or require sameness.

The organization environment can encourage or dissipate effort. Indeed, it has been argued that a work environment can influence "an inner passion to solve problems"[2] and that "great ideas dry up when people are hurting or focused on organizational dysfunction."[3] A good environment, often shaped by a strong culture, is productive and focused on results.[4] A bad environment diverts meaningful effort into meaningless distractions: turf issues, politics, power plays, beating the system, outsmarting the process, indecisions, bad decisions, redecisions.

Finally, an environment is self-perpetuating, simultaneously reflecting and reinforcing the *tone* of the organization. The longer an organization environment evolves, the more enduring it becomes, whether for good or ill.

∎ WHAT A GOOD ENVIRONMENT PRODUCES: CLARITY, CONFIDENCE, AND COMMITMENT

I never worry about action, but only about inaction.
Winston Churchill

The desired effect of any organization environment is to ensure that people persistently take action that leads to achieving the organization's goal. Whether the organization is a Fortune 500 company, an institution of higher learning, a government agency, or a volunteer organization is of little consequence. What does matter is the commitment to take action that leads to results. An environment can encourage people to work together by emphasizing and nurturing a very simple but powerful linear relationship: *Clarity drives confidence; confidence drives commitment.*

∎ Increase clarity. (Team 524)

Why is clarity so critical? Because the extent to which there is clarity in the organization—about the goal, priorities, key issues, core business values, rewards, standards, and so forth—influences the confidence people feel in their ability to exercise good judgment on the organization's behalf. Think about your own experiences. Recall a time when you may have lacked clarity in your work environment. Maybe the goal of the organization was unclear in terms of what it was trying to accomplish and how it planned to get there. Maybe you didn't understand how priorities were established or why they changed so frequently or so dramatically. Maybe you didn't understand why priorities kept accumulating but the availability of resources never changed.

Or maybe objectives and rewards seemed at odds. Perhaps the organization asked you to be a good team member, but rewarded you only on your individual performance. Maybe decisions involving your expertise occurred without you. Maybe you felt out of the loop with what was going on—the key issues, the broader challenges faced by the organization, important changes that were occurring or yet to come. Maybe what you thought to be your role and responsibilities turned out to be tasks that other people were also performing. Perhaps some people followed policies while others didn't, and it didn't seem to matter.

The problem is that if you don't know what your role is, it's hard to be fully confident about what you are supposed to do and, equally important, not do. If you don't know what the priorities are, it's hard to know where to put your time and energy. If objectives and rewards are in conflict, it's hard to feel sure you're doing the right thing. If the facts are unclear, it's hard to feel confident in making a reasonably sound decision. Without clarity it's easy to find fault, cast blame, and lose confidence in your ability to exercise good judgment.

Just as clarity drives confidence, confidence, in turn, drives the commitment to act. It is confidence—that feeling of self-assurance—that often provides the added resolve necessary to commit to a decision, to voice an opinion, to take action. Without the confidence that comes from being clear, people are less willing to raise difficult issues that may seriously affect the organization's success. All this is true not only of individuals but of teams as well.

Clarity drives confidence. Confidence drives commitment. This dynamic is clearly reflected in the three dimensions of organization environment that emerge from the comments of some 6,000 team members. These dimensions characterize the types of environments that support, or fail to support, effective teamwork and collaboration.

▪ THREE DIMENSIONS OF ORGANIZATION ENVIRONMENT

The environmental barriers to effective teamwork seem limitless. Perhaps this is the reason the team members in our database frequently referred to organization environment when responding to the following three questions:

1. If you could change one thing to help the team function more effectively, what would it be?
2. If you could discuss one issue in an open way, involving the total team in the discussion, what would that issue be?
3. What one norm or practice does the team accept that keeps the team from functioning better?

Whenever the responses to these questions focused on any aspect of the organization environment, we set aside these responses and analyzed them separately. These responses afford an exceptional insight into team members' thoughts about how an organization's environment makes teamwork and collaboration easier or harder. The respondents' observations cluster naturally into three organizational dimensions:

1. Management practices that set direction, align effort, and deliver results
2. Structure and processes that enable the best decisions to be made as quickly as possible by people who know
3. Systems that provide useful information and drive behavior toward desired results

These three dimensions are merged in Figure 5.1, with the underlying dynamic of promoting clarity, confidence, and commitment. As our research and experiences teach us, a collaborative environment smoothly combines and institutionalizes these three dimensions to maximize clarity, encourage confidence, and instill commitment toward delivering results. Let's explore these relationships from the vantage point of team members and team leaders.

1. Management Practices

Far and away, management practices have the greatest influence on shaping an organization environment that supports teamwork and collaboration. Team members' comments reveal that this is best accomplished by how well management practices are able to:

- Set a clear direction and focus on priorities
- Balance resources and demands
- Establish clear operating principles

Setting a Clear Direction and Priorities

The launch point for effective management practices is to *clearly define the goal and related priorities*. An organization's goal may seem clear,

Organization Dimension	Clarity	→ Drives →	Confidence	→ Drives →	Commitment
Management Practices that set direction, align effort, and deliver results.	**Clear about:** • The overarching goal and direction of the organization. • Strategic priorities for achieving the goal. • Resources. • Operating principles.		**Confident in:** • The leadership and direction of the organization.		**Committed to:** • Delivering results.
Structure and Processes that facilitate the best decisions as quickly as possible by people who know.	**Clear about:** • Roles and responsibilities. • How to participate in decision-making processes. • The organization's performance and key issues that must be addressed.		**Confident in:** • Thinking and acting in the best interest of the business.		**Committed to:** • Identifying, raising, and resolving all issues that can affect the success of the organization.
Systems that provide useful information and drive behavior toward desired results.	**Clear about:** • Critical information for making decisions and monitoring results. • Rewards. • Policies.		**Confident in:** • Being fact-based, current, and knowledgeable. • Knowing how to get things done according to standards.		**Committed to:** • Running an organization that: - makes fact-based decisions. - aligns systems and standards with desired outcomes. - is in sync internally and with its marketplace.

Figure 5.1. Three Dimensions of Organization Environment

SOURCE: © 1998 Frank M. J. LaFasto, Ph.D. and Carl E. Larson, Ph.D.

but all too often it is not. Team members repeatedly surface the need for goal clarity by asking about the overall direction of the organization or by asking for clarification on particular aspects of the strategy.

- What is the direction/vision/goal/ future of our company? (T36)
- We need clear, consistent direction, with continuous management follow-up. (T16)
- What is the strategic importance of being successful internationally? (T7)

Goal clarity must have deep roots. In fact, it should be a preoccupation. Organizational leaders should reiterate the goal frequently and with passion. After all, it's unlikely for anyone to stand face-to-face with the leader of an organization and say: "I don't understand the goal of our company. The words you are using make little sense to me." No one is likely to "dumbwaiter" that piece of criticism up the organization. Furthermore, if the goal becomes unclear along the way, it's leadership's responsibility to clarify it. The same is true for the path toward the goal. Although it may well zigzag from time to time, no one should have to wander around looking for a harbinger of what the objective is or how to get there.

> "We need clear, consistent direction, with continuous management follow-up."

If a goal is to be meaningful, it must be manifested in clear, well-focused *priorities.* This requires an organization to align all effort toward those tasks that will lead to achievement of the goal. One study of 193 high-technology companies found an interesting pattern among those identified as high performers in terms of time to market, innovativeness, success rate, and revenue contribution from new products:

High performers have established formal processes for managing and setting priorities among the entire portfolio of product development efforts. They set a clear overall agenda for company-wide new product development, and, on the basis of criteria tied to that agenda, carefully distribute resources among the various projects.[5]

Some of the most frequent complaints of team members focus on how poor management practices diffuse organizational effort. At the broadest level, we hear comments like these:

- The norm of "fire drill" management must be eliminated. (T360)
- Less interference by management. (T228)
- Why are we managed as inefficiently as we are? (T312)
- There is a basic distrust of corporate management and its "real" goals. (T464)

More specifically, team members are critical of how common it is to mismanage and muddle priorities and demands.

- Eliminate conflicting department priorities. (T112)
- Too many priorities, all of which are A-1! (T464)
- Balance individual goals and responsibilities for the business unit (or position) with the demands placed by the corporation. (T4)
- Does our organization really support the multiple goals we seem to have? (T192)

In many ways environment is an outcome of leadership—good or otherwise. As reflected in the tone of team members' comments, there is little reprieve for leaders who endlessly cause confusion and disarray. Team members simply ask those who run the organization to manage a productive shop, one that is more efficient and less intrusive. We all want our contributions to make a difference. No one likes to waste time and energy. As one team member, having become thoroughly frustrated by the organization's persistently changing goals and priorities, commented: "I hate to be cynical, but I'm given such great material to work with." Unfortunately, once an organization's management practices cause cynicism to set in, trust and credibility in leadership begin to unravel. Hope that changes in management practices will make the situation better is met with a saltshaker of skepticism and finally by cynicism—the downsizing of hope.

The goal must be the starting point for finding relevance in every initiative and priority—old or new. This is particularly true when an organization attempts to transform old patterns of behavior into a more relevant and productive environment. Consider, for example, the impressive cultural change initiative at Sears, the large retail chain. As reported by Rucci, Kirn and Quinn, the five-year effort was based on a "chain of cause and effect running from employee behavior, to customer behavior, to profits."[6] In our interview with Tony Rucci, then chief administrative officer who helped lead the effort, he described Sears's focus on the goal and alignment of priorities as follows:

> CEO Arthur Martinez sent a very clear message that focused the attention of the top 200 managers on the employee-customer-profit chain. He then charged them with articulating this goal to the remaining 300,000 employees. All priorities were aligned with employee and customer satisfaction. Whether CEO or forklift operator, when you came in at 8:00 in the morning you could answer this question: How does what I do over the next eight hours contribute to the strategic goals of the company? All rewards were aligned with this objective. In the course of a 24-month period, employee satisfaction scores improved, causing a 3-percentage point improvement in customer satisfaction. That, in turn, drove revenue growth to nearly twice the competitor average. Total shareholder return of 26.9% for that period well exceeded the S&P Index average. The market capitalization of the company increased by nearly $10 billion.

In a productive and efficient organization, management directives and requests are selective and aligned with the overarching objective. As such, they are more likely to be trusted as making sense rather than one more dartboard attempt at the right strategy. Aligning effort with priorities increases the likelihood of making sufficient progress toward the goal.

Balancing Resources and Demands

Sufficient progress toward the goal can be hard to come by without sufficient resources. Team members identify failure to *balance resources and demands* as a key source of frustration. As a director of information technology within a Fortune 500 company put it: "Eventually our team gets the resources it needs, but it seems it has to hit the fan first."

Indeed, part of human happiness depends on not feeling overburdened—at least not for too long. Few things are as debilitating as feeling frazzled by having too much to do and too little in the way of resources to do it. But team members' complaints about an imbalance of resources and demands are more than justified gripes about being overburdened. The theme that emerges from their comments is one of disappointment about teams not being able to hit the running stride they know they could achieve if resources (additional people, higher budgets, sufficient training) and work requirements were more equitable. In other words, team members want their teams to succeed. That desire to achieve the goal, not just personal discomfort, motivates comments like these:

PEOPLE

■ Give us the staff necessary to get the job done—we are desperate! (T272)

■ More people needed in the field. (T44)

■ We need to hire more support staff. (T192)

BUDGET

■ How can existing resources be targeted at strategic initiatives when we recognize the priorities exceed our capabilities? (T126)

■ More resources are required to comply with all the programs on our menu. (T540)

■ We need more realistic discussions on budget. (T16)

TRAINING

■ We need to spend a larger amount of time on education and training. (T352)

■ We need better cross-training. (T352)

■ We need to develop our people who do the work. (T38)

Balancing resources and demands presents a difficult dilemma that ultimately creates a push-pull nightmare between managers and employees. Whether overt or subtle, the pleas are the same: "It must get done!" versus "Give us more resources!"

From time to time it's going to happen: Workloads, priorities, and demands will exceed the available muscle, resulting in stretch and strain on a team. That's the nature of the world of work. In fact, managed properly, limited resources can help weed out unnecessary activities and outdated habits that have become part of the routine but have outlived their usefulness to the organization. Well-focused, limited resources can even breed a hardy bunch of team members, add interest and meaning to their efforts, and build their confidence in their ability to achieve.

But a steady diet of doing way too much with way too few resources is bound to have repercussions. What could otherwise be seen as challenging opportunities to achieve can easily become overburdening assignments that are dolefully carried out. New projects are met with justifiable apprehension. Eventually, discreet resentment is nurtured into a dominant theme. Occasionally, passive resistance will occur in the form of a subtle moratorium on doing anything new or outside the plan. Standards may slip from the high-water mark. And every so often—even though it seems nothing would predict it—cards are passed around, a vote is taken, and a collective bargaining unit is born.

Given that temporary imbalances in demands and resources are inevitable but that a sustained imbalance is debilitating, what is the bottom-line message from team members? Simply this: It's okay to have limited resources as long as priorities are pruned and deadlines are achievable. In other words, over the long term, the equation needs to be balanced. That can be done by scaling back demands or by increasing resources.

> "Reduce the number of priorities to allow key successes."

- ▪ We spread ourselves too thin trying to do too many things. (T316)
- ▪ Reduce the number of priorities to allow key successes. (T499)
- ▪ Obtain sufficient resources to complete our projects. (T424)
- ▪ More ruthless prioritization. (T519)
- ▪ Combine our priorities into one list and attack them as a team. (T56)

The dazzle of a lot happening with limited resources can be exciting, but over time an organization environment ought to be relatively reasonable. To be sure, it's not always easy to distinguish the background noise of hard work from the continuation of too many demands with too few resources. And it's not always easy to know when the line has been crossed.

One thing that leaders can do, however, is listen more carefully to their teams. If the organization succeeds in creating the kind of responsible collaboration described in this book, then team members' views are unlikely to be mere griping. The team members will be dedicated to their goal and invested in the organization's success. That should earn them a significant measure of trust. If they say they are consistently being asked to do too much with too little, they deserve a hearing. Moreover, they can be put to work on ways to adjust priorities or reallocate resources. In other words, they can take on a considerable share of the responsibility for problem solving.

In our right-sized, re-engineered world, balancing resources and demands will continue to be one of the great challenges to be met by good management practices. These practices must include active listening and staying in touch with real resource needs. As a member of a hospital surgical team commented, "When demands are real, resources shouldn't be imaginary."

Establishing Clear Operating Principles

Once there is clear direction and a focus on priorities, as well as a realistic balance between resources and demands, *operating principles* emphasize what is important to the organization. Operating principles are strong messages from the top that establish clear expectations and minimize any confusion about how the organization will conduct itself on a day-to-day basis. Although a full complement of operating principles for any organization is obviously unique, the responses of team members suggest that there are at least four common messages from the top that can make teamwork and collaboration more effective.

Message 1: We will take action toward the goal. Leaders must be clear "in thought, word, and deed" that the organization expects and trusts individuals and teams to take action toward the goal. Everyone must be prepared to assume responsibility, take initiative, and act in the best interest of the business. No one can be a spectator.

- Allow teams to make decisions and implement change more rapidly. (T436)
- Give teams more authority. (T164)
- Give teams more responsibility. (T392)
- Empower people more. Push decision making down to the lowest possible level. (T272)
- Delegate more to team leaders. (T60)

With a strongly stated expectation from leadership about taking action toward the goal, teams are more likely to demonstrate a desire to solve problems and move forward. Without such a message from the top, it's easy for teams to feel the weight of indecision. An organization must choreograph its feet to match the message. It does little good to pontificate on the virtues of risk taking while micromanaging everything and heaping heavy criticism on minor judgment calls. That kind of double message suppresses risk taking. And once the willingness to take risks is buried, it's difficult to exhume.

Message 2: We will be accountable for results. Consider this scenario. You are a member of a results-oriented team. Reliably, your team achieves its objectives and delivers results as promised. There is another team in the organization, one that misses its commitments often enough to draw the attention of any casual observer. It confuses effort with results, missing deadlines and placing other teams under time constraints. All this happens repeatedly and without consequences for the offending team. Question: How does it feel? If you are like most people, it's safe to say you will feel frustrated and disillusioned with the entire performance process.

Put simply, any management practice that leaves out accountability is useless. Lack of accountability—for some or for all—causes slippage in performance and impedes teamwork and collaboration. No one likes to work with individuals, teams, departments, or businesses that cannot be

> "Create an atmosphere of consistent accountability."

counted on to meet commitments, and for whom there are no consequences. Team members' comments clearly reveal an attempt to point out such inequities in accountability in the hope that the message will catch an updraft to someone who can and will do something about it.

- Create an atmosphere of consistent accountability. (T44)
- Hold the marketing function more accountable. (T16)
- We should constantly be striving for excellence at every position. This means continuous review of everyone's performance, eliminating mediocrity wherever it exists. (T392)
- Institute a more rigorous peer evaluation process. (T98)

Accountability elevates all performance. Teams are more productive when team members know that the organization holds everyone to the same standard: "We are all accountable for results." This must be a clear expectation from the top, and it must be consistently applied.

Message 3: We will work together as a team. To promote collaboration, an organization must establish clear chalk lines for the field of play. The message must be unambiguous: Work together. Collaborate. Cooperate with one another. Combine forces to address the real issues standing in the way of our success. It's good for our business. It's good for our customers. It's good for us to solve problems together, share resources, and help each other to make our business stronger. If being a good team player doesn't make good sense to you, then it doesn't make good sense for you to be here.

This isn't just warm, fuzzy thinking. We're talking about concrete, tangible success. Throughout this book we've referenced research that points to concrete outcomes from collaborative teamwork. Consider an additional study: Ancona has found that successful new product development teams are more actively involved than unsuccessful teams in creating and maintaining working relationships with other teams and work groups.[7]

Management cannot rely on an abstract dedication to collaboration. Team members must be continually reminded of its importance. Without a strong message from the top, collaboration can be easily treated as an organization virus, and all the systems and processes—and even some people—can act like antibodies.

- Get the zone VPs to reduce the size of their egos. (T28)
- We cannot function effectively as a team until the conflict between regulatory affairs and quality assurance is resolved. (T60)
- We must eliminate the barrier between clinical staff and the front office. (T328)
- We must improve our ability to work collaboratively at all levels of our organization. (T96)

Even with a strong message, there still will be some degree of organizational friction that must be smoothed. And there still will be people who see their work as an isolated project unrelated to any larger picture. And, of course, there always will be those who think collaboration is a fad that will go away or topple from its own weight. But that doesn't change the overriding message from team members. For those leaders who believe there is good business value in people working together collaboratively, there are no partial approaches. Collaboration must be an expectation that is wholeheartedly articulated and owned from the top down as *the* way of conducting business.

Message 4: We will avoid the politics. Let's face it: In the broadest sense, politics happens. By politics, we mean whenever someone is more concerned with furthering his or her own interest than with achieving a collective goal. If we were to eliminate everyone who has ever indulged in some form of organizational politics, there probably wouldn't be anyone left standing. Most of us are inclined to follow our evolutionary urge to be self-protective, and sometimes we may cross the line by not being completely open about our feelings, or by trying to position ourselves in a favorable light, or by simply wanting to be included. And as most people discover, whether through a slight faux pas or by completely "stepping in it," being sensitive to political realities can make life a good deal easier. The guilt of a little political posturing is much easier to live with than a public mea culpa or putting oneself at a disadvantage.

But when the team members we have studied refer to organizational politics, they are not referring to minor oversights and inclinations. They are referring to behavior that suffocates the real issues before they have a chance to be surfaced by the right people in the right way. They are referring to people and self-interest groups that make a challenging task much harder than it already is by confounding a business issue with a personal agenda.

- ▪ Reduce politics and redirect that energy to getting the job done. (T272)
- ▪ Remove profit plan politics from the management of joint activities. (T4)
- ▪ Eliminate objectives that are primarily political in nature. (T371)

Indulging in organizational politics is antithetical to collaboration. It chokes the ability to identify, raise, and resolve real issues in the best interests of the organization. Real issues get reconstructed into self-interest issues. Open discussion breaks down under the added burden of sifting through subtle ambiguities and taking sides. The search for good business solutions deteriorates into acceptance of half-baked decisions that satisfy some personal need or group need instead of the organization's business need.

Further, organizational politics diverts valuable time and effort. It creates schisms, often mangling and wasting good talent. Interestingly enough, all this can occur while those at the top optimistically believe that great teamwork is happening across the organization.

Avoiding politics cannot be a mumbled message. It must be a clear and forceful leadership expectation in at least three ways. First, whenever there is a discussion of organizational values or the importance of teamwork, leaders should emphasize and elaborate how politics can undermine the business by diverting effort, damaging relationships, and disrupting decision making. Second, for any decision-making process, leaders must require and ensure that all business issues are raised openly by inviting different points of view and looking for fact-based thinking at every turn. Third, leaders should make a conscious attempt to avoid participating in politics themselves.

The message from team members is clear: Politics must be avoided at all costs. It breaks the rhythm of clarity, confidence, and commitment by creating winners and losers. When that happens, the organization is always shortchanged.

As we bring our discussion of management practices to a close, we offer a simple observation: Confidence and trust in leadership are perishable. To ignore this truth is to invite disappointment. Members of organizations require a clear direction. They also require a well-managed, productive environment, and they are ill at ease when it is lacking. An organization's management practices can either build on or destroy team members' confidence and trust in those who lead.

2. Structure and Processes

Although there has been a steady migration toward teamwork and collaboration, expectations have often outstripped organizational structure and processes. Broadly, structure is the formal pattern of relationships among the various roles and responsibilities of an organization. Processes are the dynamic means by which goals are established, tasks are accomplished, and problems are resolved toward an end objective.[8] Both structure and processes need to be aligned with the requirements of collaborative teamwork for teams to succeed.

> "We need an objective and honest discussion about our organization structure."

Team members' comments reflect how efforts at teamwork and collaboration can quickly surface disenchantment with an outmoded structure.

- The organization structure could be better aligned with the team's objectives. (T360)
- Less structure, more sense of urgency with less bureaucracy and rigidness. (T400)
- We need an objective and honest discussion about our organization structure. Is it most effective? (T28)
- Change from the "old" structure to a more management-driven, smaller, quicker-to-respond organization. (T128)
- How do we operate with so many reporting structures? (T76)

When structure works well, it adds clarity, stability, and discipline to the coordination of effort. Organizational layers, spans of control, divisions of labor, reporting relationships, roles and responsibilities, and so forth provide guidance. However, when structure does not work well, it can dramatically undermine success. Indeed, even great organizations have faced periods when their responsiveness was encumbered by their own structural weight. As General Motors CEO Jack Smith commented, "The problem was never the people. It was the screwed-up structure. We had to change it."[9] In other cases, the change has been in the form of major initiatives such as General Electric's "Work-Out," an aggressive process designed to eliminate the maladies associated with structural boundaries and bureaucracy.[10]

Team members tell us that an overly fortified or entrenched structure can come to serve itself rather than the organization's goal. It can overly control access to decision making, bottleneck the flow of information, create deep demarcations along boundaries, and turn departments into gated communities. A self-serving structure can also cause roles and responsibilities to become isolated, vague, and confusing.

- What is, or is not, corporate marketing's role vis-à-vis everybody else's? (T7)
- Clarify roles. (T376)
- How do we make other areas aware of what we do and what we don't do? (T348)
- Get team members out of their silos. (T534)
- The team needs to understand all functions and how they interrelate. (T487)
- The functional structure promotes conflict between roles. If that conflict can be reduced or eliminated, team trust and effectiveness would be increased. (T140)

On its own, structure will do what it does best, seek stabilization.[11] Unattended, structure will likely overstabilize and steadily erode its own relevance to achieving the organization's goal. Team members' experiences reinforce this insight. Their positive comments about structure are related, more often than not, to a recent change.

- The new organization structure is promising. (T160)
- Our recent re-organization is a step in the right direction. (T272)

It should not be assumed, however, that even a clear and disciplined structure will promote the necessary teamwork and collaboration that lead to effective decisions. These dynamics are the domain of organizational processes.

At the broadest level, processes are the nervous system of an organization. They integrate talent, tasks, and information to produce an outcome. These include, for example, the processes that result in the strategic or operating plans for an organization, or the acquisition of a new business, or the use of money for capital expenditures, or the allocation of charitable contributions, as well as the full range of formal and informal, written and face-to-face communication that must occur to keep everyone focused on the goal.

Processes can work within or transcend the constraints of structure as they serve any of the following functions. First, processes should bring the right people together to make a decision. Second, processes should keep interrelated tasks, as well as people with interrelated responsibilities, appropriately connected with one another. Third, processes should communicate what the organization is trying to accomplish and how well it is performing, as well as focus attention on key issues that must be addressed in order to achieve the goal.

Effective Processes Foster Effective Decision Making

In the end, there is only one concern that ought to occupy our attention. *Are the right decisions happening fast enough to move us toward our goal?* A good decision-making process brings together the *right people*, at the *right time*, to talk about the *right problem* or opportunity in the *right way*, in order to take the *best action* available.

The *right people* usually means those people most relevant to the issue, in terms of both technical knowledge and managerial responsibility. The right people may be part of an intact work group, such as a board of directors, an operating management team, or a business development team evaluating an acquisition or a divestiture. But, when necessary, a good decision-making process should overarch the boundaries of structure and tap into the right talent for making a decision. Truly collaborative decision making begins by identifying with a problem, rather than with a structure. The value of this practice is perhaps best seen in a cross-functional task force, where people from different parts of the organization are brought together, perhaps unexpectedly, to coalesce into a common perspective and solve a problem. Whatever the necessary mix of talent, effective decision making begins by bringing the right people to the table.

The *right time* usually means early enough to give the right people a chance to frame a problem or an opportunity and to explore critical issues by gathering relevant facts. Sometimes a decision-making process has the built-in luxury of bringing the right people together in a formal and predictable way. For example, a strategic planning process is an attempt to map the course of an organization over an extended period. It is usually a fairly methodical process, based on thorough preparation through well-defined stages of activities. Months are spent gathering and then analyzing data before alternative long-term strategies are generated for positioning the organization on the most successful path. In such a process, the right people are usually involved at each stage, and the most useful information available is assembled in a timely way for deliberation.

But decision making is not always such a tidy process, and the unique rhythm of decision making for any organization can range from fire drill to overanalysis. Often the early stages of a decision involve one person, or a few people making an observation or simply experiencing a hunch. As the observation or hunch is developed and refined, a few more people are brought into the process. An informal decision-making process such as this—which experience teaches us occurs most frequently—is more subtle than the formal process associated with strategic planning.

Whether decision making is a formal or informal process, it's important to get the right people involved as early as possible. Good timing promotes a better analysis and understanding of the problem or opportunity at hand. It also lets people know that they will be involved in decisions that pertain to their expertise, sending a strong message that they are valued. After all, when someone feels they were not involved in a decision-making process at the right time—if at all—they may see it as betrayal.

The *right issue* is a problem or opportunity that, if left unaddressed, places limits on achieving the goal. It might be an overwhelming technical challenge related to a goal, such as minimizing gross weight when building the world's largest airplane, or controlling infection when transplanting a human heart. It might also be a strategic or operational issue. How can we improve revenue? What are new ways of generating growth? To what extent should we expand nationally or globally, or into new product lines? How should we increase membership in our charitable organization? Issues that are critical in reaching the goal are often complex and difficult to unravel. They are prime candidates for collaborative work that brings together a variety of perspectives and sources of knowledge. The key is to clearly define the really important issues and attack them systematically.

There is also another type of right issue, one that is not only difficult to unravel but also difficult to raise. These are issues that concern the workings of the organization or team itself—problems with ineffective leadership, favoritism, mistrust within the team, or a lack of competence by a team member, and the like. As we discussed in Chapter 3, effective teams must be able to raise and resolve this kind of highly sensitive issue. More broadly, the organization needs to have processes in place—such as an anonymous and confidential survey—that make it safe to surface delicate issues. Failure to confront the real issues tends to be obvious to all, as reflected in this comment from a disheartened team member:

▪ No one will address the issue, not even top management. (T400)

Unless the right issues—problems or opportunities—are surfaced, discussed, and resolved, any energy spent on decision making is probably wasted on peripheral cha-cha: It might feel like forward movement but it's just a lot of motion back and forth. Only the right issues improve the organization's positioning to achieve the goal. And, generally speaking, groups and teams that are aggressive or productive in watching for the right issues tend to be more successful, as Ancona and Caldwell discovered when they compared teams that probe their relevant environment for key issues with other teams that were less active and engaged.[12]

The *right way* usually means putting people on as close to an equal footing as possible for discussing issues openly and supportively. Good process fully recognizes that decision making is often a conflict-crammed set of circumstances, frequently laced with unequal levels of status, competing drives, difficult topics, and differing views. Such a collision of variables is either made better or worse by the process for dealing with them. It is not an effective decision-making process when the ideas of some people are always presumed useful and important, whereas the ideas of others are treated like clay pigeons. It's not an effective process when some people are embraced with warmth and acceptance, whereas others who are eager to contribute are scared into silence. It's not an effective process when it's hard to distinguish whether a rejected decision is dead-dead, or Lazarus-dead, waiting to be resurrected by someone more credible or "in favor." Such moments of imaginary openness and supportiveness eventually cause decision making to spiral into dysfunction.

Team members tell us that the issues that get in the way of good decision making most often are barriers to an open and supportive discussion of a problem or opportunity. For example, it is a failure of process when openness is suppressed or input is denied.

- In a decision-making process, everyone directly involved in the process should have a chance to give his or her input. (T487)
- We need greater group problem solving by eliminating turf protection. (T128)
- How do we get more facets of the community involved? (T320)
- There are bottlenecks at higher levels of management. (T396)

It is equally a failure of process when some people feel support for their involvement and ideas, whereas others feel marginalized by a lack of cooperation.

- A general lack of support from the other divisions for the distribution function. (T1)
- More support and understanding from our internal customers. (T516)
- Better support and cooperation from outside agencies and greater caseworker involvement. (T48)

An effective decision-making process, in contrast, banishes all that by offering an open and supportive setting in which everyone can be equally outspoken. It's not enough to ask whether the process is efficient in the short term. As you evaluate the process for decision making, ask yourself questions like these: Does the process promote an interactive environment? Does it encourage asking "why"? Do people feel free to express their ideas and opinions? Is there a supportive and cooperative climate for exploring an issue? Is the discussion fact-based rather than politically driven? Are good ideas recognized regardless of who offers them?

Confidence in the process creates confidence in the decision. In this connection, a structured approach to problem solving, as discussed in Chapter 3, can be an invaluable aid in decision making. But neither the Single Question Format nor any other structured approach to problem solving is sufficient in itself. Its value depends on an overall process that ensures that the right people are brought together at the right time to discuss the right issues in the right way in order to take the best action.

Effective Processes Keep People Connected

The importance of being connected is easily seen in a manufacturing process in which each task must be in sync with the task before it and the task that follows. There is a simple, linear clarity to this picture. To even a casual observer, it is the connectedness—task-to-task—that makes the process succeed or fail.

Similarly, process should also keep people with related responsibilities connected with one another. Team members point to two factors that help keep people in sync: time together and common physical location.

> "The team needs more opportunities for interaction."

TIME TOGETHER

- The team needs more opportunities for interaction. I do not know most of the people on this team . . . I would like to build relationships, establish trust, and benefit from their expertise. (T400)
- Provide more time for group interaction. (T348)
- Give the team more time and experience in working together. (T4)

PHYSICAL LOCATION

- ■ All members should be located together to facilitate communication and informal interaction. (T416)
- ■ Move all members of the group to one physical location. (T352)
- ■ Move us closer to the business unit. (T424)

People's connectedness should not depend on a patchwork of coincidental encounters. It should be planned and expected that people will come together in ways that make it possible to carry out—with confidence—their interrelated responsibilities and achieve common goals. But, as team members' comments reveal, connectedness is more than people interacting, which in our dot-com world can be accomplished in any number of ways from e-mail to video conferencing. It's people spending a sufficient amount of time together, in person, face-to-face.

Edward Hallowell, professor of psychiatry at Harvard Medical School, describes "the human moment: an authentic psychological encounter that can happen only when two people share the same physical space."[13] He argues that such moments are essential in organizations. Among the benefits of the human moment are that it bolsters the brain chemistry that stimulates emotional health; it decreases the likelihood of confidence being replaced with a toxic worry that comes from too much isolation; and it reduces the number of little misunderstandings that dissolve trust.

Trust, of course, is essential to all levels of social transaction. In his extensive scholarly work *Trust*, Francis Fukuyama describes the centrality of the expectation of honest and cooperative behavior to all social structures—from families to nations. Insightfully, he compares the presence and absence of trust in the workplace:

> If people who have to work together in an enterprise trust one another because they are all operating according to a common set of ethical norms, doing business costs less. Such a society will be better able to innovate organizationally, since the high degree of trust will permit a wide variety of social relationships to emerge. . . .
>
> By contrast, people who do not trust one another will end up cooperating only under a system of formal rules and regulations, which have to be negotiated, agreed to, litigated, and enforced,

sometimes by coercive means. This legal apparatus, serving as a substitute for trust, entails what economists call "transaction costs." Widespread distrust in a society, in other words, imposes a kind of tax on all forms of economic activity, a tax that high-trust societies do not have to pay.[14]

We made similar observations as a result of our three-year examination of teams that achieved high performance and teams that failed: "Trust is one of those mainstay virtues in the commerce of mankind. It is the bond that allows any kind of significant relationship to exist between people. Once broken, it is not easily—if ever—recovered."[15] Since then, our assessments of more than 600 teams underscore the relationship between building trust within a team and the need for members to spend time together—time to come to know one another as people, time to appreciate each other's capabilities, time to understand the underlying motivations that might influence how decisions are made, time to develop a common perspective on how problems should be approached by the team and how difficulties should be handled.

Organizational processes, then, should bring people together in ways that build trust in each other and in their capability as a team. Robert Eaton, CEO of Chrysler Corporation, commented in an interview with *Industry Week* that Chrysler's "Technology Center is a huge part of our competitive advantage because instead of having people scattered all over in different buildings, they can literally be co-located in one room." Chrysler even includes some of their suppliers as members of ongoing teams, with office space in the Technology Center.[16]

For people who work in the same location, sitting together at monthly or weekly meetings, face-to-face time is fairly easy to accomplish. Usually an ad hoc meeting or a quick question can be resolved by a short jog down the hall. For those who normally work in different locations, it's not as easy, but it's equally desirable and perhaps even more important to connect in person on a regular basis. For a group of regional managers spread across the country or around the world, ensuring adequate "face time" might mean meeting together every quarter to calibrate major initiatives, explore common challenges, and confirm relationships. For an expatriate who holds an international assignment, it may mean arranging a visit with key counterparts once a year to reaffirm mutual trust in the ability to make a good decision, allowing subsequent interactions through video conference or over the phone to be more productive. Whatever the process for keeping people with related responsibilities connected, it should be as simple as possible, and it should serve the goal of the organization, not bureaucratic ritual.

Apart from working meetings, team members point to the need for opportunities to get to know one another as people.

- Get to know each other better socially or outside the business environment. (T464)
- See that managers get together from time to time outside of the work environment. (T92)
- I don't think we really know each other and that may lead us to question each other at times. (T368)
- Have more informal nonbusiness group outings in which everyone participates. (T236)

Many organizations recognize the value of instituting processes that allow people to spend time together away from the work environment. Attending a group dinner or a sporting event can help people make new or deeper connections. Some organizations create opportunities to build trust by sharing outdoor adventures. Climbing poles, rappelling down the sides of mountains, or hanging from a zip line across a ravine can help team members develop a broader appreciation for each other as well as build their confidence in one another.

Effective Communication Processes Align Information, Understanding, and Effort

From the perspective of management, the power of effective communication processes lies in their ability to mainstream messages critical to success—the goal of the company; strategic priorities; the values for guiding how the organization will conduct itself; the financial targets—thus scoreboarding progress and publicizing accomplishments.

"We need information on what the company as a whole is trying to do."

We cannot overemphasize the importance of regular communication that clearly conveys the information necessary to build the organization's confidence to succeed and solicits everyone's commitment to address critical issues and achieve results.

- We need information on what the company as a whole is trying to do. (T156)
- Improve communication between upper management and the team. (T296)
- Better communication. It is hard to know the status of key issues. (T552)

The communication of useful information serves an insatiable need. That is why the organizational grapevine, although rarely sufficient, is always alive and well. The grapevine addresses the psychologically grounded need, and perhaps inalienable right, to know what's really going on and what it means for individuals and teams.

- Much needed information is communicated via the grapevine. (T424)

This need to know is so powerful and universal that when official communication is lacking, rumors will probably be created to fill the void. For quite some time, it has been known that rumors emerge when people feel they do not know what is going on, or when they feel they have little control over their destiny.[17] The simple take-away is this: If an organization does not communicate the facts, people will create them.

The experiences of team members suggest that disruption to the alignment of effort is most often the result of insufficient communication between the various parts of the organization.

- Our team needs help in the area of communication between departments. (T72)
- Better communication could help prevent team members from "tripping" over each other's work. (T64)
- Open the lines of communication. We waste time duplicating efforts. (T92)

- Often two or more team members are assigned to a project without knowing it, resulting in double work, mixed messages, and looking disjointed. (T192)

Teams are particularly vulnerable to a failure by management to emphasize the importance of clear communication between functions or departments. Too often, little or no effort is devoted to bringing functional units together to clarify roles and responsibilities, for example, by having them make presentations at each other's monthly meetings in order to combine effort, or at least avoid duplicating it. No one thinks to route critical reports outside the department or to hold combined meetings that bring together related areas of responsibilities. Instead, structural lines create ever-widening gaps in communication. Apart from the inevitable inefficiencies and frustrations caused by such gaps, it doesn't take too long for a department, function, or business to become isolated, and eventually feel a diminished sense of relevance. All this is antithetical to collaborative teamwork.

- Each of the team members works in an isolated area. Cross-pollination of ideas might lead to a more cohesive company. (T464)

Although effective communication is clearly everyone's responsibility, the formal process of day-to-day communication falls most squarely on the doorstep of those above—leaders, managers, and supervisors. This means that the effectiveness of communication will vary from manager to manager. Some managers are more likely than others to make communication a priority, especially across functional lines. Some may have difficulty being clear, causing people to pinball onto an unexplainable path. Others may take a need-to-know approach, leaving people to wonder what's really going on. So, for a variety of reasons, an overall communication process that relies solely on the efforts of individual managers is likely to produce variable results and will probably prove to be inadequate for communicating a clear and uniform message across the entire organization.

If relying on the chain of managers to carry important messages is insufficient, what should organizations do to ensure that everyone gets the same vital information? Although the answer varies with the type and size of the organization, the fundamental guideline must be: *Use every means at your disposal to ensure that goals and priorities are clear. Leave nothing to chance. Communicate repeatedly in a variety of media. And when you think you're done, do it again.*

Keep in mind, too, that effective communication doesn't mean only making sure that messages flow smoothly from the top down. Good communication needs to happen in all directions, from the bottom up and across functional lines and other structural divisions. What means do you have in place for people at all levels to communicate in all directions? What information tends to get stored in functional silos, unknown to other people and teams who would benefit from it? To whom do reports circulate? What mistakes get made because the right information didn't reach the right people at the right time? One way to answer such questions is to put them to teams themselves—and listen hard to what they have to say.

An effective communication process also includes knowing when to bring people together face-to-face to hear the same message, ask questions, and offer input. Functionally, geographically, by plant or by shift, there are times when only a face-to-face meeting will allow the right type of communication to occur. However, any strategy for effective meetings should be determined by the communication need and an overriding penchant for common sense. We suggest asking a simple question before bringing people together: *What business need would not be served if this meeting did not occur?*

Overall then, an effective communication process is a blueprint for information flow that leaves people with the comfort that they will be kept informed of plans, priorities, and progress and that they are coordinated appropriately with other internal efforts. Effective communication processes align information, understanding, and effort toward the ultimate goal of the organization. The only way to ensure that you have such processes is to make them a high priority and continually monitor how well they are working.

As we conclude this discussion of organizational structure and processes, we offer this thought. In the end, the goal is to combine the stability of structure with the responsiveness of process. The objective should be clear roles and responsibilities, clear communication of priorities, and access to decision making by the right people at the right time. Any tradeoffs within this mix should be in favor of encouraging people to address the real issues that can affect the success of the organization and then to take action.

3. Systems

An organization's systems provide information, set standards, and drive behavior toward desired results. The extent to which these systems are useful is determined by their reliability and relevance. Here we focus on two systems singled out by team members as frequently hindering their ability to work together effectively: information systems and reward systems. We then consider the importance of a system's standards in promoting consistency and fairness.

The Necessity of Reliable Information

In the 1990s, the end-of-the-millennium panic over the Y2K computer bug brought home to everyone, even average consumers, the critical role that information plays in contemporary society. People worried about failures in nearly every system they depend on: computerized cash registers at grocery checkout counters, bank records and transactions, power supplies, air traffic control, even weapons systems. Even though the anticipated crisis over the inability of older computer code to distinguish the year 2000 never materialized, no one could mistake the lesson: The lack of reliable information can be devastating to an organization, a country, or even the globe.

As if the lesson needed any more reinforcement, the United States was treated to another vivid demonstration of the necessity of reliable information in the presidential election of 2000. Not once, but twice, television networks incorrectly "called" the election based on faulty information, leading one candidate to concede to the other and then withdraw that concession minutes before he was about to make it public. The election night snafus contributed significantly to the uncertainties and legal actions that followed. Indeed, the controversy over the voting results itself represented a problem of allegedly unreliable information in the form of machine-processed ballots that brought into question the ability to record the intentions of thousands of voters.

No less than consumers, investors, or presidential candidates, teams dislike trying to make decisions in an environment in which information is suspect or insufficient. Teams depend on information to establish the facts that are the basis for decision making. Without reliable and relevant information, clarity evaporates, confidence dwindles, and commitments are hard to make. As such difficulties mount, so does cynicism. A lack of reliable information only encourages greater caution in any attempts to move forward.

Judging from the comments of team members, deficiencies in information systems are frequently a fundamental barrier to success in working together. Team members repeatedly point to the usefulness of sound information systems for making and monitoring decisions.

- Develop an effective, integrated corporate database. (T360)
- We need to exploit the new computer system to dramatically improve responsiveness and decision making. (T288)
- We need to change the way we handle paper and information flow. There must be better ways to disseminate information. (T348)
- Team members should all have ways to leave messages for one another. (T1)

Notice that information systems include not only elaborate computerized database systems but also such seemingly mundane matters as a way for team members to communicate with each other efficiently. Team leaders and members know how much they depend on information systems to provide the data they need to make informed decisions. In a collaborative team environment, it's critical to have access to reliable, well-integrated information. As always, the best way to find out if current systems are meeting that need is simply to ask the team members themselves. They are likely to be eloquent in their responses.

Relevant Rewards Drive Required Results

The second systems issue highlighted by team members is the need for relevant rewards to drive behavior toward desired results. Here, team members offer a nearly uniform perspective: Team success is not rewarded.

- ▪ Revamp the reward system to make team victory more important than individual victory. (T126)
- ▪ We should more carefully align compensation with our performance measures. (T392)
- ▪ Link personal, financial, and psychological rewards to our group goal. (T316)
- ▪ Do not make us compete against each other. There will never be a true team effort until we are not measured against each other. Set an objective for us to compete against and reward everyone who achieves it. (T405)

Systems often drive behaviors that once seemed relevant but that are no longer in sync with the desired outcome. This is especially true when an organization tries to establish collaborative teams. It is not unusual to find organizations that ask, and even require, people to work in teams toward common objectives, but then offer a traditional reward system that focuses only on individual performance rather than the achievement of a team goal. Such failure to align rewards with the desired outcome creates disincentives for engaging in collaborative effort.

Instituting team-based rewards is practical as well as effective. The Corporate Leadership Council has documented many systems used to reward teams for performance. These systems are varied and creative. Though it's not always easy to do, especially in large, complex organizations, making sure that rewards are tied directly to results usually promotes higher outcomes.[18] As an example, consider the 20-year evolution of one team-based selling process.

Team-Based Selling/Team-Based Rewards: A Short Story

American Hospital Supply Corporation (AHS), a well-respected Chicago-based healthcare company, was a distributor of a wide range of products—from tongue depressors and needles to self-manufactured intravenous solutions and heart valves—to hospitals throughout the world. Until the late 1970s, sales were made primarily, and successfully, by the selling efforts of individual salespeople.

By 1978, then CEO Karl Bays reasoned that with more than 20 operating units in the corporation, it was becoming more important than ever to offer "one-stop shopping" to hospitals. His message to the organization was straightforward: "Sell the way a customer wants to buy." At the same time, the healthcare industry began showing early signs of consolidation with the emergence of Group Purchasing Organizations (GPOs). GPOs began attracting the membership of individual hospitals with the prospect of lower cost products through volume purchase agreements with manufacturers and distributors. As Bays suspected, this trend toward consolidation continued, with 96.91 percent of the 6,788 hospitals in the United States participating in some type of GPO purchasing relationship by the beginning of the year 2001.[19]

Observing this convergence of events, in 1978 AHS established a corporate sales program designed to transcend the internal structure of the corporation, creating a unique platform of product offerings for GPOs to extend to their hospital constituents. During the next five years, the corporate sales program gained momentum, focusing attention on the executive suite of the hospital and the GPO. Externally, it worked well. After all, cost reduction was more important than ever to hospitals, particularly in light of new legislation in October 1983 that limited Medicare and Medicaid reimbursement for surgical procedures.

But whereas the corporate sales strategy matched well with the evolving marketplace, within AHS it wasn't so eagerly embraced. Individual operating units often viewed the corporate sales program as giving away profit margin through the volume and mix of product across several business units. Before this dilemma was resolved, however, AHS was acquired by Baxter Travenol in November 1985. As a previous competitor, Baxter appreciated the strength of the corporate sales program and anticipated including the combined company's many offerings under this now-larger-than-ever umbrella.

Within the next 15 months, the newly created Baxter International, with approximately 40 operating units, recognized the dysfunctional dynamic between the business units' accountability for profitable sales and the desire to continue the one-stop logic of the corporate sales program. In some cases, as many as 15 Baxter salespeople from different operating units were calling on the same customer. In some instances, they met each other for the first time in the hospital lobby. More than once, the customer introduced them to one another.

In an attempt to bridge this gap, Terrence J. Mulligan, corporate vice president of corporate sales, invited 120 salespeople and sales managers from across the organization to the corporate headquarters for a "Team Selling" meeting held in April 1987. Chairman and CEO Vernon R. Loucks, Jr., along with his three group executive vice presidents, described how the marketplace was accelerating the need to present one voice to the customer, while preserving the profitable integrity of each business.

The 120 salespeople were then assigned to seven different teams and provided a full day of training on teamwork. They were asked to work together toward addressing the needs of an agreed-on customer, to help one another, to put aside individual agendas, and when necessary, to delay pushing their own product (e.g., IV solutions, surgical gowns, latex gloves) and do whatever was in the mutual best interest of the customer and Baxter overall, as both short-term and long-term partners.

The seven teams outperformed historical results, encouraging the creation of 10 teams within each of the nine sales regions. For the next two years, these 90 teams made giant strides toward working together, strengthening sales, and improving customer satisfaction.

Each of the nine regions selected their own best team, and the nine best teams gathered at the corporate headquarters for a Team-Work Day. They shared their efforts and results with one another and with a teamwork board consisting of corporate officers. Much was learned by these "best practices," and the board of corporate officers selected the best-of-the-best team. This team was featured in the corporate magazine highlighting the people, their customer, and their accomplishments.

But there was still a fundamental limitation, and it continued to show. People were asked to work together in teams, but they were still rewarded as individuals. Although there was individual recognition for sacrificing a sale for the good of the team/customer goal, there were no rewards. The first attempt at addressing this mismatch between the goal of working together and an individual-oriented reward system confirmed that this was the right problem to fix. In 1990, Baxter made available 12,000 shares of stock for the teamwork selling process. Each region was given 1,000 shares for the winning team to distribute among its members as they deemed appropriate. The additional 3,000 shares were reserved for the "best-of-the-best" teams selected by the teamwork board on TeamWork Day. This change in the reward system helped drive a rather dramatic growth in sales and gross margin that continued for the next several years.

The success of the corporate sales teamwork approach was expanded to the entire salesforce in 1995. To strengthen the teamwork ethic, Lester B. Knight, executive vice president of the hospital business, led 2,200 salespeople through the Pecos River outdoor training experience. In the midst of pole climbing, a ropes course, zip lines over ravines, and rappelling down the sides of cliffs, they were asked to adopt a team approach to the marketplace. They were then provided with a full day of intense training on the principles of teamwork and methods for building team relationships, including techniques for giving constructive feedback to one another. And, once again, the compensation system evolved to meet this broader approach to teamwork.

In October 1996, the Distribution and Medical/Surgical businesses that were originally the core of AHS spun off from Baxter International as a publicly traded company known as Allegiance Corporation. The new company's leadership, with Lester B. Knight and Joseph F. Damico at the top, drove clarity, confidence, and commitment deep into the company's culture with particular emphasis on a clear message of teamwork and corresponding rewards within the salesforce. The sales vice presidents reinforced teamwork at every turn, with center stage awards for teamwork at each national sales meeting.

Two years later, on October 7, 1998, Allegiance merged with Cardinal Health, Inc., a leading provider of services supporting the healthcare industry. Immediately, Chairman and CEO Robert D. Walter and President and COO John C. Kane saw the value of cross-selling Cardinal's products and services through teams. Within 60 days of the close of the deal, the Cardinal corporate sales organization, headed by 30-year veteran John Hatcher, was reconfigured into four regions, staffed with the most qualified people and retrained in the principles of teamwork. Equally important, the new corporate sales organization was equipped with a compensation system that properly aligned rewards with the desired results.

This example illustrates the power of aligning rewards with the desired way of achieving results. It's not enough to say, "Let's work as a team." The rewards system needs to be revamped in accordance with this way of doing business. As the example also shows, arriving at such an alignment can mean doing significant work over an extended period to overhaul rewards systems, publicize them, and drive the desired consciousness deep into the organization's culture. And once in place, the reward system—like any other—needs continual monitoring to ensure that it is rewarding the right behaviors and getting the desired results. Yes, it's a lot of work, but the investment can reap rich rewards.

Standards Lead to Consistency and Fairness

At its most basic level, a system defines performance standards. Standards, which most often are reflected in policies and procedures, attempt to ensure some degree of consistent and reasonable judgment from one person to the next as they perform the same activity. In some cases, standards are fairly stringent, as in legal or financial or regulatory systems, which require conformity to the laws of fair business practice, adherence to general accounting principles, and accountability for product safety. In other cases, standards serve more as guidelines for behavior, such as the standards for hiring people, valuing jobs, or managing performance.

Standards are designed to prescribe relative consistency in what might otherwise be a rather wide band of individual judgment. After all, an organization is composed of a wide variety of people and their behaviors that, if left unharnessed, would most likely move in the direction of self-interest. And self-interest is contrary to the essence of teamwork. Without standards, individual judgment and coordinated effort can swerve from the desired path, resulting in confusion, underachievement, wasted resources, and unfair advantage.

Teams need standards no less than individuals do. On countless occasions we hear some version of the following lament: " They tell you to be creative, passionate, and results oriented, but then they come down on you for taking risks." Interestingly, when we dig far enough, we often find that the "creative approach" or "risk-taking event" or "passion" ignored a standard, at times putting the organization in jeopardy.

Simply put, a system of standards requires that we delay an impulse and follow a few steps. In the case of human resource issues, for example, standards may require us to hire the best person according to established selection criteria, avoid nepotism, and seek diversity in hiring practices. Standards may prescribe that we value jobs according to the marketplace, pay for performance as measured against results, and avoid favoritism. More broadly, they may enforce the mandate to create a climate that is safe, respectful, and prohibits any form of employee harassment.

- More clearly defined standards of measurement for performance. (T36)
- Everyone needs to be consistent when conducting reviews. (T38)
- We must address balanced work force issues. (T148)

In this regard, standards promote a sense of consistency and fairness. There is something reassuring about going through the required steps for a hiring decision, or a performance appraisal, or a salary increase. Almost always, standards offer greater clarity and more confidence in the fairness of the process, and a higher commitment to a decision than a hard-to-explain series of idiosyncratic choices.

When a system of standards is unreliable or irrelevant, two things happen. First, it takes a while to know it. For example, if selection standards slip, it is eventually reflected in the performance of people hired. But, it takes time for people to perform and have their performance evaluated. It takes time for them to demonstrate an ability to learn and develop, or not. Or consider the problems created if quality and regulatory standards are allowed to slip. Eventually, the slippage could be reflected in a product recall or a lawsuit, but such consequences are unlikely to surface immediately.

Second, when standards fail, we often have to live with the consequences for quite some time. A hiring decision, for example, is a fairly enduring decision. Just as good people beget more good people, the opposite is also true. And an organization's culture—which might be built on customer service or quality or innovation—can be strengthened or slowly undone by the hiring standards during prior years. At that point, the consequences have already surfaced in terms of a decline in quality or customer churn, or a bubble in the creative pipeline—whether the company is making heart valves, automobile tires, or animated films. Likewise, if there is a problem with product reliability, usually the repercussions won't disappear overnight. It may take a while to recapture customer trust or rebuild the reputation of a company or institution.

Team members know that a system must define standards that are reliable, relevant to the desired results, and well publicized. And, every so often, a system should be scrutinized to determine if the right standards are still driving the right results.

- Set definite policies and procedures. (T296)
- Procedures can benefit from being revisited on a regular basis to see if they can be improved. (T412)
- Some procedures are not fully documented and need to be spread by word of mouth. (T292)

The standards embedded in an organization's systems are the last piece in the puzzle that we have been assembling in this chapter. To sum up the message as a whole: The three key dimensions of an organization environment are management practices, structure and processes, and systems. We have dwelled on the subject of organization environment because an environment breeds habits. Collaboration may never become the rule without making it a requirement. It's easy for managers and leaders to say, dismissively, as did an executive of a Fortune 500 company:

> It's the nature of an organization. A lot of people doing a lot of stuff, at high velocity in order to produce some result. They're bound to bump into each other, or find themselves at cross-purposes, or compete against one another to get *their* stuff done. People just need to hash it out and get on with it.

But "c'est la vie" does not help us improve our reach. We must not be seduced by this easy, self-satisfying conclusion. Instead, we must work hard to stack the deck in favor of a collaborative environment: one that promotes clarity and minimizes confusion, one that builds confidence over caution, and one that makes everyone energized and committed rather than fatigued and detached. Achieving such an environment requires management practices that set the expectation that collaboration is not an option; a structure and processes that provide an unencumbered, interactive blueprint for addressing issues; and systems that provide good information and drive collective behavior toward the desired goal.

▪ PUTTING IT TO WORK

Although the following assessment can be performed by the team leader or any of the team members, we suggest it be a discussion held by your entire team. It shouldn't require more than 30 to 60 minutes.

1. Using Figure 5.1 as a guide, discuss any of your organization's management practices, structures and processes, or systems that seem to keep the team from being as successful as it could be. For example, teams we have worked with have used this exercise to explore such issues as the mismatch between the organization's goal and the team's priorities, the inability of the team to participate in relevant discussions and decisions, and the lack of alignment between required team performance and established rewards.
2. Of the organizational issues you identified, choose the one issue that creates the greatest problem for your team's performance.
3. What can your team do to minimize the negative impact of the organizational issue you identified? In addition, do you believe the impact of this issue affects other teams in the organization as well? If so, how might your team surface the issue and help your organization resolve it?

A FINAL WORD

The best time to plant a tree was 20 years ago.
The second best time is now.

Chinese proverb

In this book, we have presented five keys to success in collaborative teamwork, distilled from the experiences of team members themselves.

- Expect collaborative behavior from each team member.
- Require people to build collaborative work relationships.
- Practice collaborative problem solving.
- Demonstrate collaborative leadership.
- Build a collaborative work environment.

Does all this add up to collaborative teamwork? Our research says it's the way to bet. The benefits are clear and worthwhile—but they are not achieved without effort.

Although our unique individual ability to think may be our species-specific gift, it is our capacity to organize and integrate our collective thinking that will continue to determine our evolutionary niche. More than ever, it is important that we refine and maximize this elevating capability to work together. After all, no matter how remarkable our individual talents, only our ability to collaborate will allow us to address and solve the most meaningful issues.

At this point in our journey, we believe the word *collaborate* will continue to be the most powerful verb within the human story. We are also fairly certain that the likelihood of collaboration occurring haphazardly—by chance alone—in any organization setting is relatively small. Collaboration must be a conscious choice. We hope that we have helped to make it an informed one.

NOTES

■ PROLOGUE

1. Logsdon, J. (1991, March). Interests and interdependence in the formation of social problem-solving collaborations. *Journal of Applied Behavioral Science, 27*(1), 23-27.

2. Holusha, J. (1987, December 29). A new spirit in U.S. auto plants. *New York Times,* pp. 25-26.

3. Reich, R. (1987). *Tales of a new America.* New York: Time Books, p. 126.

4. Peterson, J. (1991, July 3). Labor Department panel urges teaching of new skills for jobs. *Los Angeles Times,* p. D-1.

5. Reich, R. (1987). *Tales of a new America.* New York: Time Books, p. 126.

6. Parr, J. (1994). Foreword. In D. Chrislip & C. E. Larson (Eds.), *Collaborative leadership: How citizens and civic leaders can make a difference* (p. xi). San Francisco: Jossey-Bass.

7. Williams, B., & Matheny, A. (1995). *Democracy, dialogue, and environmental disputes: The contested languages of social regulations.* New Haven, CT: Yale University Press.

8. Bateson, G. (1979). *Mind and nature.* New York: Dutton.

9. Moore, J. (1996). *The death of competition: Leadership & strategy in the age of business eco-systems.* New York: HarperCollins.

10. Bower, B. (1995, November 18). Return of the group. *Science News, 148*(21), 328-329.

11. Larson, C. E., & Sweeney, C. (1994, November). *Team excellence: An assessment of team effectiveness.* Paper presented at the National Conference of the Speech Communication Association, New Orleans.

■ CHAPTER I

1. Larson, C. E., & LaFasto, F. M. J. (1989). *TeamWork: What must go right/What can go wrong.* Newbury Park, CA: Sage.

2. Robbins, H., & Finley, M. (1995). *Why teams don't work.* Princeton, NJ: Peterson's/Pacesetter Books.

3. Chrislip, D., & Larson, C. E. (1994). *Collaborative leadership: How citizens and civic leaders can make a difference.* San Francisco: Jossey-Bass.

4. Phillips, E., & Cheston, R. (1979, Summer). Conflict resolution: What works? *California Management Review, 21*(4), 76-82.

5. See, for example, Bettenhausen, K. L. (1991, June). Five years of groups research: What we have learned and what needs to be addressed. *Journal of Management, 17*(2), 345-381.

6. Blomberg, D. (1996). *A theory of dual-role effectiveness: Friendship in a workplace.* Unpublished doctoral dissertation, University of Denver.

7. See, for example, Chlewinski, Z. (1981). Group and individual decisions in task situations: Aspirations and achievement. *Polish Psychological Bulletin, 12*(2), 115-124.

8. Kouzes, J., & Posner, B. (1987). *The leadership challenge.* San Francisco: Jossey-Bass.

9. Bennis, W., & Nanus, B. (1985). *Leaders: The strategies for taking charge.* New York: Harper & Row.

10. Morris, C. (1956). *Varieties of human value.* Chicago: University of Chicago Press; Morris, C. (1964). *Signification and significance.* Cambridge: MIT Press.

11. Driskell, J., & Salas, E. (1992, June). Collective behavior and team performance. *Human Factors, 34*(3), 277-288.

12. Cooke, R., & Szumal, J. (1994). The impact of group interaction styles on problem-solving effectiveness. *Journal of Applied Behavioral Science, 30*(4), 415-437.

13. Kameda, T., Stasson, M., Davis, J., Parks, C., & Zimmerman, S. (1992). Social dilemmas, sub groups, and motivation loss in task-oriented groups: In search of an "optimal" team size in division of work. *Social Psychology Quarterly, 55*(1), 47-56.

14. Goldberg, A., & Larson, C. E. (1992). *Successful communication and negotiation.* Gardena, CA: International Right of Way Association.

15. Katz, R. (1988). High performance research teams. In R. Katz (Ed.), *Managing professionals in innovative organizations* (pp. 315-324). Cambridge, MA: Ballinger.

▪ CHAPTER 2

1. One portion of our database on working relationships is based on data from an instrument called Interpersonal Impact, created in 1983. This instrument, which provides a team member with 360° feedback from supervisors, peers, and support staff, comprises more than 35,000 assessments of more than 4,500 participants in the process. Participants received feedback on 19 behaviorally anchored dimensions, along a Thurstone scale, as well as the identification of three perceived strengths and three perceived opportunities for improving their work relationships.

2. Employee tiffs twice the hassle of decade ago. (1996, June 5). *Denver Post,* p. 2G.

3. Scott, K. D., & Taylor, G. S. (1985). An examination of conflicting findings on the relationships between job satisfaction and absenteeism: A meta-analysis. *Academy of Management Journal, 28*(3), 599-612.

4. Moretti, D. M. (1986). The prediction of employee counter-productivity through attitude assessments. *Journal of Business and Psychology, 1*(2), 134-147.

5. Leiter, M. P., & Maslach, C. (1988). The impact of interpersonal environment on burnout and organizational commitment. *Journal of Organizational Behavior, 9*(4), 297-308.

6. Shilling, D. (2000, September). How to find and keep top talent in today's tight labor market. *Medical Marketing & Media, 35*(9), 125.

7. The meta-analysis, performed on 98 investigations, was conducted by Dr. Glen Clatterbuck and Omni Research and Training of Denver. Meta-analysis is a method for statistically integrating the

results from different studies of the same or similar variables. The works that did the most to promote the value of meta-analytic procedures were: Glass, G. V., McGraw, B., & Smith, M. L. (1981). *Meta-analysis in social research.* Beverly Hills, CA: Sage; and Rosenthal, R. (1984). *Meta-analytic procedures for social research.* Newbury Park, CA: Sage.

8. The second factor was originally labeled "affection" and dealt with aspects of warmth, caring, and supportiveness. We changed its label to "supportiveness" because our early discussions with teams revealed that many teams understood the concept of "supportiveness" more clearly than the concept of "affection."

9. Degman, F. M (1996). *The perceptions of sons and daughters who are caregivers of an elderly parent.* Unpublished doctoral dissertation, University of Denver.

10. Chaiken, S. (1980). Heuristic versus systematic information processing and the use of source versus message cues in persuasion. *Journal of Personality and Social Psychology, 39,* 752-766.

11. Campion, M., & Medsker, G. I. (1993). Relations between work group characteristics and effectiveness: Implications for designing effective work groups. *Personnel Psychology, 46,* 823-850.

12. Herold, D. M. (1979). The effectiveness of work groups. In S. Kerr (Ed.), *Organizational behavior* (pp. 95-118). Columbus, OH: Grid.

13. LaFasto, F. M. J., & Larson, C. E. (1990). *A study of diversity within Baxter Healthcare, Inc.* This study is reported by T. A. Svehla & G. C. Crosier in *Managing the mosaic* (American Hospital Publishing, Inc., 1994).

■ CHAPTER 3

1. Sellers, P. (1999, September 6). Ogilvy's rules for business. (As found in *Nightmare on Net Street* by Marion Warner.) *Fortune,140*(5), 286.

2. Parker, G. M. (1996). *Team players and teamwork: The new competitive business strategy.* San Francisco: Jossey-Bass.

3. See, for example, O'Reilly, C., III, & Roberts, K. H. (1977). Task group structure, communication, and effectiveness in three organizations. *Journal of Applied Psychology, 62*(6), 674-681.

4. Buchanan, K. (1996). *Control and openness: Communication in group decision making.* Unpublished doctoral dissertation, University of Denver.

5. Brannick, M. T. , Roach, R. M., & Salas, E. (1993). Understanding team performance: A multimethod study. *Human Performance, 9*(4), 287-308.

6. Saphiere, D. M. (1996). Productive behaviors of global business teams. *International Journal of Intercultural Relations, 20*(2), 227-259.

7. In *The Wisdom of Teams* (Harvard Business School Press, 1993) John Katzenbach and Douglas Smith linked team success with a challenging goal and a clear purpose. Pinto and others have discovered that superordinate goals in the healthcare industry are directly related to the amount of cooperation that occurs on cross-functional healthcare teams (Pinto, M. B., Pinto, J. K., & Prescott, J. E. [1993]. Antecedents and consequences of project cross-functional cooperation. *Management Science, 39*[10], 1281-1296). Abbott and Warren have found goal clarity to be closely associated with team performance (Abbott, J., & Warren, R. [1991, December]. Turning management groups into management teams. *Journal of Quality and Participation,14*[6], 70-72). Hirokawa and Keyton, in their study of organizational work teams, concluded that "[It] is especially crucial for group members to be interested in, and committed to, the goal(s) or purpose(s) of the group." (Hirokawa, R. Y., & Keyton, J. [1955]. Perceived facilitators and inhibitors of effectiveness in organizational work teams. *Management Communication Quarterly, 8*[4], 424-446). West has argued that vision is a primary factor in the innovation and creativity of workgroups (West, M. A. [1990]. The social psychology of innovation in groups. In M. A. West & J. L. Farr [Eds.], *Innovation and creativity at work: Psychological and organization strategies* [pp. 309-333]. Chichester, UK: Wiley). One of the most interesting discussions of goals can be found in Schrage, M. (1989). *No more teams! Mastering the dynamics of creative collaboration.* New York: Doubleday.

8. Schrage, M. (1989). *No more teams! Mastering the dynamics of creative collaboration.* New York: Doubleday, p. 217.

9. Schrage, M. (1989). *No more teams! Mastering the dynamics of creative collaboration.* New York: Doubleday, p. 31.

10. Katzenbach, J. R. (1998). *Teams at the top.* Boston: Harvard Business School Press, p. 113.

11. Gruendfeld, D. H., & Hollingshead, A. B. (1993). Sociocognition in workgroups: The evolution of group integrative complexity and its relation to task performance. *Small Group Research, 24*(3), 383-405.

12. See Latane, B., Williams, K., & Harkins, S. (1979). Many hands make light the work: The causes and consequences of social loafing. *Journal of Personality and Social Psychology, 37*(6), 822-832.

13. Hackman, J. R. (Ed.). (1990). *Groups that work (and those that don't).* San Francisco: Jossey-Bass.

14. Hirokawa, R. Y., & Keyton, J. (1995). Perceived facilitators and inhibitors of effectiveness of organizational work teams. *Management Communication Quarterly, 8*(4), 424-446.

15. Larson, C. E., & LaFasto, F. M. J. (1989). *TeamWork: What must go right/What can go wrong.* Newbury Park, CA: Sage.

16. Silver, W. S., & Bufanio, K. M. (1996, August). The impact of group efficacy and group goals on group task performance. *Small Group Research, 27*(3), 347-359.

17. Katzenbach, J. R. (1998). *Teams at the top.* Boston: Harvard Business School Press, p. 113.

18. Karlsson, G. (1963). *Adaptability and communication in marriage.* Totowa, NJ: Bedminster Press.

19. Janis, I. L., & Mann, L. (1977). *Decision-making: A psychological analysis of conflict, choice, and commitment.* New York: Free Press.

20. Shultz, B., Ketrow, S. M., & Urban, D. M. (1995). Improving decision quality in the small group: The role of the reminder. *Small Group Research, 26*(4), 531.

21. Hirowaka, R. Y., & Rost, K. M. (1992). Effective group decision-making in organizations: Field test of the vigilant interaction theory. *Management Communication Quarterly, 5*(3), 267-288.

22. Larson, C. E. (1969). Forms of analysis and small group problem-solving. *Speech Monographs, 36*, 452-455.

23. Early, J. F., & Godfrey, A. B. (1995, July). But it takes too long. . . . *Quality Progress, 28*(7), 51-55.

24. *Efficient healthcare consumer response: Improving the efficiency of the healthcare supply chain.* (1996, November). Sponsored by American Hospital Association/American Society for Healthcare Materials Management (AHA/ASHMM), Health Industry Business Communications Council (HIBCC), Health Industry Distributors Association (HIDA), National Wholesale Druggists' Association (NWDA), Uniform Code Council (UCC).

25. Fortune 500 Largest U.S. Corporations. (1999, April 26). *Fortune, 139*(8), F-14.

26. Barker, J. R., & Thompkins, P. K. (1994). Identification in the self-managing organization: Characteristics of target and tenure. *Human Communication Research, 21*(2), 223-240.

27. Souder, W. E. (1987). *Managing new product innovations.* Lexington, MA: Lexington Books.

28. Franz, C. R., & Jin, K. G. (1995). The structure of group conflict in a collaborative workgroup during information systems development. *Journal of Applied Communication Research, 23,* 108-127.

29. Chrislip, D., & Larson, C. E. (1994). *Collaborative leadership: How citizens and civic leaders can make a difference.* San Francisco, CA: Jossey-Bass.

30. Littlepage, G., Jones, S., Moffett, R., Cherry, T., & Senovich, S. (1999, May). *Relationship between leadership, potency, group processes, and work group effectiveness.* Paper presented at the Society for Industrial and Organizational Psychology Annual Conference, Atlanta, GA.

■ CHAPTER 4

1. Jackson, P., & Delehanty, H. (1995). *Sacred hoops: Spiritual lessons of a hardwood warrior.* New York: Hyperion, pp. 98-99.

2. The Jack and Herb Show. (1999, January 11). *Fortune,* p. 164.

3.   Csoka, L. C. (1998). *Bridging the leadership gap* (Report Number 1190-98-RR). The study of 400 Fortune 1,000 companies indicated that 64% of the companies used team performance as a measure of leader effectiveness. New York: The Conference Board.

4. Ulrich, D., Zenger, J., & Smallwood, N. (1999). *Results-based leadership.* Boston: Harvard Business School Press.

5. Schultz, H. (1997). *Pour your heart into it.* New York: Hyperion, p. 19.

6. Bennis, W. (1997). *Organizing genius: The secrets of creative collaboration.* Reading, MA: Addison-Wesley.

7. Goodman, A. (1999). *Public leadership: Practitioner and educator perspectives.* Unpublished doctoral dissertation, University of Colorado, Denver.

8. Bowman, M. A. (1997). Popular approaches to leadership. In P. G. Northouse (Ed.), *Leadership: Theory and practice.* Thousand Oaks, CA: Sage.

9. Ulrich, D., Zenger, J., & Smallwood, N. (1999). *Results-based leadership.* Boston: Harvard Business School Press.

10. Bryman, A. (1992). *Charisma and leadership in organizations.* London: Sage.

11. Chemers, N. M. (1993). An integrated theory of leadership. In N. M. Chemers & R. Ayman (Eds.), *Leadership theory and research: Perspectives and directions.* San Diego, CA: Academic Press.

12. House, R., & Shamir, B. (1993). Toward the integration of transformational, charismatic, and visionary theories. In N. M. Chemers & R. Ayman (Eds.), *Leadership theory and research: Perspectives and directions.* San Diego, CA: Academic Press.

13. Hollander, E. (1993). Legitimacy, power, and influence: A perspective on relational features of leadership. In N. M. Chemers & R. Ayman (Eds.), *Leadership theory and research: Perspectives and directions.* San Diego, CA: Academic Press.

14. Kogler-Hill, S. (1997). Team leadership theory. In P. G. Northouse (Ed.), *Leadership: Theory and practice.* Thousands Oaks, CA: Sage.

15. Heifetz, R. (1994). *Leadership without easy answers.* Cambridge, MA: Belknap Press.

16. Littlepage, G., Jones, S., Moffett, R., Cherry, T., & Senovich, S. (1999). *Relationship between leadership, potency, group processes, and work group effectiveness.* Paper presented at the Society for Industrial and Organizational Psychology Annual Conference, Atlanta, GA.

17. Moment, D., & Zaleznik, A. (1963). *Role development and interpersonal competence.* Boston: Harvard University Press.

■ CHAPTER 5

1. Wellins, R. (1991). Taking the mystery out of self-directed teams. *Tapping the Network Journal, 2*(1), 19-23.

2. Amabile, T. M. (1998, September/October). How to kill creativity. *Harvard Business Review, 76*(5), 76-87.

3. Frost, P., & Robinson, S. (1999, July/August). Toxic handler. *Harvard Business Review, 77*(4), 99.

4. Kotter, J., & Heskett, J. (1992). *Corporate culture and performance.* New York: Free Press. Over an 11-year period of analysis, "firms with cultures that emphasized . . . customers, stockholders, and employees

... outperformed firms that did not have those cultural traits by a huge margin. ... the former increased revenues by an average of 682 percent versus 166 percent for the latter, expanded their work forces by 282 percent versus 36 percent, grew their stock prices by 901 percent versus 74 percent, and improved their net incomes by 756 percent versus 1 percent." See also Ulrich, D., & LaFasto, F. M. J. (1995). Organizational culture and human resource management. In G. R. Ferris, S. D. Rosen, & D. T. Barnum (Eds.), *Handbook of human resource management* (pp. 317-336). Cambridge, MA: Basil Blackwell; Schwartz, N. D. (1999, September 6). The secrets of Fortune's fastest-growing companies. *Fortune, 140*(5), 72-86.

5. Deck, M. (1994, November). Why the best companies keep winning the new product race. *Research and Development Magazine* pp. 4LS-5LS.

6. Rucci, A. J., Kirn, S. P., & Quinn, R.T. (1998, January/February). The employee-customer-profit chain at Sears. *Harvard Business Review, 76*(1), 84.

7. Ancona, D. G. (1990). Outward bound: Strategies for team survival in an organization. *Academy of Management Journal, 33*(2), 334-365.

8. Adapted from Kast, F. E., & Rosenzweig, J. E. (1970). *Organization and management: A systems approach.* New York: McGraw-Hill, pp. 23, 170-171.

9. McWhirter, W. (1993, December 13). Back on the fast track. *Time,* p. 69.

10. Ashkewas, R., Ulrich, D., Jick, T., & Kerr, S. (1995). *The boundaryless organization.* San Francisco: Jossey-Bass.

11. Katz, R. (1988). High performance research teams. In R. Katz (Ed.), *Managing professionals in innovative organizations* (pp. 315-324). Cambridge, MA: Ballinger.

12. Ancona, D. G., & Caldwell, D. (1990, March/April). Improving the performance of new product teams. *Research Technology Management, 32*(2), 25-29.

13. Hallowell, E. (1999, January/February). The human moment at work. *Harvard Business Review, 77*(1), 59.

14. Fukuyama, F. (1995). *Trust.* New York: Free Press, pp. 26-28.

15. Larson, C. E., & LaFasto, F. M. J. (1989). *TeamWork: What must go right/What can go wrong.* Newbury Park, CA: Sage, p. 85.

16. Bell, J. (1996, September 16). Building the new Chrysler. *Industry Week, 245*(17), 10-15.

17. Allport, G., & Postman, L. (1947). *The psychology of rumor.* New York: Holt.

18. Corporate Leadership Council. (1996). *At the fault line: The struggle to align individual and team interests.* Washington, DC: The Advisory Board Company.

19. SMG Marketing Group, Inc. Chicago, IL. As of February 15, 2001, there were 6,788 total U.S. hospitals, of which 6,578 (96.91%) participated in a GPO purchasing relationship. Of the total number of hospitals, there were 5,179 community hospitals, of which 5,138 (99.21%) participated in a GPO purchasing relationship.

APPENDIX

Reliability of the Collaborative Team Leader Instrument

The Collaborative Team Leader Instrument presented in Chapter 4 was developed from the research described in that chapter. The six themes discussed in Chapter 4 comprise the six dimensions of the instrument. Here we report on the reliability of the instrument.

The items in the collaborative team leader instrument were constructed for each of the various ways that the themes were expressed by team members. For example, there were different ways that the team leaders were seen as "ensuring a collaborative climate." "Ensuring a collaborative climate" is the label that we put on these different ways that the team leader was seen as promoting open and supportive communication that helped the team succeed.

Our preliminary tests of this measure included two separate reliability studies involving two different samples of people. The first sample involved 86 healthcare consultants who help healthcare delivery teams improve the quality of patient care while reducing costs. The second sample included 99 members of a financial institution from the president through loan officers and bank tellers. In each of the two samples, participants were randomly assigned to one of three approximately equal groups, who described three leaders. One group of participants described their present or a past team leader of their choosing. One group described a team leader they had worked with who was a good leader. One group described a team leader they had worked with who was a poor leader.

First, Chronbachs alphas were calculated on the reliabilities of the six dimensions for the group describing their present or a past team leader. The results are shown in the accompanying table.

TABLE A.1 Internal Reliabilities for the Six Leadership Dimensions

Dimensions	Sample One	Sample Two
1. Focus on the Goal	.92	.90
2. Ensure a Collaborative Climate	.94	.90
3. Build Confidence	.90	.92
4. Demonstrate Technical Know-how	.90	.79
5. Set Priorities	.92	.88
6. Manage Performance	.94	.94

These alphas mean that, within a given dimension (e.g., Focus on the Goal), the items seem to be consistently measuring the same thing. Next, one-way ANOVAS were run to determine whether the scale scores significantly discriminated between positive and negative team leaders. All scale scores were significantly different in all comparisons. This means that the six dimensions (or scale scores) were sufficiently sensitive to differentiate good from poor team leaders.

Although we continue to examine the properties of the instrument, we believe you can use it to obtain feedback from your direct reports on your collaborative team leadership characteristics.

NAME INDEX

Abbott, J., 72
Allport, G., 183
Amabile, T. M., 158
American Hospital Association/American
    Society for Healthcare Materials
    Management (AHA/ASHMM), 86
Ancona, D. G., 170, 177
Andersen, S. O., 1, 2
Ashkewas, R., 174

Barker, J. R., 91
Barnum, D. T., 158
Bateson, G., xix
Bays, K., 129, 189
Bell, J., 181
Bennis, W., 18, 133
Bettenhausen, K. L., 16
Blomberg, D., 16
Bower, B., xix
Bowman, M. A., 147
Brannick, M. T., 71
Bryman, A., 148
Buchanan, K., 71
Bufanio, K. M., 78

Caldwell, D., 177
Campion, M., 46
Chaiken, S., 46
Chemers, N. M., 148
Cherry, T., 92, 148
Cheston, R., 13
Chlewinski, Z., 17
Chrislip, D., 9, 25, 91
Churchill, W., 159
Cooke, R., 25

Cooley, D., 132, 134
Corporate Leadership Council, 188
Csoka, L. C., 123

Damico, J. F., 191
Davis, J., 25
DeBakey, M., 132, 134
Deck, M., 163
Degman, F. M., 43
Delehanty, H., 103
Driskell, J., 25
Dykstra, J., 75

Early, J. F., 84
Eaton, R., 181
Eisenhower, D. D., 17

Farr, J. L., 72
Ferris, G. R., 158
Finley, M., 8
Franz, C. R., 91
Frost, P., 158
Fukuyama, F., 180, 181

Gates, W., 97
Glass, G. V., 42
Godfrey, A. B., 84
Goldberg, A., 26
Goodman, A., 147
Greenspan, A., 97
Gruendfeld, D. H., 76

Hackman, J. R., 77
Hallowell, E., 180
Harkins, S., 77
Harvard Business School Press, 72

Hatcher, J., 191
Health Industry Business Communications
    Council (HIBCC), 86
Health Industry Distributors Association
    (HIDA), 86
Heifetz, R., 148
Herold, D. M., 46
Heskett, J., 158
Hippocrates, 146
Hirokawa, R. Y., 72, 77, 83
Hollander, E., 148
Hollingshead, A. B., 76
Holusha, J., xvii
House, R., 148

Jackson, P., 97, 103
Janis, I. L., 83
Jick, T., 174
Jin, K. G., 91
Jones, S., 92, 148
Jordan, M., 102

Kameda, R., 25
Kane, J. C., 191
Karlsson, G., 82
Kast, F. E., 173
Katz, R., 27, 174
Katzenbach, J. R., 76, 79
Kerr, S., 174
Ketrow, S. M., 83
Keyton, J., 72, 77
Kirn, S. P., 165
Knight, L. B., 191
Kogler-Hill, S., 148
Kotter, J., 158
Kouzes, J., 17

LaFasto, F. M. J., xxiv, 3, 29, 47, 59, 78, 85, 152,
    154, 158, 162, 181
Larson, C. E., xxii, xxiv, 3, 9, 25, 26, 29, 47, 59,
    78, 84, 85, 91, 152, 154, 162, 181
Lasorda, T., 100
Latane, B., 77
Leiter, M. P., 35
Littlepage, G., 92, 148
Logsdon, J., xvii
Loucks, V. R., Jr., 190

Mann, L., 83
Martinez, A., 165
Maslach, C., 35
Matheny, A., xix
McLeod, G., 65

McGraw, B., 42
McWhirter, W., 174
Medsker, G. I., 46
Moffett, R., 92, 148
Moment, D., 148
Moore, J., xix
Moretti, D. M., 35
Morris, C., 21
Mother Teresa, 97
Mulligan, T. J., 190

Nanus, B., 18
National Wholesale Druggists' Association
    (NWDA), 86

Ogilvy, D., 66
O'Reilly, C., III, 71

Parker, G. M., 70
Parks, C., 25
Parr, J., xviii, xix
Peterson, J., xvii
Phillips, E., 13
Pinto, J. K., 72
Pinto, M. B., 72
Plinio, Alex, 97-98
Posner, B., 17
Postman, L., 183
Prescott, J. E., 72

Quinn, R. T., 165

Reich, R., xvii, xviii
Ringelmann, M., 77
Roach, R. M., 71
Robbins, H., 8
Roberts, K. H., 71
Robinson, S., 158
Rodman, D., 102
Rosen, S. D., 158
Rosenthal, R., 42
Rosenzweig, J. E., 173
Rost, K. M., 83
Rucci, A. J., 165

Salas, E., 25, 71
Saphiere, D. M., 71
Schrage, M., 72, 75, 76
Schultz, H., 128
Schwartz, N. D., 158
Scott, K. D., 35
Sellers, P., 66
Senovich, S., 92, 148

Shamir, B., 148
Shilling, D., 35
Shultz, B., 83
Silver, W. S., 78
Smallwood, N., 123, 148
SMG Marketing Group, Inc., 189
Smith, J., 174
Smith, M. L., 42
Souder, W. E., 91
Spielberg, S., 97
Stasson, M., 25
Sutter, J., 78
Sweeney, B., 81
Sweeney, C., xxii
Szumal, J., 25

Tabone, D., 82
Taylor, G. S., 35
Thompkins, P. K., 91
Tolstoy, L., 28

Ulrich, D., 123, 148, 158, 174
Uniform Code Council (UCC), 86
Urban, D. M., 83

Voltaire, 47

Walter, R. D., 191
Warren, R., 72
Welch, J., 97, 122, 133
Wellins, R., 157
West, M. A., 72
Williams, B., xix
Williams, K., 7
Winter, T., 103
Wukasch, D., 134

Zaleznik, A., 148
Zenger, J., 123, 148
Zimmerman, S., 25

SUBJECT INDEX

Accountability, 169-170
  feedback and personal, 46
Action orientation, xxviii, 5, 8, 14, 18-22, 24,
    111, 144
  success and, 21-22
  teams with, 19-20
  versus passive orientation, 18, 19
Action plan, reviewing, 150
Active listening, 168
AIDS epidemic, collaborative strategies and,
    xix
Allegiance Corporation, 191
  cost-reduction initiative, 87-88, 89, 90
  Cardinal Health merger, 88, 191
American Hospital Supply Corporation
    (AHS), 129, 188-189, 191
  Group Purchasing Organizations (GPOs),
    189
  See also Baxter International; Baxter
    Travenol
Approach-avoidance syndrome, 46
Aspirations:
  supportiveness and, 17, 18
  team performance and, 17
Attitudinal climate, team performance and,
    17. See also Organization environment

Baxter International, 87, 189
  team-based rewards story, 188-192
  TeamWork Day, 190, 191
  See also American Hospital Supply Corpo-
    ration (AHS); Baxter Travenol
Baxter Travenol, 189. See also Baxter Inter-
    national Behavior:
  as contagious, 24

"Best practices," 190
"Big Problems," 75

Chrysler Corporation, 181
Clarity:
  in expressing expectations, 140-141, 147
  of direction/priorities, 161, 163-165, 168
  of operating principles, 161, 168-173
  See also Clarity, goal; Clarity, role
Clarity, goal, 101-105, 108, 124, 161-165
  in good organization environment, 159,
    161, 162, 172, 194
  in setting priorities, 137, 163
Clarity, role, 11-12
Collaborative approach, demanding, 110-112,
    121
Collaborative attitudes/competence, contin-
    uum of, 25-28. See also High-impact team
    members; Middle-range team members;
    Noncollaborative team members
Collaborative behavior:
  expecting, 197
  rewarding, 112-113, 121
Collaborative climate, determining, 109. See
    also Organizational environment
Collaborative climate, ensuring, 108-121, 148
  demand collaborative approach, 110-112,
    121
  guide team's problem-solving efforts,
    113-116, 121
  making communication safe, 109-110, 121
  manage leader ego/personal control
    needs, 116-120, 121
  reward collaborative behavior, 112-113, 121
  See also Organizational environment
Collaborative decision-making groups:

school management, xvii
  See also Decision making, effective
Collaborative leadership, demonstration of,
    198. *See also* Leadership; Leadership
    thought, contemporary; Team leaders;
    Team leaders, competencies of effective
Collaborative problem-solving:
  in healthcare industry, xvii
  practice, 197
  See also Problem solving
Collaborative strategies:
  industrial adoption of, xvii
  science/technology adoption of, xvii
Collaborative style, setting expectations and,
    140, 141
Collaborative team leaders, 151-154. *See also*
    Team leaders; Team leaders, competen-
    cies of effective; Team leadership
Collaborative Team Member rating sheet,
    28-30
Communication:
  insufficient, 183-184
  making safe, 109-110, 121
  organization process, 175, 182-186
  problem-solving teams and, 64, 67, 70-71,
    72
  See also Communication processes, effec-
    tive; Organizational grapevine; Organi-
    zational rumors
Communication processes, effective, 182-186
  leaders' roles, 184-185
  power of, 182
  See also Communication
Confidence:
  as perishable, 173
  in good organizational environments,
    159-160, 161, 162, 172, 173, 194-195
  in leadership, 173
  See also Confidence, building
Confidence, building, 121-130
  accentuate positive, 128-129, 130
  achieving results, 123-124, 130
  assign responsibility by exhibiting trust,
    125-126, 130
  be fair/impartial, 126-128, 130
  effective team leaders, 96, 99, 121-130
  inform team members about key
    issues/facts, 124-125, 130
  say "thank you," 129-130
Connectedness, team member, 179-182
  common physical location, 179, 180-182
  time together, 179

trust and, 180-181
Connect Model, 32, 36, 38, 50-59, 142
  benefit of to team relationships, 60-61
  change one behavior each (step 6), 51,
    57-58, 59
  commit to relationship (step 1), 51, 54, 59
  explain/echo each perspective (step 5), 51,
    56-57, 59
  narrow to one issue (step 3), 51, 55, 59
  neutralize defensiveness (step 4), 51, 55-56,
    59
  optimize safety (step 2), 51, 54-55, 59
  track behavior changes (step 7), 51, 58, 59
  versus traditional team processes, 60
  See also Constructive conversation; Rela-
    tionships, good
Connect Model-type conversation, 112
Constructive conversation, 51
Contention:
  dealing with, 43-47
  difficulty in, 43-44
  poorly managed, 47-48
  See also Defensiveness
Core competency, xxviii, 7
Corporate Leadership Council, 188
Corporate retreats, 182. *See also* Pecos River
    outdoor training experience
Creative process, 75-76
Cross-functional teams, 90-92, 176. *See also* Al-
    legiance Corporation; Universal Product
    Number (UPN) initiative

Decision making, effective:
  effective organizational processes and,
    175-179
  formal, 176
  informal, 176
Defensiveness, 17-18, 44-45
  avoiding, 62
  counterattack, 44
  most common forms, 44
  withdrawal, 44
  See also Fight-or-flight syndrome
Differentiation, integration versus, 24
Drug use, collaborative strategies and illegal,
    xix
Dyadic effect, 24

Efficient Healthcare Consumer Response
    (EHCR) study, 86
Entrenched team, 20
Expectations, dimensions in setting:

collaborative style, 140, 141
management skills, 141
personal development, 141
specific objectives, 140, 141
Expectations, making clear, 140-141, 147
Expert silos, 116

"Face time," 181-182
Facilitative language, 51-52
Facilitators, language, 52
Fannie Mae, 103-104
Federal Express, 107
Feedback:
anonymity and, 149
approach-avoidance syndrome and, 46
as gift, 45-47
as threatening, 46
compromising supportiveness and, 46
confidentiality and, 149
enhanced performance and, 46
focused, 143
giving, 32, 34, 46, 48
giving constructive, 141, 142-143, 147
personal accountability and, 46
receiving, 32, 34, 46, 48
seeking, 149
team relationship growth and, 46
worker satisfaction and, 46
Fight-or-flight syndrome, 44
Focus:
in feedback, 143
on team goal, 100-108, 136
organizational politics and team, 105, 108
problem-solving teams, 64, 67-68, 71, 72, 94, 136
team leader goal, 96, 99, 100-108, 136

General Electric, 122, 133
"Work-Out" process, 174
General Motors, 174
Global business teams, 71
Goal, team, xxii, 4, 72, 73-75, 79, 81, 93, 94
adjusting, 107-108
ambiguous, 74-75
compelling, 74
defining in clear/elevating way, 101-105, 108
focus on, 100-108, 136
helping see relevance of, 105-106, 108
ill-defined, 101
inspiring, 102
keeping alive, 106-108

politics and, 105, 108
pressure for adjusting, 107
See also Clarity, goal; Management practices
Goal-setting process, 82
Great groups, 133
Group efficacy, 78
Group potency, 78, 148
Group processes, xii

Harvard Medical School, 180
Hazardous waste disposal, collaborative strategies and, xix
Helpless team, 19-20
High-control team leaders, 119
High-impact team members, 25-26
High performers, 163
Homelessness, collaborative strategies and, xix
Human moment, 180

"I" language, 55
"Informal exploring," 91-92
Informal leader, 148-149
Information, reliable, 186
critical role of, 186-187
lack of, 186, 187
Inhibitors, language, 52
Institutional memory, 132
Integration, differentiation versus, 24
Interpersonal reflex, 24
Interpretive cues, 47

"Kicking around the problem," 91-92

Leaders. See Informal leaders; Leadership; Team leaders; Team leaders, competencies of effective
Leadership:
confidence in as perishable, 173
organization environment as outcome of, 164
trust in as perishable, 173
See also Leadership thought, contemporary; Management practices; Team leaders; Team leaders, competencies of effective
Leadership thought, contemporary, 147-149
leader-constituent relationships, 148
leaderless teams, 148-149
leadership as vision, 147-148
See also Collaborative climate; Group potency

Lockheed Skunk Works, 133
Lock-in effect, 24

Management messages as operating principles, 168-173
  "avoid politics," 171-173
  "be accountable for results," 169-170
  "take action toward goal," 168-169
  "work together as team," 170-171
  See also Management practices
Management practices, 156, 161, 162-173, 194
  active listening, 168
  balancing resources and demands, 161, 165-168
  cognizance of resource needs, 168
  establishing clear operating principles, 161, 168-173
  poor, 164
  setting clear direction/priorities, 161, 163-165, 168
  See also Management messages as operating principles
Manhattan Project, 133
McDonald's, 81
Middle-range team members, 26

National Civic League, xviii, 9
Negative personal style, 23-24
Newark Collaboration Group, 98
New product development teams, 170
New York Times, The, 98
Noncollaborative team members, 15-16, 27-28
  ethically/morally deficient-type, 27-28
  immature/game playing-type, 27
  stabilization-type, 27
Nordstrom, 107
Norm of reciprocity, 24

Openness, xxviii, 5, 8-14, 16-17, 24, 41-42, 70-71, 93, 109, 111
  pitfalls, 43
  principle, 17
  supportiveness and, 16-17, 42-43
  versus defensiveness, 45
  See also Openness problems
Openness problems, 10-12
  passive conspiracy, 13-14
  performance issues, 12
  planning, 11
  policies/bureaucracy, 11
  product/outcome results, 11
  role clarity, 11-12

team's communication climate, 11
Operating principles, 168
  establishing clear, 161, 168-173
  See also Management messages as operating principles
Organizational friction, 171
Organizational grapevine, 183
Organizational resource needs, cognizance of, 168
Organizational resources, balancing demands and, 165-168
  possible repercussions of, 167
Organizational rumors, 183
Organization environment, xii, xxiv, 156-158
  as leadership outcome, 164
  as psychological atmosphere, 158
  assessment, 195
  bad, 158
  See also Management practices; Organization environment, good; Organization processes; Organization structure; Organization systems
Organization environment, good, 158, 159-160
  clarity in, 159, 161, 162, 172, 194
  commitment in, 159, 160, 161, 162, 172, 195
  confidence in, 159-160, 161, 162, 172, 173, 194-195
  See also Collaborative climate, determining; Collaborative climate, ensuring; Organization environment
Organization processes, xxv, 156, 161, 162, 173, 175, 194
  effective communication, 175, 182-186
  effective decision making, 175-179
  failure, 178
  keeping people connected, 175, 179-182
  responsiveness, 185
Organization structure, 156, 161, 162, 173-175, 194, 173-175
  stability, 185
Organization systems, 156, 161, 162, 186-195
  case study, 188-192
  consistency/fairness and performance standards, 192-195
  relevant rewards, 186, 187-188
  reliable information, 186-187
Ozone layer problem, depletion of, 1-2

Passive orientation, 18, 19
Pecos River outdoor training experience, 191
Performance appraisal, 113
Performance categories:

collaborative style, 140-141
management skills, 141
objectives, 140
personal development, 141
Performance issues, confronting/resolving,
141, 143-144, 147
Performance management, 138-147
confronting/resolving performance issues,
141, 143-144, 147
giving constructive feedback, 141, 142-143,
147
making expectations clear, 140-141, 147
requiring results, 140-141, 147
reviewing results, 140, 141-144, 147
rewarding results, 140, 145-147
subtle, 139
time involved, 139
Performance objectives, 4
Performance outcomes:
aspirations and, 17
attitudes and, 25
group process factors and, 92
interaction patterns and, 25
positive, 71
styles and, 25
team attitudinal climate and, 17
Performance standards:
consequences of failed, 193-194
consistency/fairness and, 192-195
human resource issues and, 193
irrelevant, 193
necessity of, 192
occasional evaluation of, 194
system-defined, 192
unreliable, 193
Personal style, positive, xxviii, 5, 8, 14, 23-25,
111
Politics, organizational, 171-172
avoiding, 171-173
team goal focus and, 105, 108
Priorities:
alignment of individual effort and, 138
commitment to goal, 137, 138
goal clarity and, 137, 163
setting, 135-138
setting clear, 161, 163-165, 168
to reach goal, 136-137, 138
urgency toward goal and, 136
when priorities change, 137-138
Problem solving, xxiv, xxvii, 5, 6-8, 114
dynamic in teams, 73
effective, 88-90

guiding team's, 113-116, 121
practice collaborative, 197
productive, 7, 66-67, 72
steps to effective, 84-92
unproductive, 7
vigilant, 83
See also Problem solving, systematic; Problem-solving groups; Problem-solving
teams; Single Question Format
Problem solving, systematic, 179
making priority, 81-83
presence of reminders, 83
Problem-solving groups, 71
improving performance of, 83
Problem-solving teams, 67-72
climate, 64, 67, 68-70, 71, 72
communication, 64, 67, 70-71, 72
exercise, 93-94
focus, 64, 67-68, 71, 72, 94, 136
See also Goal, team; Single Question Format; Team energies
Process problems, 92-93
Prudential Insurance Company, 97

Recognition of superior performance, 145-147.
See also Rewards
Relationships. See Relationships, good;
Relationships, good versus bad; Team
relationships
Relationships, bad, 38
Relationships, good, 37-38
mutually constructive, 37, 48
mutually trustful, 37
mutual understanding in, 37, 49, 52-53
perspective taking in, 53
productive, 37, 48, 51-52
requirements for building, 49-50, 51-53
self-corrective, 38, 49, 50, 53
Relationships, good versus bad, 36-39
characteristics of, 37
Rewards:
aligned with goal, 145
as celebration of standards, 146
fair, 146
for collaborative behavior, 112-113, 121
for results, 140, 145-147
required results and relevant, 187-188
team-based, 188-192
Ringelmann effect, 77

Sears, 165
Single Question Format, 64, 84-92, 94, 179

create collaborative setting (step 2), 85, 88-89, 92
   identify/analyze issues (step 3), 85, 89-90
   identify possible solutions (step 4), 85
   identify problem (step 1), 85, 88
   real-life use, 86-88
   reasons for using, 84
   resolve single question (step 5), 85
Social loafers, 16
Social loafing, 77
Strategic planning process, 82, 176
Supportiveness, xxviii, 5, 8, 14-18, 24, 36, 41-42, 93, 109, 111
   achievement and, 17
   aspirations and, 17, 18
   feedback and compromising, 46
   openness and, 16-17, 42-43
   pitfalls of, 43-44
   principle of, 17

Tactical teams, 71
Team climate, 24
Team energies, 72, 75-81
   diverted, 79-81, 93, 94
   mental, 75-77, 93, 94
   physical, 75, 77-78, 93, 94
   spiritual, 75, 78-79, 93, 94
Team Excellence database, 99
Team failure, reasons for, 8, 157
Team leaders, xii, xxv, 6
   aversive, 70
   encouraging the heart, 17, 26
   inspiring shared vision, 17
   managing ego/personal control needs, 116-120, 121
   personal style of, 69-70
   problems with, 100
   See also Collaborative team leaders; Team leaders, competencies of effective; Team leadership
Team leaders, competencies of effective:
   builds confidence (dimension 3), 96, 99, 121-130
   demonstrates technical know-how (dimension 4), 96, 99, 130-135
   ensures collaborative climate (dimension 2), 96, 99, 108-121
   focuses on goal (dimension 1), 96, 99, 100-108, 136
   manages performance (dimension 6), 96, 99, 138-147

   sets priorities (dimension 5), 96, 99, 135-138
   See also Collaborative team leaders; Team leadership; Team leaders
Team leadership, xxiv
   dimensions of, 98-100
   See also Team leaders; Team leaders, competencies of effective
Team members, xxiv, xxviii, 2-3
   closed, 9
   collaborative, xii
   collectively oriented, 25
   competent, xxii
   dysfunctional, xii, 3-4, 81
   egocentric, 25
   experience, 6
   inexperienced, 6
   open, 9
   supportive, 15
   using talents of, 125
   See also specific types of team members; Team members, behaviors of; Teamwork factors, team success and
Team members, behaviors of, 3, 4, 41-43
   diversity of, 66
   See also Teamwork factors, team success and; Working knowledge factors
Team mission, 100
Team problem solving. *See* Problem solving; Problem-solving teams
Team processes, traditional, 60
   versus Connect Model, 60-61
Team relationships, xxiii-xxiv, 33-36, 61
   bad, 36
   benefit of Connect Model to, 60-61
   building effective, 50-59
   complicated, xii, 33
   dysfunctional, 47-48
   effective, 36
   feedback and growth of, 46
   healthy, 36
   individual self-assessment of, 39-40
   most common shortcoming, 34-35
   objective introspection and, 40
   require building of collaborative, 197
   simple, xii, 33
   warm/caring, 16
   See also Connect Model; Feedback; Relationships, bad; Relationships, good; Relationships, good versus bad; Team relationships, team member assessment of

Team relationships, team member assessment of, 40-50
 building/sustaining collaborative, 48-50
 greatest challenge, 43-47
 most important behaviors, 41-43
Teams:
 effective versus ineffective, 64
 increase in collaborative, xvii
 primary objective of, 100
 prime directive of, 100
 successful, 73
 unsuccessful, 73
 See also specific types of teams
Team spirit, 78-79
 absence of, 79
Team strategy, 100
Team vision, 100, 147-148. *See also* Vision
Teamwork/collaboration, dynamics of, xxii-xxvi, 32
Teamwork factors, team success and, xxviii, 5, 8, 14-25, 197. *See also* Action orientation; Openness; Personal style, positive; Supportiveness
Technical competence, 4, 115
 from study/direct experience, 131-132
 versus collaborative process, 116
 See also Technical competence, demonstrating
Technical competence, demonstrating, 130-135
 analyzing complex issues, 134, 135
 inability in, 132
 get help, 133-135

know available resources, 133, 135
 "know your stuff," 132-133, 135
Trust:
 as perishable, 173
 assign responsibility by exhibiting, 125-126, 130
 in leadership, 173
 in upper management, 35
 mutual in good relationships, 37
 team member connectedness and, 180-181

U.S. Environmental Protection Agency, 1
U.S. Justice Department, 2
Universal product number initiative, 86-87, 88, 89, 90
 Group Purchasing Organizations (GPOs) and, 86, 87
Upper management, developing trusting relationships with, 35

Vision:
 inspiring shared, 17
 leadership as, 147-148
 See also Team vision

Walt Disney Studios, original animation team of, 133
Worker satisfaction, feedback and, 46
Working knowledge factors, xxviii, 5-8
 problem-solving ability, xxvii, 5, 6-8
 sufficient experience, xxviii, 5-6, 7

"You" language, 55

ABOUT THE AUTHORS

FRANK LaFASTO, Ph.D., is Senior Vice President of Organization Effectiveness for Cardinal Health, Inc., a multinational healthcare company. An internationally recognized author and lecturer on management issues, LaFasto has more than 25 years' experience helping organizations build and sustain successful teams and collaborative processes. He is the coauthor, with Carl Larson, of the best-selling book *TeamWork: What Must Go Right/What Can Go Wrong* (Sage Publications, 1989).

CARL LARSON, Ph.D., is Professor of Human Communication and past dean of Social Sciences at the University of Denver. His most recent work includes *Successful Communication and Negotiation* with Al Goldberg (1992), and *Collaborative Leadership: How Citizens and Civic Leaders Can Make a Difference* with David Chrislip (1994). Larson consults in both the public and private sectors. He received the Driscoll Master Educator Award given by the students at the University of Denver to the university's outstanding professor.

NOTES

NOTES

NOTES

NOTES

NOTES

NOTES

NOTES